# REINHOLD MESSNER
## To the Top of the World
*Challenges in the Himalaya and Karakoram*

**Translated by Jill Neate**

Published by
The Mountaineers
1001 SW Klickitat Way, Suite 201
Seattle, WA 98134

First published in 1992 by
The Crowood Press Ltd
Ramsbury, Marlborough
Wiltshire SN8 2HR

Paperback edition 1999

Title of the original German edition:

*Bis ans Ende der Welt* © 1998 BLV Verlagsgesellschaft mbH,
Munchen

**Library of Congress Cataloging in Publication Data**

A catalogue record for this book is available from the Library of
Congress.

ISBN 0-89886-677-4

**Picture credits**
Pages 33–36 and 221–224: paintings by Jean-Georges Inca,
photographed by Richard Fonti.
All other colour and black and white pictures are from Messner
Photo Archives

Typeset by Acorn Bookwork, Salisbury, Wiltshire

# Contents

# The Summit of our own Experience

Mountaineering, especially on the highest mountains in the world, is by the sport's own standards neither measurable nor describable. Metres above sea-level, grades of difficulty and the duration of climbs say less and less about a mountain as its size increases. Drifted new snow on the summit wall of K2 or Nuptse means not only enhanced danger, but also increased difficulty. It is often a shallow hollow of snow which stops the high altitude climber below the summit, not a vertical section of rock.

All those who dismiss this branch of alpinism as just snow-plodding, are showing that they know nothing about it. Those, too, who with all manner of tricks, want to get into the *Guinness Book of Records* – speed climbers without a timekeeper on the ascent, 'soloists' in single file – are only counterfeiters. The experience at the top end of the world improves with the effort, the difficulty, the danger, the exposure and, above all, with the self-reliance. This kind of experience could be described, painted, as the Frenchman Jean-Georges Inca shows in his pictures, and stored in one's sub-conscious.

It's not the success of the summit which has remained engraved in my memory, it is the mountain which, after the Nanga Parbat tragedy, breaks apart, the pressure of the storm on Manaslu, the first sight of the sublime Hidden Peak, the view through the shreds of mist from the highest mountain in the world, the apathy after a 48-hour snow storm on the South Saddle and the bodies beside the path.

Death and life, courage and fear, highs and lows, are all one up there, halves of an inseparable whole – and only in the balance between strangeness and familiarity do we climb on to the summit of our own experience.

# My Eight-Thousander Ascents – Seen Through the Eyes of the Artist Jean-Georges Inca

This book begins and ends with some pictures by the French artist Jean-Georges Inca. For two decades he has lived in Tende, in the French Maritime Alps, and owns a gallery there; his works have been exhibited in France and in several other countries. Through the stories in my books of my trips to the limit in the realms of the eight-thousanders, J.-G. Inca has been stimulated to create a series of pictures – modern, large paintings in powerful, glowing colours. In this he has succeeded, as scarcely anyone has previously, in expressing, in painting, the mountain–man relationship. There have been few statements of this, especially not recently and particularly with regard to the highest peaks.

J.-G. Inca's pictures have brought me back once more to a theme which has occupied me for sixteen years of my life and throughout all phases of my life. On many points they have restored emotions and situations to me, which today form part of the story of my life.

When I saw the first of the pictures I was captivated. I realized that here is someone who has insinuated himself into my own actions, has read all my writings, has understood the background. Consequently, J.-G. Inca has succeeded in making his pictures more outspoken than photographs and films can ever do: in other words, the mountain demands its price from he who delivers himself up to it unconditionally.

(For the explanatory text to the themes here, and the others at the end of the book, *see* page 255.)

# Not the Summit and not the Route – the Roundabout Way is the Goal

For fifteen years I have tried to extend the boundaries of the possible in eight-thousander mountaineering. To start with I first made ascents of hard routes in traditional expedition style. I then learned to do without partners and technical aids more and more, and finally, I thought of bold, roundabout ways, so as to experience what one used to call 'adventure'. For me it was nothing to do with conquest, but more about inner experience, the limit of my abilities and myself. Repeatedly, I went 'to the top of the world' to experience the limits of my strength and fear, and my ability to suffer. Adventure as an end in itself, as an approach to myself.

The fact that I have climbed all fourteen eight-thousanders is of secondary importance for alpine history. Perhaps it will stand as a footnote, like the completion in 1911 of all the four-thousanders in the Alps by the Vorarlberg mountaineer Dr Karl Blodig. Both have little to do with the development of mountaineering. I wonder how many climbers have stood on all the Alpine peaks over the magic 4,000m mark since then?

In 1987 the Polish climber Jerzy Kukuczka climbed his fourteenth eight-thousander. Sadly, he fell to his death from the South Face of Lhotse in 1989. Swiss mountaineer Erhard Loretan made it in 1995, after a string of extraordinary enterprises – the traverse of Annapurna, a non-stop climb of Everest during the monsoon, the South West face of Cho Oyu – and he rounded off his eight-thousanders with Kanchenjunga. The fact that the Frenchman Benoît Chamoux hoped to follow in Loretan's footsteps had nothing to do with this ascetic Swiss who had been making his own routes all his life. Chamoux failed to reach the summit and never returned.

The tragic loss of this speed climber, who preferred to put up records on prepared routes, is the result of a development for making the mountain a symbol of human hubris, which commercial risk-merchants call 'no limits' for advertising purposes – a dangerous ideology. It's not the mountain which is dangerous, rather human behaviour which ignores the sublimity of the mountains and assumes boundless human capabilities.

High-altitude climbing is not dead, it is even more demanding, but only in the remoteness away from the more fashionable mountains and without the ever increasing so-called record-making. In ten years' time maybe a dozen climbers will have 'knocked off' all fourteen of the highest summits on earth. By the year 2100 there will be 100 of them.

Himalayan mountaineering does not come to an end with the achievement of this 'record', which is only superficially interesting: '14 × 8,000m' is no more than a catch-phrase.

Just as Himalayan mountaineering has developed over the past twenty years, through ever harder routes and with ever fewer climbing aids and outside help, so in the future it will continue to be developed, by a young mountaineering elite.

In order than this form of mountaineering should remain an adventure at the most extreme limit of what is currently considered possible, the participants must face new problems and create new ways to the goal. In 1924, when George H. Leigh Mallory set out for Mount Everest, 'because it is there', *the summit was the goal*. For Chris Bonington and his team, who climbed the steep South West Face in 1975, *the route was the goal*. Now, when the mountain has been climbed without artificial oxygen, by the hardest routes, solo, during the monsoon and also in winter, *the roundabout way* to the summit is what counts – or record climbs. However, not everyone who takes it into his head to do something 'new', or 'storms' the summit faster than any of his predecessors, is an innovator.

Wanda Rutkiewicz, the most successful female high-altitude climber of my generation, could actually climb more eight-thousanders than many of her male colleagues – her pioneering achievements, however, were firsts only for women. On the mountain she followed the line of others and those calls for persistence which macho mountaineers have been advocating/pronouncing as their credo since the start of 'high altitude madness'. In the end she went too far.

Her death on Kanchenjunga affected me so deeply because she, like Alison Hargreaves on K2 in 1995, followed our trodden hero's path into catastrophe.

Even now, confusion in high-altitude climbing still exists. Most mountaineers today join large-scale commercial expeditions which aim to get to the summit by every possible means. Not 'by fair means' but 'by any means' is the motto. Also, the numerous small expeditions which combine into one big expedition at the Base Camps under K2 or Nanga Parbat, are further removed from alpine-style in their way of going about things than were the national expeditions of the 1950s, which performed self-imposed pioneer work on the mountain, and from which we still derive benefit today.

Erhard Loretan is the exception as he traverses the three-summit pinnacles of Annapurna I with Norbert Joos or ascends Mount Everest via the North Face in the monsoon with Jean Troillet – up and down in forty-eight hours.

This sort of 'record' has my complete respect. The fastest ascents *à la* Eric Escoffier, who ran to the summit of Hidden Peak in one day, up a prepared track and via a chain of camps provided by others does not, however. When the trail-blazers have to give up, he turns back too – as in the autumn of 1986 on Mount Everest, which he wanted to climb in his parasitic style in a new record time.

It may be that sponsors, who are more interested in publicity slogans than in authentic adventures, back records of such a kind. However, we must not believe them when it comes to authenticity at the frontiers of sport and adventure. Pioneers are not 'men without limits', rather people who set out into limitless uncertainty. The fastest ascent of K2, via a prepared route, says less to me than slow failure on a long and unknown route.

In mountaineering, speed has never impressed me as much as style and the formulation of a problem. The two together lead to a stride which the new generation of climbers can and must make over what has been reached so far if they want to prove their abilities.

There are still plenty of unclimbed faces, not only on the eight-thousanders – the

South West Face of K2, the East Face of Kanchenchunga's central summit, several routes on the South Face of Lhotse, Makalu West Face, Dhaulagiri South Face, Manaslu West Face – but also, above all, on 6,000m and 7,000m peaks. It depends on the style in which these 'problems' are solved. The manner in which V. Kurtyka and R. Schauerer climbed the West Face of Gasherbrum IV could be a model for all those who have devoted themselves to big-wall adventure.

Am I perhaps to blame for the 100 and more expeditions that take place each year now at the feet of the eight-thousanders? Certainly, the boom in high-altitude mountaineering is partly a result of my activity. It is not my fault, however, if the governments in Pakistan and Nepal issue so many expedition permits that it has become difficult to carry out first ascents independently from beginning to end. It lies with us, however, to formulate new problems. Innovation is only people with imagination going where many others do not.

We – my climbing contemporaries and I – have climbed alpine-style, without oxygen, without set camps and without outside help to the top of the world – alone to the top of Everest. We have ascended the highest peaks in the world by new routes, up steep faces and over the longest ridges. We have traversed the eight-thousanders and have climbed them in all seasons. We have traversed two, one after another, in tandem, without descending to Base Camp in between, after the 'hat trick' – three eight-thousanders in one season – had been achieved. Everything that has been done once can be repeated. Repetition is easier than pioneering in all walks of life.

Since alpinism generally has split into three types – competitive climbing, classic mountaineering, and expedition or high-altitude climbing – so high-altitude mountaineering if now also disintegrating unequivocally into two different disciplines: commercial and pioneering.

Why not? High-altitude climbing more and more will come to mean a possibility for travel rather than a sport at the limit of possibility. Organized by travel companies, led by tour leaders, supported by local high-altitude porters, one will be conducted to the summit. One will book for Mount Everest just as one might for Majorca: full-board, leadership and insurance inclusive.

I don't want to devalue organized eight-thousander tourism: I only want to make it relative. It is just as strenuous to ascend Shishapangma with a leader and a track to follow but it destroys adventure. 'Organized adventure' is indeed a contradiction yet a possibility, in every respect. For the time being it is just as remarkable as were the deeds of the earlier pioneers, and it promises success – certain success. Perhaps eighty per cent of those who have climbed eight-thousanders in recent years have succeeded within the context of a commercial expedition. That says more for the organizers than for the ambitious participants, as well as for the spirit of the times.

With great stamina, the high-altitude climber Marcel Ruedi from Winterthur has ascended ten eight-thousanders in this way. It would not have occurred to him at all to make his 'adventures' remarkable if it had not also occurred to him to make new routes. Industry offered him contracts. Animated by the local press, he let himself be forced into this 'race', which he could not have won and which was to cost him his life on Makalu on 24 September 1986. Obviously he had not withstood the pressure of publicity. I lament him as a sacrifice, not as a failure.

True adventure includes the possibility of failure; the commercial expedition should exclude it. Why do professional adventurers buy their way into an Eiselin Expedition to Mount Everest? Because that is and remains the surest way to the top, and because financial backers and the public back home still cannot distinguish between adventure and show. A television public greedy for adventure leaves everything to its adventure-greedy proxy, even if he is only setting out to fill a gap in the market.

In principle, I have nothing against multiple-summit successes; I am disturbed only by the inexact reporting. Anyone who really believes he has climbed one of the Gasherbrums 'alpine-style', when at the same time a dozen other groups were operating on the same spot, is deceiving only himself. But he who knows the state of play and, in the example given, nevertheless babbles about 'alpine-style', deceives others too. He who brings a 'limit-adventure' live into a television programme may be a good actor, a performer of adventure, but he is not a pioneer in the argument about man and wilderness. True adventure cannot be staged, it can perhaps be documented in a few films, but the rest will more or less be show.

Who is to arbitrate between show and real alpinism now? There are no generally accepted rules governing high-altitude mountaineering. There are only constraints which one person or another imposes on himself and a common language. *Alpine-style* means an ascent from scratch, without outside help and without preparation. A *solo ascent* begins at the foot of the mountain, at the point where the valley porters can go no further or may not according to local custom. *Without oxygen* means to climb renouncing bottled oxygen at all times, even while resting and sleeping.

Who controls all that? No one. And that is what makes exact statements so important. In order to be able to write the history of the eight-thousanders over the past five years, I have read over 100 reports. If in so doing I discover that a person was on Gasherbrum II 'alpine-style' on exactly the same day as Frenchmen and Spaniards, I amend this report for my history. When a person claims to have climbed Nanga Parbat 'super-alpine-style' after he has used the chain of camps and ropes of other climbers on the Diamir Face, I call his style 'super-parasite'.

I don't want to discredit anyone by my findings, only to point out that concepts are elastic and also can be deliberately falsified.

In 1975 Peter Habeler and I climbed Gasherbrum I via its North-West Face: a new route, no preparation and no assistance. From the Gasherbrum Valley to the top and back, relying on ourselves completely. Until then all eight-thousanders had been climbed after the setting up of several high camps. The chain of camps and fixed ropes constitutes 'expedition-style', and less so high-altitude porters and heavy-oxygen apparatus which merely make expedition-style necessary.

My first step towards my solo ascent of the highest mountain in the world was an alpine-style climb. The second was my Everest ascent without oxygen. The third step was a small eight-thousander climbed solo. The 'last step' could only be contemplated after these three.

It was a logical objective to go alone to the top of the world, above all because this world has only one top.

Much more than '14 × 8,000m', my Everest solo ascent marked a turning point in high-altitude mountaineering.

If we have sought relatively easy routes for ourselves in order to push to the top of the world alone (and thus by necessity with few aids), it is now necessary to do it by the hardest routes. Apart from the South West Face of Mount Everest, there are also such devious ways as the ascent via Lhotse Shar to Lhotse main summit with the subsequent descent to the South Col and thence to the summit. Or a spiralling ascent via the West Col (6,000m), North Col (7,000m) and South Col (8,000m) to the summit.

Our mountaineering was not conquest mountaineering like that of Hillary, Buhl and Bonatti. It was the quest for limiting values; at first glance illogical but full of uncertainty, like the mountaineering of the pioneers. The great mountaineering of tomorrow will be even crazier because it will be more preposterous.

However, anyone who advances knowledge by this sort of mountaineering and wants to achieve more than the 'conquest of the useless' should get into a low-pressure chamber or circle the earth in a satellite. Those people for whom it is not enough 'happiness' to start over and over from the bottom like a kind of Sisyphus, should not babble to me of 'mountain passion'. And anyone who has not learned to distinguish between adventure and show can go to the cinema instead of Mount Everest.

One rule of thumb remains: the harder it becomes to document an adventure, the more it is worth. For while one can stage, film and act, uncertainty is slight. An adventure to the limit begins where the show gives up. I was always sceptical of great documentation and great show, even my own. But when it is a matter of survival, we forget the camera and everything which comes after that. It is no longer a matter of success or failure — it is a question of life or death.

Only on ever-bigger roundabout ways may we find those contemporary limiting values which the common fund of experience and previous achievement dictate. Youth desires to do what is feasible, and in a sporting context I have nothing against that, especially not when youth seeks new horizons without technology and without drugs. But when, with the pretext of serving humanity, people exploit, ruin and thereby make this world uninhabitable, I always dig in my heels.

However, 'sick', 'crazy' or 'foolish' it may appear to laymen to go into the wilderness with self-imposed constraints on aid and security, we shall do it nonetheless, until each of us, in his roundabout way, reaches the top of the world and strives to the pinnacle of his possibilities.

# A NEW EPOCH HAS BEGUN

The world's eight-thousanders were the focus of worldwide interest for a long time. They were reconnoitred, besieged and assaulted, in fact, attacked over and over again. In 1895 Albert Frederick Mummery ventured a first attempt on Nanga Parbat. In 1950 Maurice Herzog and Louis Lachenal stood on the summit of Annapurna, the first eight-thousander to be climbed. In between there were many expeditions, the members of which paved the way for later successes.

Within fifteen years all fourteen eight-thousanders had been climbed – the run on the 'Third Pole' was over. For us young climbers in 1970, however, the ice giants in high Asia were still a dream and a goal. We looked for new problems on their flanks and dreamed of solving them. Whereas thirty or forty years before one had reached the top by the easiest way, opening up the so-called ordinary routes, we made it our job to climb the biggest and hardest faces.

The history of Alpine mountaineering repeated itself in the Himalaya. Just as the big walls of the Alps had been conquered in the 1930s, so now the new generation of climbers besieged the enormous, untouched faces of the eight-thousanders.

In the summer of 1970 a team of British and American climbers succeeded in overcoming the 3,000m South Face of Annapurna. Some weeks later my brother Günther and I climbed the Rupal Face on Nanga Parbat. In the summer of 1971 a French team ascended the extremely difficult 3,200m West Pillar on Makalu. As members of a small South Tyrol team, we set out in 1972 for our 'problem', the South Face of Manaslu.

At that time my experiences were based, above all, on the tragic Rupal Face expedition, on which my brother and I had reached the summit and Günther was to lose his life. I knew how a classic eight-thousander expedition was organized and carried out. Also, I suspected that it would be more dangerous to climb a difficult face on an eight-thousander without fixed ropes, high camps and high-altitude porters, than with all these aids.

I had not yet the courage to plunge myself into the risks of a mini-expedition. First of all everything should go well on Manaslu.

# Storm on Manaslu – a Classic Himalaya Expedition

We began the ascent to the summit of Manaslu on 23 April 1972 from Camp 3. Franz Jäger and I wanted to reach the highest point in two days and then return quickly to the lower camps. However, despite Sherpa assistance, on the first day we managed only about half of the ice ramp which leads to the summit plateau. The Sherpas went back to camp. Franz and I installed ourselves roughly in the tent. Nevertheless, we slept well and Franz declared enthusiastically the next morning that he was in cracking form.

On 24 April everything worked out according to plan. By the time the Sherpas arrived, we had taken down the tent and packed our rucksacks, except for the cooker which we had left out so that we could prepare tea for the porters. Shortly before midday, we gained the summit plateau after exiting from the South Face. The last rope lengths were over bare ice and, because the slope there was very steep, we had to help the Sherpas.

Just below the ridge, and still on the south side, we erected Camp 4, anchoring the tent to the ground with an 8mm rope. Ten metres above us was the divide between north and south. We had reached the ideal exit point for a summit push.

In good time, we lay down and I cooked the whole evening. Outside a strong wind was blowing. Over the radio we went through all the details of the summit plan once more: if we did not make contact at 6 a.m., we were already on the move and two people would at once ascend from below to give us back-up.

Our doctor, Dr Oswald 'Bulle' Oelz, recommended that we inhaled over the steaming kettle. The weather promised to remain fine. Franz and I ate as much as we could, drank tea and Ovomaltine, then placed our rucksacks under our legs, the better to rest. I slept until day-break.

In the early morning, when all the others presumably were still asleep, I got up softly and got the cooker going. Inside my sleeping bag I put on my second inner boots, then I made the tea. During the night masses of snow had been driven into the tent and now lay hard pressed between our sleeping bags. I threw some lumps into the pot and rummaged at the head of the tent amongst clothes and snow for bread and jam.

Franz's sleeping bag was drawn right up to his nose. He had laid his curly head on his rucksack and was still alseep. I woke him up. From habit he undid the zip in the tent door but the wind blew a handful of ice crystals into his face, so he quickly shut it again.

'It'll stop soon', he said. 'The weather is still fine. But the wind needs to die down.'

The tent walls flapped and at regular intervals fine snow-dust flew through the triangular opening in the gable end which we had not covered sufficiently the evening before.

'We can't go in this wind', I said.

'It'll clear up soon', repeated Franz, 'meanwhile we can get ready.'

We slipped out of our sleeping bags and put on the things we had laid out the previous evening for the summit climb – an outer suit of coated Perlon fabric, our heavy outer boots and gaiters.

Franz had kept on his down jacket; his woollen cap had white spots, was full of snow and a little too big. As the day promised to be cold, he put a hood over it, and this made him look like a polar explorer. He tied his bivouac bag around his waist under his anorak rather than on the outside, so that the wind would not tear it away. He stuffed his spare gloves into the big thigh pockets in his long Loden breeches, which were full of odds and ends such as camera films, sun-cream and goggles.

We drank the lukewarm water, which tasted of wool and tea, and tried to eat but we weren't hungry. I fetched my thin woollen gloves out of the inner pocket of my rucksack, pulled them on and opened the door of the tent. My grandmother had knitted these special gloves for me; I had asked her for them because there is nothing better to take to these high altitudes.

Outside it was already daytime and the wind had stopped raging across the plateau. The sun was peeping from behind the summit of Peak 29.

One after the other, we crept out into the open. Franz closed the zip while I tied our 15m rope on my back. We wanted to take it with us in case of unexpectedly difficult climbing on the summit ridge. We were both wearing down gloves now over our other pairs. As we stood face to face, all muffled up and clumsy, we had to laugh.

After the long hours in the tent our initial movements, awkward as they were, filled us with buoyancy, self-confidence and a feeling of strength.

We made haste to get on so that we would not be delayed at the last moment. We dismantled the tent, tying it firmly to the ground so that the wind could not blow it away, picked up our ice axes and marched away.

On the faint ridge between the North and South Faces we stopped. Franz breathed deeply; it was windless, and the air was cold and pure. He looked around – there were no clouds in the sky and the world lay below us. It was the right day for the summit. Franz pointed over towards Himal Chuli, to Peak 29. The as yet invisible rising sun covered the sky with bright streaks.

Before us there extended a gigantic snow plateau, rising slightly eastwards; hump-backed sastrugi covered the white expanse. Only to the right of us, below the rock towers of the South-West Ridge, did a gentle hillock block the view. Once we had climbed up this ridge we would be able to see the summit, then after a few more hours' climbing we would be on top. Perhaps the summit was really behind this hill!

We moved fifty or a hundred metres at a time, past the delicate pointed edges of the sastrugi, then stopped for a breather. The storm had swept away the loose snow, so that our boot soles scarcely penetrated the surface. Only in the hollows and shadows of the sastrugi was there looser powder snow. Behind us, still recognizable, was the narrow, dark track back to our tent: it seemed to swim on the wavy surface.

The conditions were ideal. The weather had held for so long that the wind had been able to sweep bare all the ridges. There were no more obstacles in the way of our summit assault; we must use this opportunity.

14

The summit block of Manaslu. At 4,000m, its South Face is one of the biggest and hardest walls in the world.

On the ridge, far to the right above us, hung small, shining snow plumes. Filled with pleasure in anticipation of the summit as Himalayan climbers in particular feel, Franz came along behind me. During the rest stops, he often beamed at me as if he wanted to say 'We'll soon be there!' His eyes raced far ahead, along the many waves of snow. Counting the hillocks and slopes in front of us, he said once: 'The top must lie behind there!' Time and again he looked ahead. Behind the cold snow expanses the summit towers would rise up. For more than an hour we had been approaching – step by step and stop by stop – the hump from behind which they must emerge. Sharply drawn shadows now hung from the edges of the snow waves. Out of the valleys mist was rising, mixing with the white of the foothills. It was still not warm but in Butterfly Valley it must already have been unpleasantly hot.

Behind each ridge we expected to see the summit but each time fresh snow slopes and ridges lay ahead of us. As there were no technical climbing difficulties to overcome and the ground was free of crevasses, we proceeded unroped. To the north, above the mountains of Tibet, lay a cloudless sky. Gradually we became impatient: still no sign of the final rise!

With each ridge reached we were in despair. Franz suddenly abandoned his initial plans and decided to give up, to return to camp at once and to wait there for me.

'Reinhold', he said gently and stopped to draw breath. I turned round to him and saw renunciation in his eyes.

'I'm going back', he said resolutely, 'we shan't make the top today.'

'It can't be much further', I tried to encourage him.

'That's what we thought three hours ago', he replied.

'Are you tired?' I asked.

'No, it's not that, but I don't want to bivouac, I'd rather go back to the tent in good time.' He persisted with his decision.

'I don't want to bivouac either. But we still have time, plenty of time before dark.'

'You go on alone, you're faster, perhaps you at least can make it.'

'And what about you?'

'I'm going back, I'll wait for you in the tent.'

It was late morning. We were standing directly below the first two steep rises.

As there was only walking terrain between us and Camp 4, there was virtually no danger of falling and the weather promised to remain fine, so neither of us doubted for more than a moment that Franz would get back to camp alone. He was in good physical shape, was equipped with the best gear, and had a straightforward track which led easily downwards towards the tent.

'I'm going on, as far as I can. If I'm not up by early afternoon, I'll turn back. I'll be back in good time', I said.

'Good luck!'

'And you.' I turned back to the slope.

'I'll make some tea for you', Franz called back after descending a few metres.

He went downwards, I went upwards, we could still see each other for a while. He followed the track which he had followed step by step on ascent and reached the gentle ridge with the resting place where, twenty minutes before, he had arrived full of hope, convinced he would see the summit.

This sudden abandoning of the summit, what was the reason for it?

In the winter, when Franz's participation in the expedition was in question, the thought of an eight-thousander had made him almost crazy. But now, despite the thin air, he had the strength to renounce it. Going down in good time meant so much time gained, safety. Franz crossed the ridge, sat down and gazed up at me. He waved. I had stopped to rest. How small he looked now!

I climbed on slowly and calculated how many hours were necessary for the return: two perhaps, three at the most. I wished I knew what the summit looked like, whether it were possible solo. But the slopes above blocked the view and I had difficulty keeping a regular pace.

Suddenly, however, there were rocks above me. I sat down and looked back along the slopes, wanted to call enthusiastically to Franz. I could still see him clearly, far off, very small, then he disappeared behind the ridge.

After four more breathers I reached the South-West Ridge. A rock tower stood before me but it was easy to imagine that there was another behind it. On the edge of the ridge a sharp wind was blowing, driving isolated shreds of mist before it. Very fine snow-dust adhered to the precipitous slabs. Beneath an overhang, I bore to the left on the northern side. Here there was no wind. The face fell steeply away below me and further down stood a steep-sided rock tower – the Pinnacle. All the towers on the ridge – and there were very many of them – sloped and pointed eastwards.

After climbing for a while between rock and snow, I came to a notch. Again the wind blew hard from the south and the face there fell away almost vertically. A sharp snow edge led upwards to a rock rib. That must be the summit! I sat down in the notch. From here I could get a good view of the last part of the ridge. It was very steep, yet neither of the faces offered an easier climb.

I climbed slowly and carefully, resting more often than previously. Now I was standing, somewhat insecurely, on a rock ledge and saw once more a moderately inclined ridge in front of me. This short piece of ridge ought not to prevent me from reaching the highest point.

Meanwhile, the wind had strengthened, the air was icy and in the south there hung a bank of dark cloud. I would have liked to rest a while but here on the ridge I could neither sit down nor even stand comfortably.

I adjusted my speed to the difficulties and the thin air, going only ten paces without a breather. Then I saw beyond the ridge a rock tooth, five or six metres high, one half dark and the other bright, like a longitudinally-split pyramid. This was the summit and never before in my life had I seen one so peculiar.

I climbed up the south side, with my feet on a rock ledge and my ice axe on the snow ridge. Perhaps because of the proximity of the summit, I felt no more tiredness now. At all events I felt safe and clear-headed. Then I discovered a notch so broad that it separated the ridge from the summit tower. As I climbed down into it I had to tread on some loose bits of rock and be doubly careful.

The final few metres to the summit were hard, as the rock was very splintered and steep. Then, in the middle of the summit pinnacle, I saw a bent and rusty piton about 15cm long. Further up was another, much firmer, with a ring. Some bits of material hung from it. I held it firmly for two or three steps, then I was on top.

As a change in the weather was coming in from the south, I stayed only a few minutes. I built a cairn, took some photographs, knocked out one of the pitons and stuck it in my pocket.

I wasn't tired but the cloud bank in the south and the strong wind urged descent. I had to reach the tent before nightfall. I picked up a handful of pebbles for my comrades who were waiting for me below.

In the notch I turned around once more and looked back: a rock tooth, some wisps of mist, a little pile of stones — that was the summit. Just below, a piton and scraps of a one-time flag. The sky was all around, and to the south, heavy, bloated clouds were clinging to the summits. The wind hunted them on, closer, always northwards, away over the top of Manaslu.

The descent went smoothly and quickly to begin with, as I climbed back down my route of ascent. Suddenly and unexpectedly mist and a snow storm sprang up. Descent became a race against death. As I battled my way back, I imagined Franz safely in the tent at Camp 4.

So long as the route went down steeply, I could orientate myself excellently. Here a rock tower, there a glistening blue ice slope, and lower down I had to pass between some snow towers. I had every detail of the ascent in my head, so that I couldn't lose my way even without a track. I had ripped my windproof with my ice axe, so as not to slip if I fell. Soon the storm rose to hurricane force and it was impossible to see with goggles. My mouth and eyes iced up and the situation seemed hopeless.

The plateau was now flatter, and the storm threatened to hurl me to the ground. My eyes were stinging as I kept going straight ahead but the snow slope was endless. Where was the tent? I moved upwards, downwards, across the slope: I let myself drift with the wind, and came to a shining ice surface which had not been there in the morning. Everything was more or less altered — the snow waves and the ridges — and nowhere was a saving rock island. I moved against the storm, backwards, doubled up and fit to drop. In places the snow was already knee deep. When the storm came from the side, it overturned me.

I was reduced to crawling. I crawled across the plateau, no, not a plateau, rather a basin-shaped valley. Sharp ice crystals and snow-dust rushed towards me out of the mist. Occasionally they hit me in the face and pricked my eyes so that I could see nothing. I went on crawling and felt the weight of my body pressing me into the ground. At first I thought it was the storm which was pinning me down but it was tiredness — it was my legs which had become so heavy.

I felt my tired body and dragged it along, as if I were recovering from a bad illness. In this storm I thought I should never get on my feet again; yet it could not be much further. The main thing now was not to give up, I must find the tent. I breathed deeply and recovered relatively quickly in the rest stops. Suddenly I was standing again, with my legs straight but with my body still doubled over.

I moved with my back to the wind, without hesitation, without thinking. I struggled on, straight ahead, to the left, to the right, staggered, groped with my feet in space, found firm ground again, stood still, took a breather . . . then I groaned and began to move in the other direction. The plateau had neither end nor beginning. The tent was nowhere to be seen.

The route up the rock pillar, via which the Tyrol Himalaya Expedition attacked the South Face of Manaslu; above is the ice labyrinth.

Only as I kept coming to this same smooth-swept patch of ice did I realize that I was going round in circles. My despair grew. I didn't know where I was, imagined myself to be in close proximity to the tent, within a circle of at most 500m in diameter from it. Nevertheless, I didn't find it. I had been walking for hours but didn't know where I was going. The whole time the hurricane was chasing ice crystals ahead of itself, throwing them in my face until my skin stung. 'Keep going', hammered through my brain. Things had never looked so hopeless. But the worst thing would be to stop and lie down here in this basin, without ever getting out again, to die here . . .

Suddenly I heard someone call my name. I stopped and listened. Nothing more. Was it an hallucination? No, there it was again, quite distinct: 'Reinhold!' I was so excited that my voice shook.

It was Franz's voice, I recognized it exactly. He seemed to be calling to me from in front of the tent.

'Franz', I shouted, 'I'm over here!', not that that told him anything.

'Franz!', I called again. He did not answer.

'Hello!' Again nothing. Only the storm howling and the shreds of cloth fluttering from my body.

I began to panic. Naturally, somewhere near here lay the tent. I must hurry, hurry . . . and I rushed forwards, curved around a 2m high wall of snow. My gaze hurried on ahead but my legs wouldn't follow. I was so tired, desperately tired!

Then I saw a dark heap in the snow. Immediately I thought: 'That's it'. I wanted to run to it but my legs refused and my chest threatened to burst. Exhausted, I let myself fall on the snow.

I had no breath left to shout out. Weak and coughing I lay there, not letting the tent out of my sight.

'Franz!', I shouted after a while. 'Fra-anz!' And later: 'Hello!' Why didn't he answer?

I crawled towards the tent – if only he would come out! . . . Nearer . . . nearer . . . and at last I was there. It was a pointed mound of snow!

I lay there and wanted to give up, to dig a snow hole and dig myself in. Nevertheless, I stood up and continued searching, driven by my survival instinct.

I was so cold that my whole body shook but, as I went back, I was amazed to notice that I was no longer so tired. The snow surface under my feet was now uncertain in an odd way, so that often I groped into space. Everything around me was indeterminate, and at most I could see only 8m.

I moved almost without thinking. Suddenly I was startled, believing I was hearing shouts again. I circled around, listening, in all directions. And then, more distinctly than before, I heard someone shout.

'Reinhold!' Again it was Franz.

'Hello', I screamed as loud as I could.

'Reinhold!'

'Franz', I begged him. 'Stand still and call at regular intervals, otherwise I shan't find the tent'. No answer. I heard him call once more. I never found him again.

Later on I began to call for help but no one heard me. I stayed in the same spot for a long time and shouted out regularly. However, the storm must have swallowed up my calls.

Now I was no longer despairing – for preference I would have lain down to sleep. Then it occurred to me where I had heard Franz's voice most distinctly: on the ridge, by the smooth-swept stretch of ice. I went quickly upwards but couldn't find the place, recognized nothing again. There was no obvious upwards slope any more, only an expanse of snow around me, the circumference of which was noticeably getting smaller. The storm increased, minute by minute . . .

Again I could hear Franz's voice; it must be coming from the tent. He's trying to direct me, I thought. Only in the lulls in the storm did I hear scraps of words, my name. Again I answered and called his. Again I waited for an answer, which never came. I wandered aimlessly around the great plateau, rested . . .

At that time I thought I would die. I sat in the snow which the storm tore away from under me. I was so tired that I had given up moving, given up looking for the tent. Snow and blood stuck to my cheeks and nose. I had partly torn out my beard, from which centimetre-long icicles hung, to be able to breathe.

Now and then I thought I would die of thirst. I opened my split lips and dreamed of a gulp of hot tea. Then, lost in thought, I looked at the tiny patch of snow which was still visible in the storm. Night was coming on, noticeable by the thick, grey mist which was mixed with snow. It surrounded me like a cage.

When the storm diminished a little, I rolled on my side, stuck a fist in the snow, stood up and carried on walking – to this day I don't know where.

During my next rest, I seized on a clear thought, to which I owe my life. Again I was sitting on the edge of a sastrugi, blood dripping from my beard on the snow. There came to me the idea of moving against the storm, always against the storm. Only thus could I get out of this cage in which I was circling.

I thought to myself: 'The wind is out of the south'; sudden changes of weather on Manaslu always came from the south. That had struck me during the expedition. Thus, if I walked against the wind, I reflected, I must come down to the South Face.

Naturally, I knew that in this snowstorm I would never have been able to climb down the South Face. I didn't want to do that. Our tent stood on the plateau just above the exit from the South Face. Vertical to the supposed wind direction, left and right of the tent, were rocks, the only ones on the broad slope. I remembered it. If I found them, I thought, the tent must lie in between. The storm might rage as much as it liked, but I would not give up before nightfall. I groped my way backwards, scanning the slope and got stuck in the snow again. For a long time I walked with my back to the storm, doubled over, gasping for air. Suddenly I came to the line of the South Face, turned back to the ridge, found the rocks, went along the stretch in between twice, three times – the fourth time I saw the tent. 'Franz', I called, when I was still a few metres away. 'I'm here!' Something moved. There was the entrance. It really was the tent this time!

I was so glad that I wanted to run, yet my feet stuck in the snow and I fell over. Someone helped me to my feet and supported me. As I saw his face near mine, I asked: 'Is that you, Horst?'

'Yes, it's me, Horst!', he replied.

I had not recognized him at once. He led me the last few steps to the tent and helped me inside. Head first, I crawled through the narrow slit. Andi greeted me. Snow covered the down bags.

Camp 2 (5,850m) in Butterfly Valley.

Happy as I was to meet up with my comrades Horst Fankhauser and Andi Schlick, equally frightful was the discovery that Franz Jäger was not lying in the tent. I reckoned that he must be inside and must have been there since midday. I thought that he must have arrived at Camp 4 hours before the storm – he had been calling me!

Andi began to rub me down, to pick the snow from my face, then he held a mug of warm tea to my lips. I couldn't drink or speak, my whole body was shaking and I was breathing fast and irregularly.

'Isn't Franz here?', I uttered at last. Andi shook his head.

'I heard him calling, right around here!'

'When and where?', asked Horst, who was still standing by the tent door.

'Lots of times and only here on the plateau. I've been looking for the tent for hours.'

'I'll go and have a look', called Horst from outside and went off. Shortly afterwards he returned.

'You're right', he said, 'I heard him calling too.'

'Where?', asked Andi.

'Up there, on the plateau, he's calling "Reinhold", I'm sure of it.'

When I had arrived and told them about the shouts, Horst thought I could have been hallucinating. Now, however, he was convinced that Franz was out there calling in the snowstorm.

Andi and Horst immediately got themselves ready for a search. They didn't discuss it, for them it was a matter of course to go to Franz's aid – despite the dark and the snowstorm, and despite the cold and the altitude. They put on everything they had.

'Don't forget the bivy bag', I said to Andi before he went out.

'We'll be back soon', I heard one of them say, then nothing more. The storm howled. Shortly afterwards the crackle of the radio interrupted the icy silence in the tent.

'Camp 4, come in please!' It was Bulle from Camp 2.

'I got here alone about ten minutes ago, in a really bad way because I wandered at least five times around the tent before I found it. There's a terrible snowstorm up here, up on the big plateau it was impossible to orientate myself. During the last part of the descent I could hear Franz calling all the time. He came back down long before me because he gave up before the top. He must have got himself lost and apparently still hasn't found the tent. Horst went out and heard him shouting as well. Andi and Horst, who got here about an hour ago, have now climbed up to fetch him. Let's hope they find him soon. Over!'

'Reinhold, first of all, we hope Franz will be with you as soon as possible. Next, naturally we are terrifically bucked that you made the summit. How do you feel?'

'I'm a bit hypothermic because I've been searching for the tent for three hours. I didn't think I would find it. With a great deal of patience I finally discovered two rocks and got a fix from them, otherwise I wouldn't have made it here. It was hopeless working by compass because we have no maps. We set off relatively late because it was stormy early on. So I must have done more than 800m in six hours, to reach the summit. I was on top but it was misty, bad for photographs. Instead, I found a Japanese piton up there and photographed that, knocked out a second one and pocketed it as a summit proof. Then I came down. Franz turned back hours ago. I found one of his gloves and, as I kept hearing him call, I was certain he was already in the tent. But when

I arrived, he wasn't here. It was a terrible shock. Five minutes later Horst, too, heard him calling again. Andi and he have climbed up to bring him down. I hope they can fetch him in about half an hour. I've hung a lamp outside the tent so that it's easier to find. Over!'

'Reinhold, how are your feet? Over.'

'My feet are fine. I've checked there's no frostbite; hands are alright too. I was afraid that my nose was frozen but that is warm again as well. I've pulled out half my beard because icicles were stuck to it but that doesn't matter. I'm just rather cold but if I drink half a litre of tea, I shall be OK again. Now the main thing is for Franz to turn up, then all will be well. Then I'll call you at once.'

After this radio conversation, my friends in Camp 2 were simultaneously happy and troubled – troubled and alarmed that Franz had not come back yet. Their worries were, nevertheless, not so great because Andi and Horst were in good form. We all believed that Franz would soon be found.

I waited in vain – thirty minutes, forty-five minutes, an hour. They didn't come. Time and again I crawled out of the tent, to call, to help guide them in. In doing so, I went no more than 5m away, so that I could still recognize the tent's outline.

I was in despair, exhausted and frozen. Inside the tent the snow already lay several inches deep. The lamp, which I had hung outside the entrance, had to be wiped clean every ten minutes because the light shone only dully through its coating of snow.

Every half-hour our expedition leader Wolfgang Nairz came on the air from Camp 2. Still I could give him no positive answer. We weighed all the possibilities, hoped that the others had dug themselves a snow-hole, so that the three of them could warm each other up.

We considered why Franz had not been in the tent when I arrived at Camp 4 and came up with only two reasons. The first possibility was that Franz had reached the tent but quitted it later on account of the snowstorm in the hope of being able to lead me in. In so doing he must have lost direction and wandered aimlessly like I did around the big plateau. The second possibility was that, while descending, Franz had wanted to wait for me, as Otto Kempter had waited for Hermann Buhl on Nanga Parbat in 1953 – and that he had been surprised by the storm.

Then Bulle's voice came over the radio from Camp 2.

'Of course, we don't know how things are with Franz and the others but if possible you must come down somehow to Camp 3 tomorrow. At all events, Wolfi and I are climbing up early again to Camp 3 to arrange everything there. How far you can get down from Camp 4 by yourself, I don't think one can decide right now, we must discuss it tomorrow. Over!'

'I can make it without the others, at least I think so. But how things will be with Franz I can't say. If things are really bad, we may well have to rope him down. For that we may need some Sherpas. Over!'

'We'll discuss that tomorrow early on the climb. There's also the following problem: Andi already complained up there that his feet were numb. If he spends the whole night outside, the consequences can be bad. I don't know about Horst. But we shall see. If possible, everybody should come down to Camp 3 for proper treatment.'

Then Wolfi came on again.

'Reinhold, meanwhile you can sleep in peace again, I'll wake you with the squawk in half or three-quarters of an hour to see what's going on. Over!'

'Understood, I'll leave the radio on receive. Out.'

I lay in the tent, troubled, head covered up, so that the snow, which would press in through the window, would not touch my face. In my thoughts I was with Franz, Andi and Horst outside in the stormy night. Towards midnight, Wolfi called me again.

'Nothing new', was all I could say.

The whole night the storm raged across the high plateau, blew away rocks, excavated ice towers, filled hollows and choked everything. So much snow fell that the plateau was completely changed in the morning and the tent scarcely still showed above it.

After Franz, Andi and Horst had remained outside hour after hour, my friends in the lower camps and I had assumed that the three of them were sitting in bivy bags in a snow-hole. They would wait until morning, when they would find the way back to the tent more easily. Until 2 a.m. we were in hourly radio contact.

In the morning Horst came back. Alone. Our worst fears had come true!

As Horst stood alone in front of the tent, I could not work out what had happened during the night. The weather had seemed to improve. The storm had abated but it was still howling.

Horst let himself fall inside the tent. I shook him with all my strength, shouted in his ear, held a mug of hot tea for him but he was unable to drink. Shortly afterwards – Horst had closed the zip on the door – I noticed that he was very sad. Then he began to talk. His snow-covered face looked tired, his eyes were red . . .

After Andi and Horst had left the tent to look for Franz, they marched in the direction of Manaslu summit. The storm had briefly become bearable. Again they heard Franz's voice but could not find him. After a short while the storm increased anew, their faces were iced up but they did not think of returning to camp for the time being.

They felt afterwards that they had climbed for some hours. On account of the strengthening storm they had meanwhile lost Franz's calls and, when they wanted to return to Camp 4, this was impossible. The storm and the onset of night prevented it. Their only chance of surviving in this inferno was a snow-cave.

In order to protect themselves to some extent against the force of nature, they dug a hole in the snow. Inside, the biting cold was a little more bearable. Horst massaged Andi to warm him up. Nevertheless, Andi pressed ever more strongly for finding the tent. In vain Horst attempted to dissuade him from this dangerous undertaking as Andi was already suffering rather from the cold conditions.

After a long time, in which Horst had tended to Andi and massaged him, Andi entreated him to look for Camp 4 with him. Andi was longing for tea and his warm sleeping bag. After much insistence, Horst gave in. They quitted the snow-cave and went out into the still-raging storm. In the meantime they had completely lost their sense of direction. In addition, there came stinging pain in the face, wind tearing at shreds of clothes, icy beards and gummed-up eyes which stayed open without seeing.

After a long and desperate wander around, Horst realized that searching further would mean their certain end. Once more Horst persuaded Andi to crawl into a snow-cave and to wait there until morning.

Andi stopped insisting and so they dug a second snow-cave, for they couldn't find the first one again. With the last of his strength, Horst burrowed in the snow. It was a superhuman exertion. They hid in the cave and again Horst tried to warm up Andi with his body. Andi was completely apathetic, exhausted by the horrors of the past hours.

They spent approximately two hours in the icy hole. Horst looked after Andi again, as before – he was still extremely weak and rather cold. Once Andi spoke of Hildegard, his wife, then again of the Sherpas. He was shaking. As in a dream he saw the Sherpas in front of the rising smoke in Base Camp, and heard their prayers which he had never understood. He remembered the stone, on which the sacrificial fire burned and the frequently recurring word in the prayer, 'Manasuli'. When Andi had recovered, after rather a long time, he said to Horst in a clear voice that he wanted to see what the weather was doing. Horst believed that Andi had recovered due to his massaging and was feeling better.

Andi went outside and did not return.

After a short while, Horst began to worry and left the snow-cave. Of Andi there was no trace. Horst's shout was lost in the raging storm. Andi had disappeared. Horst screamed, yet the storm tore the words from his mouth. His face was freshly iced up. He was close to losing his reason and wanted to run out into the night. With an iron will, he forced himself to go back into the snow-cave. Several times more he crawled out; still no trace, no sound, nothing.

He could stand only with difficulty. Now and then he fell at the edge of the snow-cave. 'So this is the end', he thought, 'I shall freeze'.

There was nothing left for him to do but crawl back into the snow-cave. Only there had he a chance of surviving the night. Once more he left the hole to be on the look out for Andi. It was all in vain. If he had distanced himself from the cave in order to look for Andi, it would probably have meant death for both of them.

The rest of the night Horst fought for his own life. 'Just don't fall asleep', he said to himself over and over again. He kept moving about. The night was endless, the storm howled on. He still didn't want to believe that Andi was no longer there.

Minutes became hours, became eternities. The inferno lasted until four o'clock in the morning and still there was no sign of his comrades.

At last day dawned, and the longest and hardest night of his life was over. He had triumphed over sleep and the cold which had never relented. In ever-greater circles, he moved around the cave, looking for a sign of life from Andi. Nothing.

Horst was in despair. The weather had improved so much that he could see enough to descend to Camp 4. He burrowed around in the fresh snow which had fallen during the night.

With the tiny glimmer of hope that Andi might perhaps have reached the tent, he got on with the descent, and after three hours' wading through very deep snow he reached the camp. Now also his last hope was gone, and the last chance was buried ...

It was a miracle that Horst had survived the night. He warmed himself up a bit and drank some tea. Only because of his conscientious preparation and his fully developed abilities, as well as his clear and logical thinking in life-threatening situations, had he withstood this white hell.

Now he told me why he and not one of the others had come up to Camp 4, to cover our retreat.

Retreat from the Manaslu face in the snowstorm.

Camp 4 at a height of 7,400m. The snowstorm had abated; Andi Schlick and Franz Jäger lay buried under 2m of new snow.

Because of his cracking good form, Horst had come up from Camp 2 to Camp 3 on the morning of 25 April. After a short rest, he continued climbing with Andi up the ice face to Camp 4. Only he could have done it. Hans Hofer and Hansjörg Hochfilzer didn't feel well on this particular day and gladly handed over to Horst. Later in the day the pair descended to Base Camp to recover.

'In Camp 3 I loaded up with another can of fuel', reported Horst. 'We came up the ice face swiftly. Half-way up the weather suddenly deteriorated and the Sherpa turned back. We reached the tent in the late afternoon. The weather had deteriorated further, and the storm whistled and threatened to rip the tent to shreds. I secured the tent with a rope and ski sticks rammed deep into the snow. Then you arrived.'

On this morning the Sherpas had prayed in all the camps and throughout the night they had chanted: 'Manasuli, Manasuli . . .'

The cook in Base Camp knew nothing of the tragedy as he piled up the brushwood for the daily sacrificial fire on the stone in front of the kitchen. He did it as always and the kitchen boy repeated the prayers: 'Manasuli, Manasuli . . .'

Horst then reported over the radio everything that had happened. All the expedition members, who had hoped so very much for a happy outcome, particularly Wolfi, were shocked.

Shortly after the radio conversation, the storm diminished. The wind abated, it became bright, cold and then even windless. Only on the western edge of the sky over the Annapurna range hung a narrow, dark streak.

Half an hour later, with Horst partially recovered, the sun was shining again in the valley. The mist had evaporated and I went once more around the tent. Then we began immediately with the search. The layer of snow with which the plateau was covered seemed to be bottomless. The wind-blown waves were often 2m high, the hillocks were swept clean and the hollows were filled.

'I came down from up there', said Horst, pointing eastwards.

I could see no track. It was cold. There were walls of snow standing on the plateau. No track. The tent was covered, everything was completely covered.

We walked and walked. In our down clothing we looked like astronauts. We searched but found no sign of our friends. So we continued searching. The sun shone, it was icy cold with clouds in the south and west again. We were tired by the time we found ourselves in the middle of the plateau. In this white desert we were the only dark points.

As we moved from north to south, the wind blew in our faces. We could not recognize the tent. Half-way through the snow field was a deep trench – our track. The snow was like fine sand.

We had been on the go for some hours and there was still no trace of the absentees. We had been around the search area twice but saw nothing except hollows and snow humps. Yet we knew they must lie there somewhere – so we trudged on in order to find them.

We did not find them.

And so we went on searching. We had been over every ridge twice, yet we said to ourselves, wherever they may be, we must find them. From where we had been poking about in a snow mound, we moved across vast flats. Still we saw nothing in particular and were dead tired.

Nevertheless, we climbed upwards a long way, as far as the South-West Ridge; we didn't find anything there either. Finally we gave up and went back down to camp.

I thought of Andi. He must have died towards the morning. Before anyone could help him, the storm and cold had worn him out. He must have been completely hypothermic and in a trance, like a sleep-walker. All his instincts were directed towards the search for Franz. He would first have been conscious of the approach of death when he no longer heard Franz. He had left the cave in the snow and the raging hurricane had swallowed him up.

Franz must have died hours before Andi did. He must have waited for me and frozen to death, even though he had given up the summit for worrying about exposure. Before we separated he had promised me he would make some tea and keep it warm for my return. Like Andi, he also died in the hope of being able to help a friend.

When the tent came in sight, I looked back once more. I didn't want to accept that the two of them had vanished for ever. The snow gleamed brightly.

Then we noticed something which looked like a body and was buried under the snow. We went back again. As we approached, something dark rose out of the bright surface. Yet when we got there, only a sastrugi lay before us ... We were very sad.

Laboriously we burrowed our way back. I had a frightful thirst and imagined I saw water. I saw it as a lake with neither beginning nor end; I saw it flowing from wells; I saw it in earthenware pots and jugs. We marched in the direction of the tent, making a deep trench in the snow and having to sit down frequently.

I lay in the snow getting my breath back. Then I stood up, took some more deep breaths and pressed forward once more. Two, three paces. We sat and moved, moved and sat. I pushed my legs in front of me and kept balance with my ice axe. I couldn't see my boots because they were swimming in the snow. My breeches were encrusted with it.

At midday – we were still searching – the weather worsened again and, as there was no question of assistance from Camp 3, we had to go down. At each rest stop I thought I would never make it to the tent. Time and again I stood up and we moved three paces, just three paces. When we sat down again, the tent was still endlessly far off.

At last we arrived back at Camp 4. I glanced inside and burrowed amongst the snow and bits of clothing, perhaps in order to find something important. But I found nothing, not even my second anorak. I crawled outside. The cloud bank in the south was coming ever nearer and there were many shadows on the great, white expanse. I looked for ski sticks but there was none. Again and again we looked across the snow slopes. One could have seen a person from miles away as the air was so clear and the snow so white.

A rope hung from the tent. I uncoiled it and we roped up for the descent. I heard the tent flapping in the wind.

When I thought about my time up here, it seemed long to me – about a month – as so much had happened.

The slope to Camp 3 was covered with new snow. We traversed it and were heartily glad that no avalanche came down. I felt all done in when I thought about our dead friends. We waded downwards, rested, waded on.

Carefully the others watched our progress through binoculars, as the weather got worse and worse.

On the one hand we were happy that the expedition leadership had ordered our descent. An even longer stay up above in this bad weather could have led to further tragedy. On the other hand, we were depressed because the search for our friends had been unsuccessful.

On the ice slope between Camps 3 and 4 there was a frightening amount of fresh snow and our companions were afraid that something else might happen.

After hours of wading through very deep snow, we finally approached Camp 3 and were welcomed there by Josl Knoll. He had kept constant watch on our descent. When he saw that we were well on the way down, he came towards us and helped break trail. We were grateful for this assistance. In Camp 3, he and Urkien took charge of us in a touching way. Urkien, our Sirdar, supplied us with drinks while Josl examined our frostbite. He massaged Horst's feet and managed to get them warm again.

Sitting on the air mattress, my frozen hand on my knees, I contemplated Urkien who, with hands full of items of clothing, fetched tea for us. In his haste to help he burned his fingers when he tried to lift the can from the cooker without a cloth. Although ultimately neither of us could drink, this selfless readiness to help left behind in me the deepest impression. It seemed to me as if I had become an old man in these few days.

After some hours when Horst and I were sufficiently recovered so that we could contemplate a further descent, Josl accompanied us down to Camp 2. There Wolfi and Bulle were waiting for us. A few days later, Bulle wrote up his diary:

> When one visualizes their long and hard route, the pair of them, although they were exhausted, were in astonishingly good shape. After they had recovered somewhat, I took care of their frostbite myself. Both had second-degree frostbite but the prognosis was favourable in that the damage only dated back about twelve to twenty-four hours, so that with intensive therapy much could be saved. I administered intravenous injections to Reinhold's and Horst's arms and legs for their condition.

Fortunately this led later to a complete healing of our injuries.

Horst and I lay next to Bulle in the tent. Although our doctor was sick himself, with high-altitude pulmonary oedema, he exerted himself touchingly for us.

That night the storm began again and continued for ten days . . .

# THE STYLE MUST BE ALTERED, NOT THE GOAL

After my second eight-thousander expedition had also ended in tragedy, I was determined not to repeat this sort of climbing. I would go alone or with a small team, and only then to the summit if each would bear the risk himself. The blitzkrieg assault on the summit from the middle of the face that we had adopted on Nanga Parbat and Manaslu was obviously too dangerous with teams and therefore irresponsible.

I had led neither the Nanga Parbat Rupal Face expedition nor that on Manaslu South Face myself. Nevertheless, I felt myself co-responsible.

In 1973 I failed in an attempt to climb Nanga Parbat solo; I also failed in 1974 on a classic-style expedition to the unclimbed South Face of Makalu. Finally, in 1975, I received permission for a small expedition to climb Gasherbrum I (Hidden Peak) in the Karakoram, via the North-West Face.

I invited the Zillertal guide Peter Habeler as the only other member of my party, assembled 200kg of expedition luggage and worked out some completely new logistics. After the approach march, two to four weeks' acclimatization at Base Camp and observation of the face, I decided that I wanted to climb to the summit with Peter and back in one go, without preparing the route and without outside assistance.

This mini-expedition cost less money and time than the classic, large-scale expeditions. It was, however, full of unknowns. Today, now that this style has found many imitators, we have accumulated new experiences and know that alpine-style is not only sportier but can also be safer than the unwieldy expedition-style.

Meanwhile, the South Face of Manaslu has often been repeated via our route, with and without oxygen. To date (1989) no one has succeeded in repeating our route up the Rupal Face of Nanga Parbat; neither in expedition-style nor in alpine-style.

Nanga Parbat 1970: 'Frantic on the Diamir Glacier'.
*Overleaf*: Manaslu 1972 – 'The greatest ice desert in the world'.

Up to ten ice avalanches an hour often swept over the gigantic hanging glacier on the lower part of the Manaslu face.

Hidden Peak 1975: 'Nirvana'.

The 1972 expedition team in Base Camp on the Thulagi Glacier. From left to right: Josef Knoll, Dr Oswald Oelz, Andreas Schlick, Hansjörg Hochfilzer, Hans Hofer, Franz Jäger; in front: Horst Fankhauser and Wolfgang Nairz.

Day after day the Sherpas carried heavy rucksacks up the rock pillar on the lower part of the Manaslu face, secured with fixed ropes.

Starting the ascent of the South Face for the last time. All the Sherpas and sahibs extended themselves fully to make the expedition a success.

*Top left*: Camp I (6,000m) of the 1975 Italian Lhotse Expedition, in the classic Himalaya style. *Top right*: In contrast to that, the tiny second bivouac (7,100m) by Messner and Habeler a few weeks later on Hidden Peak; Masherbrum is behind to the right. *Below left*: Reinhold Messner and Peter Habeler on their lonely way to Hidden Peak in front of the backdrop of Baltoro Kangri. *Bottom right*: The approach march to Lhotse required 600 porters; Island Peak is in the background.

From Askole, the last village on the approach march to Hidden Peak, it is still a good 100km to Base Camp: glacier streams, bivouacs under the open sky, a sea of rubble and ice, fascinating peaks.

Skilfully the local Balti porters traversed the dangerous rocks above the rushing Braldo River.

Base Camp (5,100m) on the Abruzzi Glacier: in the background is the West Buttress of Hidden Peak.

A dozen porters accompanied the Messner expedition for twelve days from Skardu to Base Camp. They needed eight days to return.

When the angle of the face permitted, Reinhold Messner filmed the ascent of the North Face of Hidden Peak.

The tiny tent – Perlon outside, silk inside and weighing 3kg – which Messner and Habeler carried up the 1,200m high face as far as 7,100m. Here they spent the last night before their summit assault. During the night after their descent, the storm tore it to pieces.

# Gasherbrum I – Hidden Peak

## THE CHALLENGE: AN EIGHT-THOUSANDER ALPINE-STYLE

On 5 August 1975 I was sitting in Base Camp at the foot of Hidden Peak feeling sad. Since the flight from Munich four weeks earlier, I had heard nothing from my wife, Uschi. As I lay in the tent during the bad weather, often for hours, and brooded over what we wanted here and why we had set out for Hidden Peak, I found no answer. But if I gave up asking myself these questions, and read or walked some way up the mountain over the rubbish-lined moraines, suddenly everything seemed clear and self-evident. I knew it was just because I was doing something, doing it with a conscious aim and was waiting tensely for our first summit assault.

Here the weather seemed to have a regular rhythm; three to four days bad, three to four days good. It was clear to us that we must utilize the next fine-weather period for our decisive attempt. Our rucksacks were ready. Time and again we had emptied and repacked them. A pound too much could have cost us success, a trifle too little likewise.

Peter and I had to carry everything ourselves, placing no fixed ropes on the face and with no prepared high camp waiting for us. On our two reconnaissances we had determined the final route of ascent, but as yet we had not set foot on the face itself.

I struggled to my feet and stepped out of the tent. As I looked around inquiringly, I found that the summits of Gasherbrum II and Hidden Peak had emerged from the mist. Would the weather improve? Could we set off as early as tomorrow? Back in my sleeping bag, I looked at the time: no, set off today, for it was already after midnight.

The first light of the morning snatched me from my dreams. Time to set off!

The glacier was still fairly quiet. The streams, which during the day gurgled through all the crevasses in the sunshine and leaped over ice walls, were now frozen. The avalanche runnels were not yet dangerous and the serac faces were as firm as concrete walls. No icicles broke off without us touching them.

The only sounds which we made as we began to climb the lower ice-fall were the soft creaking of our boot soles on the firmly frozen snow and the swish of our protective leggings rubbing together. All the crevasses were uncovered, and we knew the way so well from our two reconnaissance trips that we could risk climbing unroped. To start with, Peter brought up the rear and I climbed ahead, paying scrupulous attention so as not to lose the correct route.

Reinhold Messner on the summit of Hidden Peak (8,068m); Masherbrum is in the background.

I looked up at the stars which were partly fading already and partly still twinkling coldly. It promised to be a beautifully clear day. Soon the dawn gave way to a glassy blue light and already the two summit ridges of Chogolisa were bathed in a warmer colour. Peter and I marched along light-heartedly, although our rucksacks, filled with pitons, ropes, crampons, provisions, cooker and sleeping bags, were heavy; more than 20kg apiece.

We didn't talk and found the silence of the early hour soothing – the quiet of the morning a part of ourselves. The feeling of fear and inevitability that had come over me several times last night had left me completely, and had made way for that matter-of-factness and calm which filled me at the start of every big climb. I felt now the strength of every muscle and, as I climbed quickly from one small step in the ice-fall to the next or when I jumped a crevasse, I felt my self-confidence grow. Effortlessly our legs overcame each rise and stepped out in the flat hollows. I enjoyed it as the ice-cold morning wind blew the last of the sleep out of my beard and hair, not once hindered by the rucksack towering high above my head.

Peter concentrated alternately on the route and on his legs which seemed to be winged. Without ever having thought about it much, I became conscious of how important these simple experiences are at the start of a climb and, with each step, I felt my strength and self-confidence grow still further. I knew, too, that it would not be strength and endurance on which success ultimately depended, rather will-power – the 'last will' – as well as my belief in a goal, that seemed to me now so convincingly near and logical.

Peter had caught up and was standing beside me.

'I think it'll go, Reinhold.'

'Yes, if the weather holds.'

'This time it must.'

I broke off the conversation, which had disturbed my simple sensations, and continued climbing, trying to find my old rhythm again.

Without resting again we climbed several steep ice steps and soon reached the flat basin above the first ice-fall. From there the glacier ascends evenly into the Gasherbrum Valley, bordered to the left and right by mighty rock and ice walls. For a few minutes we took off our rucksacks. A few metres above our resting place a long, broad crevasse crossed the glacier: the first serious danger of the morning. We decided to rope up. I got the 20m rope out of my rucksack, rummaged out my climbing harness and tied on the water repellent Perlon. Peter had done the same.

After this routine procedure, we took up our rucksacks again. Now, for the first time, we noticed how heavy they were. I shook mine to settle the weight and then began to move along the edge of the crevasse on the tightened rope. Peter followed some 20m behind. In the hope of soon finding a place from which I could jump to the other side, we traversed a fair way to the right.

Peter and I had shared out equally between us the few pitons and ice screws which we had brought, so that each could have freed himself from the crevasse and also been able to belay the other at any time. For us it was a matter of course – a long-standing tacit agreement – that we would alternate the lead, that first I then Peter climbed ahead, and that each was ready to take on the work of leading as well as of belaying.

Hidden Peak from the
north.

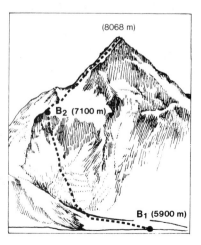

The Messner–Habeler
route: B1 = first bivouac,
B2 = second bivouac.

51

By now it was seven o'clock. The sun shone, as it did only on crystal-clear days, like an enormous bright wedge on the upper Gasherbrum Valley. In doing so, it struck the East Face of Gasherbrum V and it was not long before the first avalanches began to thunder down. Peter and I were still moving in the shade and I hesitated briefly before I ventured to leap the 2m wide crevasse. As a precaution, Peter had previously distanced himself some way from the edge, rammed his ice axe into the hard, frozen snow and promised to pay out the rope carefully without jerking it. The moment I touched the opposite side, I threw myself forwards, so that I could get a hold in the snow with my axe immediately. In this way I would have been able to hold on if my jump had been a little short. The crevasse seemed to be bottomless. Brittle ice hung from its walls and it made me shiver involuntarily as I bent forwards to peer into it. Then I moved back a few metres from the edge, rammed the shaft of my axe into the snow, took in the rope and belayed Peter as he jumped.

We continued upwards, still in the shade. During the day and in sunshine these glacier valleys were exceedingly dangerous. New crevasses suddenly opened up, ice towers collapsed and breaking trail was much harder than in the early morning hours. As long as the sun had not softened the snow, climbing was not a grind; just here and there we sank in ankle-deep. Generally, however, the snow was so hard that our soles only scratched it lightly and left scarcely a mark behind. There was no need to put on crampons for there were only a few patches of bare ice showing through the upper surface and we always went around them in time.

We were approximately in the middle of the gently rising expanse of snow when the first rays of the sun struck us. The light was very glaring and it hurt our eyes so that we had to put on our goggles before we could carry on climbing.

At first we kept to our old direction, then we curved to the right between huge serac towers and located the right-hand edge of the ice-fall. There we traversed – as we had done on our reconnaissance trips – a steep, somewhat avalanche-prone slope and reached the Gasherbrum Valley where we wanted to bivouac.

We had the time and strength to climb further up the Gasherbrum Valley as far as directly under the North-West Face of Hidden Peak, but we preferred to spend the night at our accustomed campsite. There we knew the wind, knew that the basin was safe from avalanches and also knew that in really bad conditions we could get back to Base in quick time.

The sun was fierce and burning hot on the roof of our tent, so that we had to cover it with sleeping bags. We had partly unpacked our rucksacks and left them standing outside the tent.

Peter had such a bad headache that he lay down, took a pain-killer and tried to sleep. For hours the awful throbbing pain in his head tormented him, affecting not only his speech but also his breathing. He lay there mutely, staring at the tent roof and groaning.

Meanwhile, I tried to make tea in a small aluminium pot and had trouble fixing the gas cooker so that the water didn't spill. I gave Peter some of the hot drink and he sipped it slowly. Then he tried to sleep again but neither tea nor lying quietly relieved his pain.

A strong inner unrest let him forget it later for some moments as, feeling helpless and lonely, he dozed off to sleep. I must have slept for a while too. We didn't wake up until the sun had gone down behind Gasherbrum V and it was getting cold in the tent.

Peter's headache had gone and he was again ready for action, raring to go and convinced that our undertaking must succeed. The sun blinked through the gap between Gasherbrum V and IV and shone like a beam on the summit of Hidden Peak.

We had some more tea. Later, outside the tent once more, we emptied our rucksacks, checked everything again and repacked. Some things which we thought we didn't absolutely need – such as spare gas cartridges, some provisions and several rock pitons – we left behind in the campsite. We got the two rucksacks ready, each weighing about 13kg.

Yet, with the rucksacks packed, our ice axes stuck in the snow and the uncoiled rope hanging over the tent entrance, we could not relax. My thoughts moved to and fro between joyful expectation and a vague uneasiness about the exertions and dangers of the coming days. Side by side we stood in the cold evening wind under the no longer radiant sky, which seemed to become brighter all the while.

When we returned to the tent it was already late evening and the sun had vanished. We made ourselves as comfortable as possible in the narrow tent and brewed some more tea. Drinking was now more important than everything else. We had to tank up enough liquid for the morrow, for during the day there wouldn't be any. It would have taken too much energy and time to carry along water or tea in our rucksacks.

For a while I watched over Peter's shoulder as he cooked, wielding pans and spoons. The soup was hot and very salty; the bread that we ate with it was so hard that it cracked as we chewed it. A Villnöss farmer had given it to me before our departure, as provisions for the summit. This home-made farm bread was light, nutritious and satisfying – ideal for an eight-thousander.

As we ate, we chatted, mutually encouraging each other and strengthening ourselves in the expectation that during the next day we would put the hardest part of the face behind us. Success depended now only on our fitness and whether we were sufficiently acclimatized. Our technical climbing abilities must suffice to do the face. In the Alps, albeit at much lower altitude, we had already conquered far more difficult faces.

We were both quite conscious that with this ascent we were breaking new ground. Neither of us previously had tried to tackle such a high peak without every support from below, and even if the technical climbing difficulties were no more than had to be overcome on other expeditions or Alpine ascents, we were completely dependent upon ourselves. We had no moral support from a ground team, much less the medical care of a doctor or the slightest hope that someone would rescue us if anything went wrong.

The middle part of the North Face of Hidden Peak is frighteningly steep, as steep perhaps as the North Face of the Matterhorn. When Peter and I thought about it, and thought that possibly we would find friable rock up there, we were not so sure that our courage would suffice to climb it. An experienced and well-trained mountaineer can climb a face on brittle rock as long as it isn't overhanging, and he can use the hand- and foot-holds as pressure holds. His instinct prevents him from pulling on a shaky hold or moving out of balance, at least as long as he keeps moving and doesn't climb to and fro jerkily.

We both knew that and had often practised it, yet we asked ourselves now whether we would succeed in putting this technique, which in the Alps we could do with our eyes shut, to use at 7,000m or 8,000m above sea-level. Up there not only technical climbing skill counted; it was primarily a matter of endurance and will-power. In other words, that toughness which, when paired with self-confidence, helps to endure this last limitless loneliness. Important as it was now to estimate the difficulties and steepness of the face, to focus on the emotional drain and all the possible surprises, it would be just as important the next day to wangle our way up the face from stance to stance, and to find the correct route. Even though we had decided the ascent route in outline, if there were a way up this face it lay with us to read it bit by bit the next day on the face, and to find exactly where we wanted to go and where the next usable, firm hold was.

This instinct for the right route was one of Peter's strengths as well as mine. Perhaps we are no better climbers than many others. Certainly, we had a great deal of experience, more than a dozen good mountaineers put together, but that was not decisive. As we had both been climbing for twenty-five years already, we had gradually acquired a sleep-walker-like security, a sort of instinct which did not fail us even in shock or exhaustion. However, what we had over the others to a high degree was the team-work of experience and ability, plus a mutual trust which was virtually limitless.

No false step or miscalculation might be allowed to creep in during the next few days, for every mistake could have led unquestionably to death, each wrong appraisal to demoralization and with that to failure. On an Alpine climb one usually grazes a knee or elbow in a fall, perhaps cannons off somewhere or breaks a leg. At 7,000m and above that is not the end of it. Every fall would trigger not only a dangerous shock but at the same time a considerable weakening. And even without injury, one would not be capable of rescuing the other, much less of carrying him down. If only the slightest thing happened, we were caught in the trap.

I thought of all that as I lay in the tent and tried to fall asleep. The fact that I could think these things through to the end without being afraid of them was a sign that my self-confidence was very strong, and that Peter was the best possible partner for this bold undertaking.

The route on which Peter and I had decided lies somewhat to the east of the fall line of that ice bulge which springs out from the lowest part of the North-West Face. It was, in our opinion, the only justifiable line and at the same time the most direct line.

It was far enough. We dumped our rucksacks in the snow, put on our crampons and roped up. Although the sun was shining on the projecting rock crag in the middle of the face, the gullies were still quiet, so we had nothing to fear from a stone-fall. Only later as I coiled up the rope and hung it from an ice screw in the middle of an ice bulge, did some pieces of rock and ice come leaping down the Gasherbrum Face. Hissing, they plunged into the snow at the start of the climb. The snow surface below the bergschrund was flat and free of crevasses, so that we could move to and fro unhindered. Our boot soles only scratched a few millimetres into the hard snow, and moving was not especially strenuous for the time being.

In the Gasherbrum Valley we had progressed quickly and it had been splendid to see how the sun had slowly flooded the walls to the left of us. The view which was now offered us was breathtaking: we were standing immediately between two eight-thousanders.

Peter and I moved a few steps, then he offered me a piece of chocolate and we stopped once more to tighten the straps on our crampons.

Peter Habeler.

There was a constant noise that resonated everywhere. During the past hours, as we had been marching through the slightly wavy Gasherbrum Valley, this sort of humming had increased more and more in strength. Our regular paces did not disturb it, and only when we spoke with each other when resting, did it fall silent. This noise did not come from the wind, nor out of the suddenly opening crevasses, rather out of the mountain itself. Out of everything around us, out of the snow and ice and rock, and out of the air which now as before seemed firmly frozen in the narrow valley.

I had been fascinated on earlier expeditions time and again by noises of this sort. Yet never before had this noisy silence of the grave, this accompanying tone of loneliness, made me feel so calm. Fully conscious of the exertions and dangers of our ascent, I was now neither anxious nor excited, but rather confident and completely filled by that noise which seemed to carry me along.

I looked at Peter to see if he sensed it as well. His movements revealed that he was in his element and completely confident. Only his face was pensive and his eyes blinked somewhat nervously. One could see that he was full of tension, body and soul.

With some mountaineers, the mountain experience obliterates all other sensations. For them there is no tension and no fear, no yesterday and no tomorrow, when they are climbing. While they are on a face, nothing roundabout exists for them; neither the valley below nor their life in the valley, simply nothing. This satisfaction and lack of concern takes me over too when I climb and when I succeed at it.

As long as we had been marching through the Gasherbrum Valley, the world had seemed to consist of nothing but the snow beneath my feet, the faces which towered up

55

steeply to left and right. There were still my ice axe, rucksack and rhythm, which I must not lose. But now, standing as we were at the true foot of the face and preparing ourselves for the ascent, my normal fears and worries set in again. Perhaps the ensuing days would bring bad weather? The weather could change suddenly and unexpectedly here and it would have been infinitely strenuous and difficult to find a way back in mist and fresh snow. We would need at least a day to climb down the face above us and two to three days to get back through the ice-fall to Base Camp if the weather changed. Also, the fact that it was now beamingly beautiful and the air calm did not exclude a turn around in the weather in five, seven or ten hours.

At the moment, certainly, we were still much too near our first bivouac to be really afraid. Here and now it would have been easy with the onset of bad weather to put into effect the decision to return to Base Camp. Further up, however, this would be much, much more difficult. In the event of avalanche danger, naturally we would have to stop and wait. Then we wouldn't have been able to climb back down the steep face. Added to which, higher up, weather changes came much faster and the storms were more powerful. Perhaps the weather would hold, however, until we were up. At great height, where often it can be months, perhaps even years, until a warm, still day guarantees a danger-free ascent, one must be more deliberate and at the same time more determined than in the Alps.

Meanwhile, we had adjusted our crampons for the third time and checked our equipment again. Everything was in order. We picked up our rucksacks, took our axes in our hands and with regular, calm steps approached the actual foot of the face.

If we wanted success, we must now climb swiftly and keep climbing. From the next bivouac site there would be only one chance to make a push for the summit.

'Each to his own pace', said Peter.

I nodded: 'We'll take it in turns to lead.'

'I think we'll make it. If the weather holds for two days, we're on top.'

We changed the lead regularly, with the one in front determining the route. The other followed, using the foot-holds of the leader. In this way the second got a rest in order to be able to break trail on the next stretch. It was not always clear where the best route ran, nevertheless we trusted each other entirely. Conversations were superfluous and would have only hindered our breathing.

Peter's feet protruded out of the bare ice surface above me. The topmost layer of ice was soft enough for the front points of his crampons to penetrate into it as far as his boot caps, and was hard enough for a safe stance — good conditions. The leverage — from the toe of the boot to the heel — was bigger than usual with our three-layered boots and the calf work was enormous.

After twenty-five paces in each case we rested, and Peter cut a few steps in the ice and rammed the shaft of his axe in as soon as he had his right foot on the hold. Only then did he lean his body over the ice, hold fast to his axe, and have a breather. He waited until I had worked up to his ledge and then climbed on the next twenty-five paces.

'What's the ice like with you?', I called up.

'It's getting better, firm snow; but the rocks look bad.' Peter was thinking now of the brittle band above him.

I had already seen from below that there were brighter patches on the face.

Arriving on the stance, I pushed some snow crystals into my mouth, leaned against my rammed in axe and rested.

I had always foreseen that Peter was the ideal man for great altitudes, and now he was furnishing me with the proof. He climbed as tenaciously and as surely as a sleep-walker, prudently and regularly even when tiring. I was convinced that nothing would happen to him and, so far as a route to the top was concerned, that he would find it.

'Do you want to rest?', asked Peter. 'We can stand here alright.'

'No, I'd rather keep going', I countered. 'As long as the ice face isn't in the sun, we should make use of it.'

Peter was in complete agreement. Even if the danger of a stone-fall was never wholly absent, in the morning hours when the stones were still frozen in high above our heads the face was safer than in the afternoon. We did not want to invite danger.

In the warmth of the midday sun and little by little, pieces of ice, rock and scree were beginning to work free, and already the first lumps were skipping down the slightly concave face in great bounds. The ways of the stone-fall were incalculable. We were constrained in our movements by the steepness of the face and could not dodge out of the way quickly. There was nothing we could do except wait until the buzzing projectiles were directly overhead, then twist out of their line of fire.

In the Alps one would normally climb such a face at night to minimize the stone-fall risk. But here it was too cold at night and we probably would not have been able to find the ideal route.

Had we stopped to consider the position in which we found ourselves, we would have been in despair. How tiny and lonely two people on an eight-thousander are! However, step by step we climbed unremittingly upwards, concentrating only on the twenty-five pace pitches between one rest stop and the next, rather than on the whole summit wall.

'We must have done 200m', I estimated.

'Yes, perhaps even 250m.'

I sensed from Peter's words that he too was satisfied with our speed. Nonetheless, we would need at least eight to ten hours to the next bivouac. The face became ever steeper and overhangs arched out far above our heads, seeming to bar every path to the summit. But – and we knew this from our observations from the Gasherbrum Valley – above these rocks there was a flat place on which we could erect our tent. Below us the face fell extremely steeply, and above us it soared up without any sizeable terraces or ledges. If only the snow cover did not get any thicker. Trail-breaking was far more strenuous than climbing on bare ice.

I attempted to photograph Peter, who was now climbing below me obliquely to the right but it wouldn't work out well. After I had replaced the camera equipment with difficulty in its foil-lined, sailcloth bag, I looked down at Peter once more. Fantastic, I thought, simply fantastic, the way he's coming up there. That I must film, this scene must be in!

'Hold on!', I called, although Peter was badly placed. 'That looks absolutely terrific!'

It was not only awkward but dangerous getting the camera out of the rucksack and shooting film. I must not lose my balance and for that reason I leaned against the face somewhat. The smallest slip of my right foot, which was standing on a hand-sized notch, or the slightest swaying of my body and I ran the danger of plunging irretrievably down the face.

Very slowly but steadily we made progress. The twenty-fifth pace, the last before the rest stop, sometimes seemed pure hell but after a few minutes' breather we climbed on each time. Now we had more than half of the first rise behind us. If we were as fast on the second half, we would reach the bivouac site above the brittle band by evening.

Thus we were able to carry on, edging our way upwards. Constantly changing the lead, mutually encouraging ourselves, bit by bit we put the face behind us. Sometimes we climbed one at a time, often we climbed at the same time, one behind the other.

Perhaps it was only our mutual trust that allowed us to forego the customary safety measures of rope and pitons. Perhaps it was also our obsession with the idea of two men on an eight-thousander, which was somewhat responsible for this extravagant climbing style. In the first place, however, it was the instinctive knowledge that, in the given circumstances, we were not capable of carrying the necessary ropes and pitons for a textbook belay. Probably ours was the only method for two people to reach the summit via the face. With confidence it was less dangerous than it might have looked from below to outsiders.

Suddenly some lumps of snow hit my left hand with which I was supporting myself on the ice. That told me that something must have happened and I looked up at Peter. He was swearing because a foot-hold had broken but was climbing on again already. Without the slightest set-back on account of this small mishap Peter had found his rhythm again at once. He was climbing so that he would not lose his balance if any one of the three fixed points, which we used with every movement, suddenly failed. As long as we had two firm holds we would not fall, yet we endeavoured, nevertheless, always to have three fixed points on every new move.

Meanwhile we had arrived directly below the rock step which blocked the face at 6,900m. We deliberated as to where we could best tackle it and spotted some gullies which ran out of the concave ice field like spiders' legs into the broken rock. After we had rested on some broader snow steps which we had scraped out of the slope with our crampons, I attempted to climb up the first rock rise. The rock was terribly friable but not wholly vertical, so that for the most part I could put pressure on the foot- and hand-holds. After a few moves it was already clear to me that I would have to take off my gloves and I located a somewhat sloping but large foot-hold, on which it was possible to stand without support. First of all I took off my left glove, stuck it in the breast pocket of my anorak, then I took off my right glove.

With bare hands I got a hold in a narrow crevice. The rock was cold but not so icy that one's fingers stuck to it, as was the case with the ice-axe shaft or karabiners – an unpleasant feeling. Every time I pulled my fingers away from my axe I left some skin hanging there.

Peter, who was holding himself on with outstretched arms, watched me attentively. After the initial moves on this broken rock I had shaken off all my inhibitions and was concentrating completely on carrying out a short traverse to the right using two supporting holds. With my hand pressed flat on a faint rock projection and crampon points dug into the gravelly rock, I shifted my weight centimetre by centimetre, only fumbling with my hands again when I believed I could complete a move safely.

Although I was climbing completely free and shaking slightly with the inhuman exertion at this altitude, I was still calm. I was so attached to Peter that I felt myself as secure as if I were moving on the rope. Time and again I had to stick my fists in narrow cracks which were filled with fine snow and inevitably it stuck to my warm skin.

Gradually the cold and snow robbed me of all feeling in my fingers. A longer rest now would have only squandered strength and concentration, so I climbed on, despite the icy lumps which were now my hands. To the right of me I spotted an ice gully which finally promised a resting place where I hoped to be able to put on my gloves again. I was wholly confident that Peter would overcome the pitch safely and gazed at him with the same concentration with which he had previously watched me. There was not the slightest uncertainty in his movements and although he had to grit his teeth on account of the icy cold, not once did a hint of fear show in his face. Instinctively his fingertips found the correct crevices and embraced rock projections, and his centre of gravity, above the front points of his crampons, always stayed put so that he could not slip suddenly.

I took some deep breaths and began to climb up the gully above the rocks, although as yet I did not know where it would go. A quick glance back over my shoulder proved to me that Peter had already finished the traverse and, breathing heavily, was now resting on my previous stance. Forehead pressed against his lower arm, he leaned against the rock wall and took a breather.

Automatically I wondered where, generally speaking, we would have belayed ourselves on this broken rock. Certainly there were cracks to hand but large pitons would have split the rock and smaller ones would not have held.

Meanwhile Peter had fished his gloves out of his pockets and put them on again. His hands no longer hurt, for he had no more feeling in them. He didn't like to say how he had held himself with them on this difficult traverse.

Head back, I gazed upwards: the sky was a matt white on blue ground. There, where it formed the horizon with the mountain chains, the blue was still more blurred. A bright light came from the westwards-inclined snow slopes and it was unbearable to look at the sun directly. Below us the valleys lay in a bluish vapour, already with a touch of violet — an almost magical gleam. Here and there the shades of vapour seemed to seethe as if the earth below were simmering.

It seemed to me as if we were suspended between heaven and earth, with unfathomable distances above and below. We were still 1,200m from the summit, but far more than 2,000m above the bottom of the valleys. My thoughts blurred like the bluish light beneath me; another 200m and we would be safe for the time being!

The gully narrowed more and more into a chimney. With my legs widespread — I now had faith in the rocks — I climbed up the cleft. I could not judge whether I could hold myself anywhere if I were to slip and, as a precaution, I pressed more firmly with my hands against the rising parallel rock walls between which I was climbing. If I slipped just a bit now I would drag Peter off with me. He could never have held a falling body. The chimney narrowed once more which was a piece of luck as we could wedge ourselves better in it.

I climbed up the next gully until I could quit it to the left to a ridge, and via this I reached a shoulder between the North and North-West Faces. Here I rested. A steep snow face rose above me, rocky in part, and with all the hollows filled with wind-drifted snow. It looked as if it might avalanche. I was undecided as to where we ought to continue and for the time being consoled myself with pushing on over the next steep rise towards our bivouac site.

Meanwhile Peter had reached my stance and immediately worked his way up the shoulder to the steep wall. Here he paused to gather fresh strength and also the fresh courage, so to speak, that he needed in order to attempt the initial moves. First of all he stuck his axe in the snow, grasped the pick with his right hand, searched with his left for a firm hand-hold on the rocks which stuck out of the snow like islands, and pulled himself up. His arms trembled with exertion. After seemingly endless seconds he found a small foot-hold with his left crampon under the snow and placed his whole weight on this invisible hold. The snow was loose but not too deep. As fast as the altitude allowed, Peter climbed obliquely upwards to the left, sticking his axe so high up in the snow that, holding firmly to it, he could make three moves in a row each time. This was not wholly without danger.

Meanwhile Peter had reached a rock step and settled himself on it to let me follow. He had performed good work and hoped that we could also use this track on descent.

'Should I go ahead now?', I asked when I had arrived below his resting place. My question came somewhat too late. Peter was already climbing on again above me and his strong movements were still as swift as they had been in the early morning hours.

On this last steep rise a trembling often ran through my legs, especially when I found only tiny rugosities on the rocks with the front points of my crampons on which I had to stand.

From our position neither Peter nor I could see what it was like above us. However, when Peter poked his head over the ridge for the first time, he called down enthusiastically that there was a flat hollow above, an ideal bivouac site. I climbed around the rock projection and reached the foot-hold from which Peter had launched himself on this last slope. Peter's face, radiant with joy on the edge of the ridge revealed that we had done enough climbing for today and that the bivouac site surpassed even his wildest dreams.

The exertion of the 1,200m climb we had made on this day, 9 August, had been enormous. However, now the strain was already gone from Peter's face, although he was no longer moving as effortlessly as he had been at the start of the climb. With the trained eyes of an experienced mountaineer, who always tries to make the best of any situation, he began to search the basin for the flattest place for our bivouac. It didn't take long and we both settled down on a slanting scree patch at a height of 7,100m.

When I had my rucksack comfortably settled behind my head, I stretched instinctively, relaxed and breathed deeply for the first time for several minutes. After a while I looked across at Peter who lay quietly next to me. I wanted to say something to him but he had his eyes shut and it seemed, judging by his expression, that he had no further worries. I closed my eyes too and lay there motionless. At last, after ten hours of intense exertion and concentration, we could simply lie there, completely forgetting the dangerous, steep face below us.

'The worst is behind us', I said after I had turned round and cast a glance up at the summit face.

There were still 1,000m to the highest point but these were less steep than the section of face below us. Also, we had a night ahead of us in which we could rest ourselves.

'We'll be OK here', observed Peter, trying to push away the stones under him with his boots. 'But we can't go back down those rock pitches', he declared decidedly.

'If we can find a gully, we can climb down directly, otherwise we'll have to . . .

Peter interrupted me: 'We should have brought a rope.'

'We'll get down. After the summit we'll get down somehow', I said after a pause, in the complete conviction that we would be able to reverse the rock pitch free if there was no other possibility.

Peter was not entirely happy at the prospect of the descent but said no more about it. In the meantime he had taken off his crampons and, still squatting, was busying himself with building a platform. He placed the bigger stones at the front edge of the scree patch and then pushed the small ones about with his feet, levelling and enlarging the platform for the tent. I helped him as best I could, using the same technique. We didn't have the strength to stand up.

'You're in great form', I said to Peter.

He was evidently satisfied with himself and knew that he had considered and carried out every move safely. He also felt that his strength would suffice to reach the summit. This was the highest he had ever been and, although he was again plagued with a headache, he continued to scrape the scree to the front edge of the platform.

Turning to me, he said casually: 'Tomorrow we shall be on top. If we take only essentials we shall be faster even than today. I think I shall leave my rucksack too.'

'So shall I, but I'm taking the camera as far as I can lug it. However, I'm not giving up the summit on its account.'

'If only I didn't have these damned headaches!'

'Is it bad?'

'It always is when I reach a new height and sit around.'

Peter, who until now had been sitting calmly on the platform, now peered, face contorted with pain and fear, down into the Gasherbrum Valley in which already the first shadows lay. His cheerfulness had vanished. He spoke no more, seemingly completely lost in thought and very cold. The sudden and unusually severe headache was so bad that he was almost sick with it.

I took the tent out of my rucksack, unrolled it, laid it on the platform which we had laboriously prepared, and spread it out. The ground underneath was still a bit lop-sided as the ice, which our excavations had soon come up against, had not allowed us to construct a completely level site. Luckily we had already marked the tent poles down in the valley, so that now we had no difficulty in putting them together correctly.

I had taken on the job of fixing the back of the tent. Peter sat by the entrance and gently massaged his temples; his head seemed about to burst at any moment.

'As soon as the tent is up, you can lie down and get some rest. You must try to get rid of your headache then everything will be OK again. If I know you, you'll be right as rain again tomorrow.'

We anchored the main guy ropes of the tent to some head-sized stones. It stood there somewhat cock-eyed. The walls sagged inwards and the slightest puff of wind made them flutter. As Peter was unpacking his rucksack, I occupied myself in building a cooking place in the lee of the tent.

Every fibre of my body was tired, worn out by the uninterrupted exertion and a tension which had taken over my whole body. The cooking, too, was an effort. My eyes were sore from the constant looking and seeking; and just above, behind my forehead, it felt as if a knot had formed.

It took a long time to melt the ice and almost as long until it was warm enough to make tea. I was now no longer in that condition between sleeping and waking, as had been the case directly after the climb and during the time when we put up the tent, rather I was mentally wide awake. With relish I sipped my tea and stood up frequently to stretch myself. The fatigue slowly melted from my muscles and that knot above my eyes dissolved.

The acute angle at which the brassy coloured rays of the sun were striking the tent indicated the approach of evening. Once more I handed Peter some tea and he swallowed down a second pain-killer, then lay down again. I sat on a pile of stones outside the tent and cooked, melting ice, and brewing soup and tea.

While the cooker buzzed, I gathered up the bits of equipment which lay strewn around the tent and arranged them so that we could put them on or pack them quickly the next morning. After a while I breathed deeply to mobilize all my available strength, pushed myself up off the ground and moved the few paces to the edge of the scree platform. There was no snow there, only ice. I chipped some pieces off and took them to the tent door. Here they would be handy for cooking when we were lying down in the tent in the evening and in the morning.

During all these ceremonies, Peter had at first lain there motionless. He had forgotten that we were camped high on Hidden Peak, that tomorrow was to be the decisive day. Only when his headache had diminished did he feel as if a great weight had been lifted from him. Suddenly he was filled with anticipated joy at the next day – an emotion such as he experienced only before really big climbs. His whole being concentrated now on the coming day, on the clothing which he would wear and on the sequence of moves. Above all he was occupied with the questions of parcelling out his strength and of tactics. He had thrust all private thoughts and feelings aside out of his subconscious.

'What time do we have to set off?', he asked after a while.

'When the sun comes up.'

Everything depended on neither of us being ill, on the weather remaining fine and on us being fast enough to reach the summit by early afternoon. We were agreed that we must be on top by three o'clock at the latest, otherwise we would turn back without making the summit. It would have been imprudent and irresponsible to have continued climbing to the top if our speed had not lived up to expectations. The descent too had to be taken into account and I knew from experience that a night descent from an eight-thousander, with the tiredness and lapse of concentration which are unavoidable up there, always carries great dangers with it.

Peter was cheerful enough all evening yet hardly spoke. He ate little but drank as much as he could and often stared into space. I made no attempt to start up a conversation and when my attention wandered from the forthcoming ascent, I gazed in the direction of Gasherbrum IV on which the sun was now setting.

The 'Brittle Band', a steep rock band between 6,900m and 7,100m, formed the crux on the North-West Face of Hidden Peak.

We didn't feel the cold although with the setting of the sun the last breath of warmth had vanished too. The sky to the west was tinged vermillion and the mountains, which in the morning had been so clear and sharp that we could see even the smallest ridges and gullies, lay buried behind a curtain of haze.

A spot of light focused on the summit of Hidden Peak as I forced my way fully clothed into the tent. Breathing heavily, I crawled into my sleeping bag, loosened my inner boots and placed a second pair of gloves under my pillow. I pushed my down jacket, a hat and the rucksack under my back and bottom and then pressed myself to one side of the tent so that Peter had space.

The small patch of scree on which we lay was scarcely suitable for a bivouac, but we had decided to make camp in daylight, otherwise we would have run the risk of not finding a site at all. Here the ground was sloping and the place exposed to the wind, but we could walk around the tent unroped and without danger of falling, and that was important.

We lay stretched out in our sleeping bags in the tent. I faced uphill and Peter faced downhill. We had both shoved some items of clothing under our mats so that the tent floor would be less sloping; only this prevented us rolling about all the time.

Alarmingly, it now occurred to me that, when setting up the bivouac, I had been able to place only one ice piton. The tent was fixed to this. All the other guy ropes were attached to loose stones. A better anchorage had simply not been possible. I could not entirely banish from my head the feeling of being carried away together with the tent in a strong storm.

Long before I began to cook for the last time on this evening, the first stars appeared in the ever-darkening sky. Up here it was still not dark although it was already night in the valleys. Naturally we had no idea what the weather forecast was but I was convinced that the next day would be fine.

On the small gas cooker, which I had set up on a rickety rock slab at the entrance to the tent, I brewed one can of tea after another. We drank alternately and without any pleasure, but we drank and had to drink. We had both eaten a few mouthfuls during the late afternoon – dried plums and a little bit of bread – yet we had not the slightest desire for a big evening meal. A sticky, insipid taste filled our dried-out mouths, which even the tea could only suppress for a few minutes. The warm drink helped against thirst and every gulp warmed not only our tummies but also our whole bodies.

With nothing to do in the bivouac for the first time in hours, I tried to recapitulate the day in order to obliterate all other thoughts. I did not succeed.

Open mouthed, Peter lay near me. From his movements I concluded that he was awake. When he slept, his breathing changed into a panting because of the lack of oxygen in the tent. Finger-thick hoar frost clung to the cloth walls.

Scraps of poetry ran through my head: 'With the Gods one should compete . . . With the Gods one should not compete . . . With the Gods . . .' I couldn't get any further. Then: 'Up this empty lane he must come.' Like telegrams, these fragments came into my head like lessons by rote at school.

'One must be free in order to be able to bring something to a peaceful end; free of women, free of material desires, free of fear.' At last a self-contained chain of thought.

What was the time? Maybe 3 a.m., or perhaps 4 a.m.? It was as dark as ever in the tent; outside it was a starry night . . .

We were resting on the 'Sickle'. The hollow, which had looked from the Gasherbrum Valley like a recumbent sickle, was in reality an enormous concave basin, steep and icy. On a tiny platform, which Peter had trodden out in the snow, we were resting for the first time since setting out at eight o'clock in the morning. From the ridge we saw far below us the yellow tent in which we had bivouacked until dawn. The small patch of scree now lay in the sun . . .

Our next rest was by a block which we reached after another twenty-eight paces. Then we climbed up the 'Basin' – technically easy terrain but strenuous. I counted paces again: ten, eleven . . . twenty-four, twenty-five. It only became steep again higher up; that I had already made out from the photographs. Now we kept to the ridge between the North and North-West Faces. After twenty-five to twenty-eight steps each time we were as exhausted as if we had run a record-breaking middle-distance race. And there were still about 200 such pitches to the summit! It was lucky that we had begun climbing so early. We were still low, it was true, but that didn't matter; we were where we were. Our goal was still imaginary but a goal; our will borne up by our belief in success.

Another twenty-five paces with little to see. Only the tips of one's own boots as they pushed into the snow and one's hands. Every step the same, as one recited the same litany: twenty-one, twenty-two . . .

When we could, we sat and gazed down into the valley: splendid scenery! Summits as far as the eye could see; mist only on the horizon. We were far above it.

Two hundred metres further on I had to take off my right boot as I could no longer feel my toes. It was a complicated manoeuvre: gaiters off, then outer boot, socks, inner boot, felt boot, more socks. Carefully I massaged my numb foot.

When we had gained the ridge between the North and North-West Faces we stopped for a while. To the left of the ridge it was steep, as well as rocky, obviously too difficult. So we quitted the ridge again to the right.

Sunlight now filled all the couloirs and valleys. In the distance a matt veil lay over the mountains like a transparent curtain.

Now and then Peter said a few words: 'Things are going well', or: 'That's Tibet over there'; and I would answer: 'Yes'.

The significance of these sentences lay more in the sounds than the words. We wanted to reassure each other that we were still there and also still capable of thinking.

For a while we climbed up an S-shaped gully but it was too strenuous and moreover avalanche prone, with too much loose snow lying on the slabs. We left it again and continued up the rocky ribs.

It was obvious that we had gained height; now we could see K2. In the distance there were isolated little clouds on the horizon, like pearly-grey fish.

As I leaned motionless against the slope after a couple of dozen steps – with my hands grasping the pick of my axe, the shaft of which I had rammed into the snow before my will-power gave out – I noticed how my heart was pounding. My body throbbed from my calves to my head. Slowly the throbbing wore off and once more I heard a very faint singing, almost a monotone. A regular, bright noise came out of the snow, or out of the rock. It wasn't the wind. Probably Peter heard it as strongly as I did. At the end of the rest stops it was clearest. Not human sounds but a singing that was only there as long as neither of us moved.

We were lucky with the weather which remained fine like the previous day. While bridging a rocky gully, Peter's right crampon had come loose. His red gaiters, which enveloped his whole foot from boot sole to knee, were interfering with his climbing as well as making the fastening of his crampons more difficult. So he took one off and simply left it lying under a cairn.

We were standing in the middle of the summit waste land head-wall. The steep, hard lines of the pyramid ran together above us, to a streak where the rock and ice walls fell back. Up above everything seemed calm and even the thin snow plume hung motionless on the corniced ridge.

Not a breath stirred although the air was light and cold. The whole white surface was untouched, as it had been for thousands of years. The voice of the mountain no longer sounded like a drowsy praying, rather like a dreamy humming that from time to time completely died away and then awakened anew.

Peter was concentrating on essentials as, in order to save his strength, he climbed upwards as straight as a die. Now he had reached a narrow rock rib above me and was staring into the depths. Mechanically he adjusted his crampons which had loosened once more during the ascent.

Next to my own safety and health I was naturally concerned about Peter's. Not in the way a guide cares for his client, more an extension of my concern for myself. I thought of us as an entity. Even if we were not roped together, we felt like a roped party, like something at one with itself. It was something synchronous in our thinking, in our way of doing things and in our plans. A brief glance sufficed to learn the intention and state of mind of the other, in order to do what he wanted. It was not only our routes together in earlier years which gave us this greater mutual understanding. It was also the extreme tension we were under which heightened this feeling of oneness and our concentration, which in the summit region became more sluggish but more marked.

Mostly we both saw the best route at the same time. Our eyes amounted to an extended sense of touch. When they scanned the wall above us, tested the snow or were on the look-out for the summit ridge, it was as if our hands reached out accordingly.

Again and again Peter said something which I had thought seconds before. But it was not absolutely necessary for us to be standing next to one another or speaking in order to sense that guidance; the stream of communication merely passed from one brain to another. Moreover, even when we were climbing up to forty paces apart, one noticed what the other was doing, seeing or thinking. As always, the leader bore the responsibility for the correct route and the best trail, while the second kept out of the way for the time being. The constant role reversal of leader and second was hardly a conscious act but was carried out after each 200m of height gained.

For hours I had noticed Peter's energy and courageous determination, knowing that we would get to the top and descend the same day to the last bivouac. All the inhibitions and worries which had beset us the day before on the steep ice slope had crumbled away from us. A calm began to spread out in us.

As in the late afternoon the height became more noticeable with every step, we rested more frequently. Peter, who was leading again, concerned himself not only with kicking regular steps in the hard snow, but also with cutting small steps.

Suddenly he interrupted the quiet of a rest stop, saying to me: 'How's it going then, Reinhold?'

I raised myself a little from my axe and, as I put my head back, managed an optimistic grin.

'We're fast enough', I said. 'We'll do it'.

Then I breathed again hurriedly and propped myself on my axe as I usually did during these breathers. Before I climbed on, I exchanged a look with Peter. I was on the point of climbing past him when I was interrupted. 'That must be the ridge up there, the summit ridge.'

Fine snow crystals floated between us and the deep blue sky, sparkling now and then. The snow-dust hung in the air in an oddly weightless manner. The soothing effect of this process was enhanced by the fact that it was totally still on the face and that, far and wide, no clouds were to be seen. For the first time on an eight-thousander the air around me seemed to be standing still, seemed to have suspended all atmospheric powers. Even the sun was relatively warm and not once did my breath freeze in the fringe of my moustache, which hung from my upper lip into my mouth. Neither of us spoke, neither broke the silence.

The steepness of the face now relented. The higher we climbed, the more the slope decreased. It literally obliged us to climb up into a notch which seemed near enough to touch.

Softly at first, then becoming ever louder, a roaring started over our heads like an enormous bellow.

As Peter reached the ridge, the sun and wind caught his hair. Down below, where I was, the air was still calm. I plodded upwards in the hope of being able to film Peter's further ascent. Totally convinced that we would soon be on top, Peter uttered only one sentence:

'This is the summit ridge!'

So saying, he tugged his axe out of the snow and climbed on. The wind was strong here but not unpleasant. It absorbed the sound of my laboured breathing and irregular footsteps in the snow.

Arriving on the ridge between the North-West and South-West Faces, a view of Tibet opened up over the east summit of Hidden Peak, a distant view beside which everything I had seen before paled into insignificance. A mountain landscape in grey and white, which fanned out rock ridge by rock ridge to eternity. The isolated high ridges looked like gigantic storm waves suddenly turned to stone. Left of that the three highest peaks in the Karakoram, all eight-thousanders: Gasherbrum II, Broad Peak, K2; frontier peaks between Tibet and Pakistan. How irrationally they reached into the blue-black sky; they paralysed my courage, and indicated to me our own height and isolation.

This loneliness was overwhelming. When I thought about it, and how long we had needed to get this far, it seemed an eternity to me. It was also still, silent like the transparent space over the summits, in which only the stars still turned. I had always wished for this solitude. Over many years I had acquired the independence for it. Now I found for the first time the peace to experience it.

Here, in close proximity to the summit, the world stood timelessly still. The roaring of the wind and the humming of the innards of the mountain carpeted the valleys like a sea, with a continuous surging noise. The gliding colours in the jagged round of peaks met at the summit in black and white. The atmosphere was stamped with calm, not the paralysing calm of death but rather the liberating calm of emptiness, which stood easy and carefree in space. All sounds were like a deep silence, every movement not work and not doing, only being. Being was peacefulness, completely undisturbed by the distant passing of the millenniums.

I could hardly make out Peter in the view-finder of the camera as his dark figure blurred with the black background of the sky. Only when he descended the West Face a few steps could I see his feet in the snow. Now he was standing up there on the highest cornice, apparently absorbed into nothingness. I couldn't say how far away he was.

At the thought of being the first to stand on the summit after this tough ascent, a feeling of triumph overcame him, a strong, inner excitement. I noticed how his tiredness fell away and how he quickened his pace without realizing it.

He noticed the fact that he was on top the moment he could see westwards to the Abruzzi Glacier. To make sure once more, he climbed down the opposite side to the first rock pinnacle and banged in the only piton which we had brought with us to the summit. As he returned to the snow top, we met and hugged each other.

Only with difficulty could Peter hold back his tears of joy. For a long time we sat there silently and gazed around. Our spontaneous excitement moderated and, with the rest, peace returned. Again sounds broke the silence and a soporific tiredness crept into our thinking, gazing and feeling. Only the marks of our crampons in the hard snow and the axe with the tiny Europa flag near my rucksack reminded me that we were sitting on the highest point of Hidden Peak.

The sky above the mountains was covered with fine patterns, patterns which collected around a central point, shot through here and there with purple and gold flecks. The peaks themselves – Baltoro Kangri, Chogolisa, Masherbrum, Mustagh Tower, the Gasherbrums, Broad Peak and K2 – made up a chaos of flanks and walls leaning on one another. Here and there they barred the view. Further back, darker rock chains and sky blurred into the horizon. Above that stood clouds and mist like white minarets, or occasionally like multi-coloured flowers.

We sat on the summit, in the centre of an endless, empty space. Far below in the valleys lay milky vapour. The horizon around me grew like the emptiness in me. And my deep breaths condensed to spontaneous events in a purely visionary circle. With an indescribable feeling of serene indifference I awoke from this state of tranquillity, as from a sort of nirvana.

We must descend, get back to the bivouac . . .

We picked our own ways down – face to the wall – back down the ascent route. Now all my planning and thinking was no longer taken up with the summit but more with Base Camp and, above all, home. Abruptly thoughts emerged from my subconscious which had not been there during the ascent: 'We did it'; 'My third eight-thousander'; 'The first man to conquer three eight-thousanders'.

Now we were resting less often and had forgotten tiredness and time.

After less than two hours we were 100m above the 'Sickle' and the ground began to get flatter. I forced myself to pay attention as I had on the ascent, putting one foot in front of the other.

In the clear light of the late-afternoon sun we stumbled up to the tent on which we had focused long since. Our evening meal consisted of soup, tea and chocolate. After that we lay in the tent, listened to the sounds of the evening and enjoyed the clear sunset. Finally we took off our heavy outer boots and crawled into our sleeping bags.

I slept well, but at day-break numbers were hammering through my consciousness: fifteen, sixteen, seventeen ... My brain was counting, starting over and over again, without result and without sense, still counting paces.

Peter awoke, gasping for air like someone who has been stuck in a plastic bag. The strong wind and the fluttering of the tent walls formed an acoustic bridge between the confined tent and the cold night at over 7,000m. Peter opened and shut his eyes a few times, looked around in the dim light and tried to orientate himself. It was about five o'clock in the morning.

Now we saw that the front of the tent was torn. The wind was driving fine powder snow inside and banking it up at the top end. Whilst asleep one of us had pushed the items of equipment which we had placed at the end of the tent in the evening against the front wall, with the result that the storm had torn it. Peter had slept deeply. The changed, dramatic situation, frightful as it was, failed to rouse him.

Slowly the heaviness on his legs began to give way to a discomfort, which brought forth a slight twitching in his feet. In order to escape the icy snow which kept blowing across my face, I pulled my down jacket, which I had placed on my sleeping bag for the night, over my head. My movements were clumsy, somehow automatic, as when in sleep someone tugs at the bedclothes. The wind blew so icily through the tent that I could stand it no longer. I half raised myself to do something about it. My hair and sweater were pasted over with snow, and at the front of the tent fresh snow-dust was constantly whirling inside and the interior of the tent resembled the outside – stormy and unpleasant. Only tiredness had made us wake up so late.

The wind was whistling over all the ridges, a rushing and roaring that drowned out our conversation and the flapping of the tent walls. It was tugging with such might at everything which lay around that I could not get rid of the feeling that it would simply carry us off together with the tent.

I opened the tent and momentarily had the feeling that I was lying in a wind tunnel. Instinctively Peter and I made a grab for our belongings which lay around loose in the tent. We looked for our rucksacks and stowed everything in them that we didn't want to put on. Then we placed them outside and in the next instant had also quitted the tent ourselves. We dragged out our sleeping bags and endeavoured to fold them up in the storm. As we pulled on our boots, items of clothing began to fly about and with a hasty glance we checked to see whether the crampons and axes were still there. Then we sat on our rucksacks and watched as the storm tore the tent to shreds.

Although still tired from our summit bid and the night which had passed in numbness, we had to continue our descent to the Gasherbrum Valley. Neither of us thought of postponing it. We knew that the longer we remained up here the more troublesome the descent would become, and the sooner we got back to the valley the better. Once more we took only the most essential items and left behind everything that we wouldn't need – gas cooker, spare rations and some climbing gear. These items would be blown away by the storm in a few days or frozen into the ice. As we were tying our sleeping mats on to our rucksacks, a gust of wind knocked down the tent.

'Lucky we moved out when we did', said Peter.

Although now free of the tension which had driven us step by step on the ascent, we were concentrating as never before. We knew that the descent demanded our whole attention. In the present conditions it would be decidedly more difficult than the ascent.

If we wanted to get down the first 1,000m alive, we had to apply ourselves completely, to work together with all our powers and with all our skills. We could afford to go all out on this face for it was important that we actually reached the flat Gasherbrum Valley. Far below we would make progress, even if not by walking, then at least by crawling.

The satisfaction of our sensational success, of having been the first two-man expedition on an eight-thousander, was now pushed into the background. In fact it was completely meaningless in view of the difficult descent. Still Peter and I sat on the edge of the small scree terrace which the slanting morning light illuminated timidly. The surrounding peaks were tinted a rose colour. In the valleys it was still night and down there it seemed to be completely calm.

Wearing the same clothes as on the way up, Peter and I picked up our rucksacks with our photographic equipment, the film camera, the exposed films and the emergency rations, and began our descent. For the few paces to the edge of the plateau we moved somewhat unsurely. The storm drove us on, tried to overwhelm us.

The face fell away terrifically steeply beneath us. It took some mental effort to leave the safe ground and climb out into the apparently endless abyss. But we had to get down. On the face the wind was less strong than it had been at the bivouac site, and even there it was now no longer raging as loudly as before. As soon as the sun got stronger it would slacken off completely.

A small stone rattled away under my crampons. It sounded uncommonly loud, the sound drowning even the hissing storm over our heads. Peter turned his head to one side and watched the stone skip into space, releasing a small avalanche with every bounce. By the speed of the stone and length of its fall, the steepness and height of the face could be estimated.

Peter's caution and determination did not quail under this disquieting certainty. After a few steps we had both found our balance and inner rhythm again and were climbing down the same route we had ascended. Faces to the mountain, we made some moves carefully holding fast to two rock-holds, then groped lower with our hands while our feet stood on the firm holds. Again we were climbing automatically, following the three-point rule. Then Peter vanished directly below me in a chimney. Looking between my legs, I could follow his movements.

This morning we had had no time to discuss the day's start calmly. Now and then shreds of words flew from one to the other.

'It's not as difficult as I expected', said Peter.

'Uh, huh', I growled.

Peter continued to climb down as in a trance. Time and again when he reached a safe rock projection, he waited and gave me the lead so that he could rest somewhat when following. When I went ahead, I endeavoured to traverse slightly out of the fall line of our descent route, so as not to be eternally exposed to stone-falls from above. However, that was not always possible and sometimes, especially when we had to stop in narrow gullies, we were climbing directly above each other. Every little stone that the top man released could have knocked the other off the face if the speed of fall were great enough. For that reason we endeavoured to keep the distance as small as possible and not to become careless in our tiredness.

'Look out, stone!'

I looked up at Peter, saw a small black dot which had slipped from directly under his feet and which was coming towards me. In the next instant I dodged and watched the fatal rolling sphere as it vanished into the depths.

'Are you hurt?' shouted Peter, shocked.

Involuntarily I held my breath for a heartbeat before I answered.

'No.'

Peter examined the rock on which he was standing, then dodged to the right to reach a gully via less dangerous terrain.

To begin with our descent was painfully slow. The snow was in part floury so that the crampons on our feet scratched the rock, and in part it was crusted and so hard underneath that our crampons could not penetrate. We had to place each foot so that it did not suddenly break in or slide off, always making sure that there was counterpressure. The snow clung tenaciously to these sixty-degree gullies and only remained there because frequently they narrowed like bottle-necks.

In contrast to the ascent we were able to take far more steps going down without having to rest. At the stops I was no longer content just to stand there. I endeavoured to kick a small step in the snow so as to place both feet horizontally. Basically this descent was not a complicated proceeding, yet it was not monotonous. It demanded a lot of energy, even though with every step downwards the air became richer in oxygen.

More and more I came to the conviction that a belay, such as we had wished for occasionally, didn't actually make much sense. We would not have been able to construct a safe stance all the time. A belay only fulfils its purpose on such faces if the belayer can place sufficient pitons to secure himself.

The last, lowest third of our descent was the most strenuous and for that reason the most dangerous. The face here was steep and bare in parts, so that we could jab in only the front two points of our twelve-point crampons. We maintained balance by holding the ice axe in our right hands and a piton in our left, resting more frequently than before. All the time we climbed without belays, relying on the psychological back-up which the presence of the other gave each of us. Any slip would have led unquestionably to a plunge, and although the face ran out flat below, there was no chance of surviving a fall into the Gasherbrum Valley. Not that we thought about this risk during these hours but we did climb with the greatest circumspection, despite the constant tension.

Although now we were descending really fast, our speed seemed a snail's pace. At each rest stop I reckoned up in my mind the distance still to go to the bottom of the face.

To hack every single step out of the ice in order to be able to rest correctly and not to lose balance whilst climbing with my heavy rucksack — these were the thoughts which time and again stimulated my will-power anew.

In four hours we had descended about 600m. Just as much remained to the bergschrund which was recognizable below as a narrow, black streak. Peter was coughing with exhaustion, the icy air of the still-shaded face stabbing his lungs. His arms were leaden from the constant pressure on piton and ice axe; now and then his feet threatened to give way. When he stopped to rest for a few minutes, one torment was exchanged for another. In each rest pause a paralysing heaviness in his legs and the stabbing of his lungs was even more strongly noticeable, and his muscles were racked with spasms of cramp. He was moaning with overtiredness. Isolated little drops of snot had frozen on his beard and upper lip.

Our goal, the Gasherbrum Valley, was still all too discouragingly distant for it to be worth while thinking about. Thus we concentrated on the things which lay immediately ahead of us, on the almost endless ice slope under our feet. Again a few steps and again some blows to the hard ice so that we had a notch on which to stand. This descent had lasted five hours already and there were still 300m to go to the bottom.

Ever more frequently we inserted rests which dragged on longer and longer. I tried to deceive my body, to seduce it into making the distances between stances longer. By suggesting to myself that once down everything would be over, that down below everything would be easier, I dredged up the last of myself.

'One more step, then you can rest again.' This 'one more step' I said over and over again and so little by little I was able to double the distances between rests.

Suddenly out of the corner of my eye I saw that Peter, who was climbing directly to the right and below me, had lost his rucksack. In fantastic leaps and bounds it rolled down the face out into the Gasherbrum Valley. Initially a cold shiver ran up and down my back at this sight but then I noticed that Peter was maintaining his balance despite the falling weight and was watching his rucksack composedly. His right crampon had apparently come loose and in order to be able to fasten it again he had had to remove his rucksack. With the awkward load on his back he had not had enough room to tighten the straps.

At this moment I noticed that one of mine was loose and I was standing on the face insecurely. Without thinking about it further, I slid out of one of my rucksack straps and turned myself somewhat – already the load had slipped away from me. Like Peter's rucksack a few minutes before, mine too rushed down the face. Firstly the red bundle rolled, and then it leapt mightily. I watched as it whizzed over the marginal crevasse and burst open below.

I was indifferent as to whether I would find the rucksack again or not, whether I would take home my belongings or not. The important thing at this moment was that my crampons should hold and that I did not plunge down the face myself.

In thought I was still with our two rucksacks as I resumed my descent. Suddenly there was a grating noise under my foot and I noticed that a big lump, an ice crust, had loosened and was moving. Just in time I was able to take my weight on my arms. A few small steps with my feet and I had hold again. The ice slid away ever faster and soon was scattered into many small pieces.

Instinctively I attempted to distribute my weight equally on my arms and legs so as to have a bigger surface to hold on to. In order to avoid the danger of sliding off at any moment, I was still descending with my ice axe and piton.

Mostly during the rest stops I thought of nothing. Peter crouched down on a relatively pleasant step and adjusted his crampons. His eyes were fixed and the snow, which stuck to his clothing overall, made him look like a piece of rock in the midst of this bare ice surface.

An hour later we gathered up our rucksacks in the Gasherbrum Valley.

Thirst! My tongue was sticking to my palate like a piece of leather. Dust and dirt were in my throat. We had had nothing to drink since the evening before and we struggled yearningly towards our bivouac where we had left behind not only a cooker but also some gas cartridges.

The sky was now the colour of water on moss-green stones. Far out in the Gasherbrum Valley I could see a small lake. No, it was a crevasse, the long, dark fleck to the right of our first campsite was nothing but a crevasse. Was I colour blind now? Crazy? Plagued with hallucinations?

Peter was just ahead of me. He was no longer moving like a human being, rather like a machine, and his will-power was his motor. He felt ready to drop but he didn't stop. He just kept going and going, with his body slightly bent forward and taking small, regular paces. He would not get up again if he sat down just once.

After resting for four hours at the bivouac site, we struggled to our feet once more, packed our rucksacks with items we believed only absolutely necessary and began the descent of the ice-fall in the direction of Base Camp.

We didn't get far. The snow was still soft and the sunshine unbearable. After 200m Peter had already fallen into a crevasse for the second time and we decided to return to our old bivouac site and to delay the descent until the following morning.

The evening and night passed in a flash. Slowly the tiredness eased out of our dehydrated bodies. Towards morning the wind had almost died down and in place of the fluttering of the tent walls there was only a gentle singing to be heard. The unaccustomed stillness made me sleepy and dazed. For a while we dozed, the howling of the storm of the past night still ringing in our subconscious ears and the tearing at the tent felt in our joints. To me it seemed as if a nocturnal journey in an open vehicle was suddenly at an end. Fine snow-dust drove through the ventilators in the bivouac tent.

When Peter and I crawled out of the bivouac, the snow which had collected during the night between our sleeping bags crumbled and now lay on our yellow insulation mats.

Peter straightened himself and tried to stretch. It remained an attempt. He looked around: rocks, mountains, a bit of sky above, and to the south the summit wall of Hidden Peak which now barred all view of Tibet.

The sky had still that bluey-white colour which indicates a lasting period of fine weather. In the east a golden tinge was spreading over the horizon, while the blue in the valleys was still transparent, the snow a dirty grey in the dawn light.

Descent to Base Camp on the morning of 12 August was no more than a stroll. Our rucksacks were half-empty, the snow was hard and all the crevasse bridges were frozen. The two ice-falls had certainly changed but we found a way through nonetheless.

The climbers in the Polish group, all those who were not sitting in the high camps with Wanda Rutkiewicz, their leader, were the first to congratulate us. They spoke of a new epoch which we had introduced to the sport of alpinism and of a new, logical method which we of a younger generation of adventurers had shown. For the first time we had succeeded in applying the sport of top-notch alpinism to altitude, to the last corners free of development and technical exploitation.

We ourselves had been led less by these thoughts in our planning and rather more by the fascination of this hardest waste land on earth, by the question of the ability of two people to live in the ultimate loneliness of a situation at the limit. This expedition had not only proved to me that two people could climb an eight-thousander just like an Alpine peak but it also gave me an answer to the question of mankind's fundamental existence, and already I had begun to see myself in a new relationship with the world.

Sometimes I wondered what would have happened if we had dozed off on the summit of Hidden Peak or if we had not got that far. For the world it had been one and the same. Only Peter and I would have missed another of life's experiences.

On 13 July we had set out from Skardu for Base Camp. On 13 August, together with Khaled, our liaison officer, we evacuated Base Camp for the return march to Skardu. We had had exactly four weeks to acclimatize ourselves for the summit and we had needed just five days for the actual climb. Thus we had made it a day before the Graz expedition under Hans Schell, although they had set out two weeks ahead of us and had used oxygen apparatus and high camps for their summit assault. Was our system on that account the better?

No, there was no one better or worse, our system was just different. Schell had operated in exemplary fashion. He could boast of having led one of the smallest expeditions ever to have reached the summit of an eight-thousander.

On the second day of the march, on the way from Concordia to Urdukas, a squall of icy rain hit us without any warning. It was impossible to estimate how long it would last. Wet and dreary, the view consisted of a broth composed of mist, whipping rain, hail and snow which the wind drove directly into our faces. The ice crystals stabbed our skin like hundreds of small needles. Apart from the pain in our faces, water which ran down from our hair into our boots brought on a numbness in the tips of our toes. Rushing streams and wet stones added to our misery along with a constant, deafening noise when we came to rivers and the uninterrupted whistling of the wind. In the distance now and then we heard the noise of avalanches which were coming down to the left and right of the glacier. We kept losing our way and, when we could not get through the crevasses, we had to go back to look for another route.

In Urdukas, where we set up our second return camp, the rain lasted less than half an hour. Then there was total peace and the break in the weather was over.

The excitement, which had gripped us during the hours of the storm, gave over like the rain and now my thoughts were as clear as the stones and grass were pure.

Water bottle in hand, I went in search of a spring. Then I heard a squishing sound in my boots and noticed that my feet were ice cold and that I had water up to my ankles. I must change my clothing first.

The spring from which we had drunk on the outward march had dried up while we had been gone. I looked further until a gentle rustling, a regular dripping between the stones, showed me the right direction. With difficulty I found an underground spring which didn't give much but at least it was water. In twenty minutes my bottle was full.

The next morning we were standing above Liligo in front of a milky-grey glacier stream. But now I no longer asked myself the approach march question: 'How shall we cross it?' Now I knew that we could. The uncertainty, which at the beginning of our undertaking had relented only hesitatingly, did not arise at all now. We became more resolute with each day and each step which we put behind us. Now the obstacles were obstacles no more, they were simply steps taken. It needed no self-conquest, and we no longer feared troubles and dangers. We had not the slightest doubt about crossing the river. On the march in we might not only have hesitated here but would perhaps have waited a whole night for the mass of water to subside.

Where did this sudden resolution come from, this toughness? Perhaps the knowledge that we no longer needed to cosset ourselves, perhaps we had learned to endure heat and hunger and the hard life. We no longer needed to go sparingly with our strength, our courage and our skin. We were inconsiderate of ourselves, calm and composed at the beginning of each new difficulty and without any doubts.

I fumbled in the icy broth in the middle of the river, legs numb. I did not hesitate, at least not until the water was up to my waist, when I stopped. The stones which banged against my shins and pushed me a little downstream at every shove, were not painful even though afterwards there were bruises.

Peter followed and we supported each other mutually with our hands, balancing. As we were still struggling against the flow in the middle of the stream, in our mind's eye we were already on the other bank. With our eyes firmly fixed on it we fumbled, holding our breath, in the deepest swirl. The water pressed us hard, nevertheless no one was carried away as we all concentrated on reaching the opposite bank.

Our return into the lowlands was one mighty march. Day by day the stages over the relentless Baltoro Glacier became longer.

'Never again!'

We moved trance-like, lips cracked, shreds of skin on nose and cheeks: 50km in ten hours.

We spent two days in Askole, the first village — meadows, trees, people! The early morning sounds were like music: the chirping of the crickets and cicadas, the singing and chattering of the birds; somewhere a cock crowing, in between a dog barking now and then; peasants driving their oxen in the fields, children bawling, girls' voices. Nevertheless we wanted to get on. Again it was an endless waste land.

'Were we ever there?'

Peter could no longer remember many sections. The temporary amnesia, which is unavoidable on every similar eight-thousander ascent, made itself apparent. I remembered a remark by Uschi. *Vis-à-vis* a curious journalist who was researching loss of vigour at extreme altitude, she had remarked:

'Reinhold goes past the point where he doesn't even recognize his own wife.'

How were things with her now?

While I had been on Lhotse, she had felt good. She had had few cares, scarcely any fear. She knew the team was experienced, and in a few weeks she would be with us, perhaps in time for the summit attempt. Now, on the Hidden Peak expedition everything was entirely different. Uschi was tense and tired. She brooded a lot over everything. I believe it is a question of inner harmony. If one feels himself a part of his surroundings, of a friendship circle, it is easy to be serene and imperturbable. But she had rather concentrated on me exclusively and although she is basically a person who can get on well alone, she felt herself forsaken, not just alone. Thrown completely off the rails by a whole mosaic of untoward circumstances, she could not endure this isolation.

During the return march I concentrated on Uschi as on a tangible vision. Her picture accompanied me during the day while walking, at night it appeared to me in half-sleep. Occasionally I had anxiety dreams, as always when I was on the way back to civilization after big expeditions.

Only in the first half-hour amongst the branches of the apricot trees in Chongo could I forget everything.

Time and again the pleasure of walking flowed through my limbs, as if my whole body had become lighter and at the same time much stronger.

'I could march on for ever and ever.'

The terraced cultivation in the valley bottom appeared marshy this afternoon, and everywhere water drains and pools glittered in the sun. A crass contrast to the brown, dried-out mountain slopes above, rising directly out of the valley. Despite the early hour the sun was already high, yet the air over the fields was still pleasant and almost cool. It awoke in my skin the memory of spring, of spring in South Tyrol. Of a day in April more than twenty years ago, with flowers on the meadows and little streams, damp earth and fresh foliage. A time which belonged to the few truly happy weeks of my life.

How many years now had I been away in spring? Six, seven? Spring was different everywhere and everywhere in the world it came at a different time. But at home it was softer, with meadows like wall-to-wall carpets and the air as clear as fresh water. Here too the earth was damp and warm — I even took off my boots — but less fresh.

'Next spring I will stay at home.' My bare feet elicited this promise from me.

It was still early morning when we left Chongo. The sound of tumbling water mixed high in the air with the wind into an on and off swelling symphony which accompanied us constantly. We had taken off our shirts and marched bare-chested through the fields, along shrub-lined water ditches. The dew-fresh foliage struck me on my chest and arms, and the drops of water stayed on my skin like flower blossoms.

How thin my arms had got, those arms, with which I had been able to pull myself up on pencil-thick ledges, looked like the arms of some untrained office employee.

I now weighed a little over 9st and had lost 16lb.

'The scree traverse shouldn't be a problem this time.'

The sight of the slope recalled once more the horrible pictures of the march in: laden porters, a rolling body, Khaled like a living stone in the tossing water, fear-driven men whom the foam engulfed and released again, far ahead in the river a lost load. Five weeks ago the stones had come from everywhere, over a distance of ten, twenty, thirty metres nothing but stones. Stones like missiles and in between them mud.

This time, too, a hail of stones whistled over our heads. Again it called for ducking and pressing ourselves under projections. The stone avalanche was hardly past when I looked up. Peter was running on ahead as the last fragments splashed into the water. Anything to get out of this slippery gorge, away before the next load came down, before it was perhaps too late! We were standing in the middle of the traverse and there was no time for hesitation. Firmly I took the one porter we had hired in Askole by the wrist and pulled him along as Peter gave me the sign to come on. I made some big strides, wobbled, regained my balance and continued, my feet barely touching the stone slope. When a foot-hold broke I was usually already over it, nearer the next shelter – another scoured-out gully. I edged my boots into the soft conglomerate, so that the stones sprayed out. The porter behind me hesitated. I could not blame him for that, nevertheless I bawled at him.

'Go!'

We had no time to lose. The pauses in the stone-fall were brief and limited. He could not go back so he rushed forwards to the end of the dangerous traverse. Still 500m, still 400m.

We climbed on, always along the Braldo, often 2m, often 50m above the bank with the treacherous scree wall above, which could come down on us at any second. Every moment it could come alive again and one never knew where the stones would then emerge. Some 500m above us a whole bunch came together. One stone dragged another with it and by the time they reached us on the traverse there were hundreds: fist-sized stones and head-sized blocks. They leaped over vertical steps, whirred through the air, and smashed and splintered into a thousand pieces.

We rested for a few minutes in each case under overhangs or projections. We could not be entirely safe there either for the whole mountain above us could disintegrate and start to slide. The porter leaned there now, panting and trembling with fear from tip to toe. He did not calm down until we were on the other side, at least 100m beyond the stone-fall zone.

The slope suddenly gave way under my feet, resilient no longer. Without me realizing it, the river had undermined the slope. Quick as lightning I sized up the situation, fixed my eyes on the rocks on the bank and leaped downwards. The water spilled over my feet and closed over my head as a room-sized chunk of earth came down behind me. My glance flashed from the porter to Peter who kept quite calm.

'Are you OK?'

'Sahib dripping wet – hope nothing comes down – hope nothing', murmured the porter timidly.

'Pig dangerous this slope', commented Peter, waving him on.

'Get a move on, we must get out of here!'

And as encouragement for me: 'Long live the crew!'

The porter still stood irresolutely under the rock projection, cowering down as if in a bunker. The steep wall changed every few inches: now muddy, then gravelly, in part vertical with hump-backed stone. Now and then I scraped steps in the muddy gravel with the blade of my axe. They were for the porter a kind of commitment to follow us.

After these last dangerous sections my tiredness had increased abruptly many fold. How far was it still to Dassu? Hours or days? I no longer had any concept of time and had given up measuring it and dividing it.

# FINALLY I HAD FOUND MY WAY

With the ascent of Hidden Peak, it had become clear to me that Himalayan mountaineering would alter radically. I knew for sure that it would be possible to climb an eight-thousander solo and I began to contemplate such a bold plan. Still more, however, I was occupied with the question of whether an alpine-style ascent of Mount Everest were feasible. Only if I could manage without bottled oxygen could I turn this idea into reality.

In 1978 I attached myself to an Austrian expedition to Mount Everest, which Wolfgang Nairz had organized and was leading. Within the framework of this undertaking, I wanted to climb to the summit with Peter Habeler without artificial oxygen. If this succeeded, as the next step I thought I could attempt the highest mountain in the world alpine-style or even solo.

My mountaineering at that time no longer had anything in common with the conquest alpinism of the 1950s and 1960s. It was an attempt to introduce the alpinism of renunciation which seemed to me appropriate after man had learned, with the help of technology, to fly to the moon.

The ideas which I had realized on my climbs in the Alps — safety through speed, risk discipline, and inner security instead of safety and climbing aids — were just as practicable on the walls of the eight-thousanders. And thereby, above all, the field of personal adventure was as great as it had been for the original pioneers who, for lack of technical aids, were exclusively dependent on their own skill, instinct and ability to suffer.

My mountaineering was not about conquest, it was an end in itself. With my gradual renunciation of all those climbing aids, which the conquerors had used to achieve success at any price, I recovered for myself a good deal of that uncertainty which alone could be the basis for my adventures.

*Right and overleaf*: In the dangerous crevasse labyrinth of the Khumbu Ice-Fall. The route was made passable for the team and high-altitude porters by some fifty ladders and over 1,000m of fixed rope.
*Next page, small picture*: Everest Base Camp (5,340m).

Ascent of the Lhotse Face: on the right are the tents of Camp 3 (7,200m).

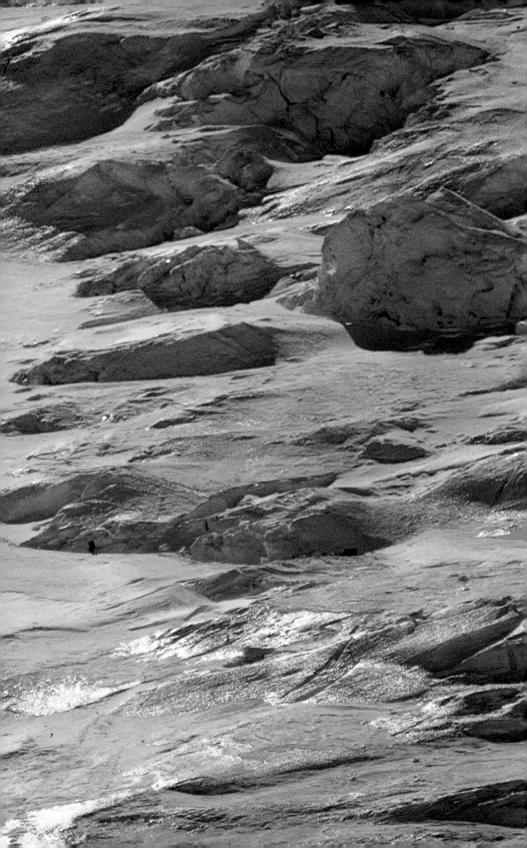

Camp 2 (6,400m), Advanced Base Camp, at the foot of Everest's South-West Face.

Peter Habeler at about 8,200 metres; in the background is our tiny camp on the South Col.

Descending from the summit over the Lhotse Face.
*Previous page*: Reinhold Messner by the survey tripod on the summit of Mount Everest (8,848m).

Approach march from Nagaton to Base Camp, with a few porters and two pack-mules, and over the rubble-strewn Diamir Glacier.

Our tiny Base Camp at about 4,000m.

On the way across the dry glacier to the foot of the Nanga Parbat face. Reinhold Messner left behind the backpacker tent (which also contained extra bivouac equipment) at the start of the climb. He photographed his solo ascent by means of an automatic self-release timer — balancing across narrow ice bridges without rope protection.

The first rays of morning sun strike the seracs; this is the best time to climb this steep ice. The dark rock ridge on the left of the picture is the top of the second Mummery Rib. Messner's solo ascent of the Diamir Face went from the centre of the picture diagonally right, then left again over the Great Ice-Fall.

Blue-grey light lay over the Great Ice-Fall.

Messner's second bivouac in the fall line, under the Mazeno Col.

Nanga Parbat at day-break.

Exposed view from the steep face away down the Diamir Valley.

# Expedition to the Final Point

## WITHOUT OXYGEN ON MOUNT EVEREST

Alone I was climbing up the Lhotse Face, my body swaying to and fro on the fixed ropes. The heat was still bearable. The sun crept behind wreathlike mists which built up out of nothing and vanished again. In the early morning I had finally decided to move in the direction from which the wind was coming. I always prefer moving against the wind as opposed to with it and sometimes use its smell as a signpost. Although everything indicated otherwise, I believed firmly that the weather would remain fine. How promptly I read a good weather sign into every alteration in wind or cloud plume! The mists had a different smell from the air up here and if wind got up everything became more sterile. That is the only reason why I don't like the wind very much.

How exacting I had found similar starts in days gone by! Psychologically strenuous. To leave behind everything to which I am attached is much more difficult for me than the climbing.

Next morning too, on the climb to Camp 3 on the South Col, things seemed almost trivial. Not that the climbing bored me, but it was not compelling. I felt it more as a deepening perception of myself.

On the Geneva Spur I overtook Dati, our second Sherpa Sirdar who, climbing without a load, had broken trail thus far. I only needed to go on when, after short breathers, the absurdity of our climb overcame me. When exerting myself at this height it felt as if each step and each breath could rescue me from my meaninglessness, as if life at this height had no meaning other than me myself.

After three-and-a-half hours I was on the South Col. Peter Habeler and I installed ourselves in the tent. The whole afternoon we brewed tea, as if many drinks alone could substitute for an oxygen mask. Occasionally we fell asleep briefly. Time and again one of us awoke gasping for air. Our life there consisted simply of a deeper and faster breathing.

In the evening — our three Sherpas had long since gone down again — the British cameraman Eric Jones, who was to film us on the South Col, dragged himself into camp. Now everything was prepared for the deciding day. The weather was fantastic. As I stood outside the tent once more at 6 p.m., after Base Camp had radioed us a good

After a snowstorm lasting thirty-six hours and at a height of 7,400m,
Reinhold Messner quit the last safe campsite and descended to Base Camp
in one day — more than 3,000m.

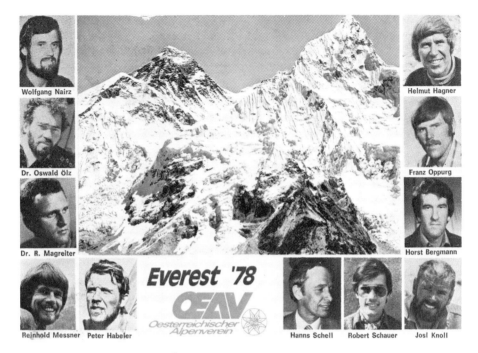

Wolfgang Nairz

Dr. Oswald Ölz

Dr. R. Magreiter

Reinhold Messner   Peter Habeler

Helmut Hagner

Franz Oppurg

Horst Bergmann

Hanns Schell   Robert Schauer   Josl Knoll

*Everest '78*

ÖAV
Oesterreichischer
Alpenverein

The official greetings card of the Öesterreichischer Alpenverein's 1978 Mount Everest Expedition with members of the team.

weather forecast, to the west I recognized the silhouette of every summit in the setting sun.

I felt as if all my wishes, all my hopes were reducing to certainty in my mind. Deeply contained within myself, I screwed myself up to that once-and-for-all burst of energy which was to satisfy my curiosity and my ambition. All the criticisms, which had preceded our 'crazy' attempt, bothered me no longer. For a year I had been ready to go to my limit, to risk every last thing.

Peter and I had known each other for fifteen years and we held each other to be infallible as regards mountaineering. That comforted me.

'7 May 1978, South Col, 8,000m. Two of us in the tent, about 8.30 p.m.', I dictated telegram fashion into my mini tape recorder.

'The tent wall is completely iced up at the bottom, the cooker is buzzing and we are waiting for our last mug of tea which we shall drink without sugar. Peter, do you think we'll get up tomorrow, right up?'

'I don't know. But certainly as far as Camp 5.'

'Possibly to the South Summit', I said, 'but the rest is in the lap of the gods.'

'It looks an awful long way to the summit from here.'

'Yes, but look here: it's 800 metres to the top, 500 to Camp 5. Today we made 800 metres from 7,200 to 8,000 metres in quick time, with poor conditions, too much snow and too much trail breaking. I'm sure that we can make it to the South Summit.'

'That certainly wouldn't be any further than today', Peter agreed, 'but higher up.'

'Would that make so much difference?' I asked.

'If things go as well as today and we can make good to some extent our fluid loss, it'll work out OK. I'm optimistic at all events.'

'It will depend on the wind.'

'Sure', replied Peter, 'if the wind gets up, we haven't the slightest chance.'

'It was really dreamy at sundown this evening', I said.

'But it was terribly cold. Today it was at least minus thirty-five outside the tent. I'm absolutely frozen. You can't get warmed up in here.' How right Peter was.

'One doesn't notice the lack of oxygen so much lying down.'

'Only because we're completely passive and not doing anything.'

'Every time I move, for example when I sit up, I get tired very quickly. If that isn't better tomorrow, I don't know what will happen.'

'The whole thing would be easy if we had oxygen bottles.'

'We're always intent on doing something unpleasant.'

'I'll tell you one thing, I'm turning back before my mind blows!'

'Me too!'

'If I sense any sort of brain damage, I'm not going on'.

'Speech or balance disturbances or the like; yes, then we must turn back.'

'If we're still relatively low down and only one of us has a problem, then the other should go on. I would like to get higher than Norton did in '24.'

'Over 8,600m then?'

'Their heights were a bit vague.'

'And one can't compare the North Ridge with this side.'

'Wolfi says it's very steep near the top, on the other side too.'

'But on a day like today, when one is going well and feeling good and the views are fantastic, it's really fascinating. Besides, as I was climbing the Geneva Spur today, I heard sounds again; not music but a murmuring and humming, like night-time in big, empty churches. Have you never heard the mountains singing?' I asked Peter.

'No, I prefer my own singing.'

'I don't sing much but I listen a lot. You have to listen hard but in some places the mountain gives off sounds, not rhythmical or tuneful, just a constant drone.'

'Like lamas praying?'

'Yes, something of the sort. Perhaps they got their hymns from the mountains.'

'I hope there won't be any wind tomorrow', Peter turned our conversation back to reality. 'That's what I fear most.'

'So long as it's tolerable and one can keep one's face free, it's OK. I'm more worried about my feet.'

'My toes are ice-cold.'

'I've had trouble with my left foot ever since I lost my toes', I said, 'because I can't wiggle the stumps very well. We were in the shade a long time today.'

'I can't imagine why Eric took so long — eight-and-a-half hours from Camp 3 to Camp 4', said Peter, changing the theme. 'It normally takes six hours.'

'Yes, that's about right. And today we did it in three to four. One really can't imagine how far away from the rest of the world we are now. Here no one can help you and if you can't go on you're dead, you've had it.'

'A retreat over the Yellow Band on the Geneva Spur would be ticklish.'

'I've made my will!'

'I tell you, that band is dangerous.'

'When I came up here the first time it was a stroll compared with today. But I could see how it would be with a little snow slab, smooth rock underneath — it would need care.'

'We haven't drunk our four litres yet today.'

'That tastes horrible', said Peter after I had handed him his mug.

'But we must drink. The wind's getting up again already.'

'Particularly higher up.'

'The wind is an advantage in that it blows away the clouds but it's also a nuisance. If it doesn't snow in the night, and I don't think it will, we'll set off early. I think we'll have a fine day tomorrow.'

'Now, how about a beer before bedtime!'

'Beer? I'd be satisfied with a decent cup of tea.'

'If not beer, then Glühwein at least.'

'That would be great. I could down four litres of that.'

'My thighs still feel strong', said Peter.

'Mine too.'

'My rotten headache gave me double-vision.'

'This isn't the ideal spot to start from tomorrow. It would be better to have a tent 200m higher — we could sleep almost as well there.'

'A night without oxygen at this height will be hard enough on us.'

'We can't recover our strength here but I don't think we shall deteriorate.'

'I'm not so sure, Reinhold, I think we will. It can't be otherwise. Sleeping at 8,000m, you can't expect to feel the same next day.'

'Last time, after the tent ripped to pieces in the night, I remember I got up and functioned splendidly.'

We had another drink.

'We ought to try and get some sleep.'

'I'm shivering again already.'

'I've got a cough and a pain under my left ribs. I had it yesterday but not so badly.'

'It'll pass off.'

'Tomorrow we shall have heavy rucksacks because we have to carry spare gear and provisions up to Camp 5. I don't think sleeping in 5 is a good idea — on the way down at a pinch.'

'We'll climb down even better, since there's no one to fetch us.'

'It's an advantage, just the two of us. There's nothing better than a two-man rope, generally speaking, when both are in harmony.'

'At a great height, a fast two-man party is the best life insurance.'

The classic route to the top of Everest via the southern side.

'And if somebody dawdles a bit, it doesn't matter because you mustn't exhaust yourself either. Each must keep something in reserve for an emergency.'

'And one must really know oneself.'

'We haven't done much together but what we have done has all been top notch', said Peter.

'If we go on talking we shall use up the little air there is in the tent. Let's try to get some sleep.'

'Good night!'

8 May: shortly after 3 a.m. I began to cook; tea and coffee. I put into the pot bit by bit the head-sized lumps of snow which lay in the tent from the previous evening. It was a long time before the water was warm. We drank it in turns.

Still in our sleeping bags, we pulled on two pairs of socks and our inner boots. I tried warming up my frozen outer boots between my legs. It's a long, breath-consuming business getting dressed at 8,000m!

Sometime after five o'clock we were ready at last. I was wearing silk underwear, a pile undersuit, a one-piece down suit, double-layer boots and gaiters of strong insulated Neoprene, plus three pairs of gloves, two hats and storm goggles. For emergencies I had another pair of gloves, and a hat and goggles in my rucksack.

Apart from that I had only the barest necessities: a length of rope, cameras, altimeter and mini tape recorder.

It troubled me less than usual that hoar frost was crumbling from the tent wall, that my sleeping bag was frozen stiff outside and that icicles clung to my beard. For six weeks – the time we had been at Base Camp and higher – we had lived with such inconveniences.

As Peter and I quitted the tent, a squall of sleet hit us in the face. Oh no, it couldn't be true: the sky was overcast, with only a thin streak of blue to the west! A sharp wind was blowing out of the south and all the valleys were filled with mist. At first we were shocked, paralysed, but then, conscious that this was our last chance, I decided to go as far as possible.

'We can always turn back', I said temptingly to the still-hesitant Peter.

When one has a wife and child to consider, as he had, such decisions weigh heavier. In the subconscious there grows up a natural barrier of fear. I know that from earlier days when I was still married. Since living alone again, I felt myself unconcerned and freer when at my limit. I concentrated totally on making progress, there was no more before and after. I had nothing to lose but my life; but I was still alive.

Despite our light rucksacks we made only sluggish progress. Then things got somewhat quicker up an ice field which was shot with crevasses. From the ice top, above which the summit pyramid rises, we could see eastwards for the first time, over to Makalu, a massive granite peak. An enormous fish-shaped cloud enveloped its summit. It was snowing there already. Above us the wind whipped up the snow and the streaks of blue on the horizon had vanished. There was a cheerless emptiness in the sky.

The snow underfoot was hard and the points of our crampons gripped well. But time and again we had to rest in order to recover in the thin, oxygen-starved air. Higher up, where the drifted snow lay knee-deep, we often switched over to the rock buttress, which was technically harder climbing but which spared us the labour of trail-breaking.

We communicated in sign language. Every time Peter drew a downward pointing arrow on the snow — 'We must go down!' — I drew one pointing upwards: a silent dialogue.

After four hours we reached Camp 5 which represented for us only a sort of back-up. Now and then the summit of Lhotse cleared — we were now at the same height — also the sharp, finely drawn Nuptse Ridge. We made tea. Again I dictated some impressions into my tape recorder:

'Peter and I are at 8,500m, in the top camp. We came up relatively quickly but the weather is extremely bad. We don't know whether we should go on or not. The snow is so deep, trail-breaking so strenuous, that we don't see much chance of making it. Just now we are trying to melt a bit of snow. Early today, when we saw that the weather was not as good as expected, we didn't bring any sleeping bags with us. We confined ourselves to essentials, so as to be as fast as possible. But now we're in a jam. To wait here and bivouac is risky, something to do only in extreme emergency. To go on — it's still pretty early — is equally hazardous. The weather fluctuates, now Makalu is in cloud, now it isn't; but while I am sitting in the tent drinking tea, I feel rather better. There's no question of talking whilst on the move, that would be too strenuous. Every scrap of oxygen is needed. That we should reach the summit is almost out of the question. But perhaps we could get a bit further yet. We shall try everything, we are both in good spirits and want to do it. And if this frightful weather is intent on upsetting our plans, well then, we are equally keen to continue.'

'Peter, what's the weather like now?', I called from inside the tent.

'Bad again.'

'Are you game to carry on for a bit?'

'We may as well risk it.'

'Perhaps there's a chance of getting to the South Summit in three or four hours if we keep up the same speed and if the snow isn't too deep. Further than that won't be easy.'

After resting for thirty minutes we continued our balancing act. Our climbing became still slower. On the eastern, Chinese side of the ridge the snow was hard but then we had to return to the Nepalese side because the other was too steep. Again we had to wallow up to our knees, treading down the snow. The steep rock pillar to the left of the Hillary Step appeared to be impassable. Nevertheless, we traversed out and felt our way up ledges with the aid of our crampon points.

Regularly, after a few steps, we propped ourselves on our axes and, with mouths wide open, gasping for air, rested thus so that every muscle and fibre could work. Yet I felt I was bursting. Higher up I even had to lie down in order to be able to continue breathing.

Above me the ground continued to rise, so I climbed on, without thinking much about it. On the South Summit we roped up for the first time. Just below the South Summit the rope tightened, I looked round but only very quickly. Peter wanted to take off his rucksack, be free of his load. He didn't want to carry anything any longer, and just wanted to be completely free in his movements.

Under the South Summit I unearthed my camera from my rucksack and filmed Peter as he climbed upwards in the raging storm. Ahead of us a mighty snow edge towered up, the most beautiful ridge I had ever seen. The cornices billowed out hugely towards

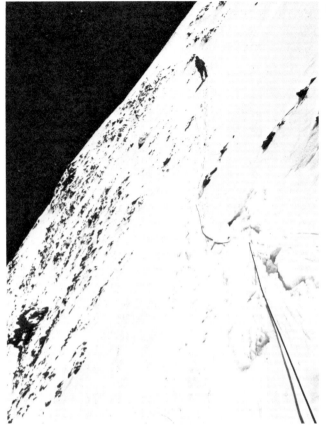

Ascent of the Geneva Spur.

Tibet; on the Nepalese side they were slightly sloping. The main summit seemed endlessly far away but I knew – as far as I was still able to understand and concentrate – that at altitude distances deceived. In the thin air everything looks much further away. By now I was sure that we would reach the summit.

The ice axe in my hand was like a balancing pole. Incessantly I stuck it in the snow or dragged its point along the snow, hour after hour. It had already become essential to support myself on my axe, for I would have fallen over if I had no longer been able to insert it in the snow.

Sensing the nearness of the summit, I could no longer look upwards; I didn't want to know how far away it still was. I had minutes of will-power and self-control when squalls blew in my face, and then again minutes in which I doubted and, despite my wide-open mouth, tried to clench my teeth together.

The storm raged over the sharp edge of the corniced ridge leading to the main summit. Peter and I tried to move carefully but we were, however, extremely clumsy and finally completely exhausted. We tacitly agreed that there was insufficient air for talking and so just made signs in the snow with our axes. Every gust of wind which threw sleet directly in my face made me clumsier.

A listlessness combined with obstinacy: did we have to be here in this weather? Peter seemed to be writing something in the air with his axe. I looked intently and finally smiled as he finished. To the south Ama Dablam was clear and the sun was shining on it. Perhaps the weather would hold yet.

I climbed down into the notch which separates the South Summit from the main peak and fumbled my way forward at a respectful distance from the corniced edge. Just below the Hillary Step, the hardest spot on the summit block, I stopped. Peter followed and then I climbed, resting three, four times, up the steep step. On top we changed the lead. From the south a cold wind blew ice crystals into our faces. What with filming and photographing, I forgot sometimes to push my goggles over my eyes.

Now, shortly after midday and at a height of 8,800m, we could no longer stay upright when resting. We crouched down, knelt and clung to the shafts of our axes, the points of which we had rammed into the hard snow. We didn't belay each other, in fact neither of us paid much attention to the other, but deep in his subconscious each knew the other was there and made no mistake. The harmony of our climbing had grown so much on repeated expeditions to the limit, that neither feared for the other.

Breathing was so strenuous that strength scarcely remained for us to continue. After ten to fifteen steps we sank down on the snow, rested, crawled on.

I was not thinking of much and just climbed automatically. It had slipped my mind that we were climbing Everest, the highest mountain in the world. It was also immaterial to me that we were climbing without oxygen apparatus. Now it was simply all about that point in which all lines merged, that vanishing point which attracted me so magically. The exertion was hellish but I didn't feel it. It was as if my shell were dead and only deeper within my head something was keeping me going. I no longer wanted to move, crawl and pant, yet I was drawn by this finite point as by a magnetic pole. Perhaps because only up there was a solution possible. My brain seemed to be switched off and dead, yet my soul was more permeable, more sensitive – it was now large and tangible. It wanted to get to the top, in order to swing back into balance.

The final metres to the summit were not difficult. Once on top, I sat down and let my feet dangle over the edge. No need to climb any more. I fetched my camera out of my rucksack and fumbled with the battery for a long time with my awkward down gloves until I got it going. Then I filmed Peter.

After the hours of torment, which I had not really sensed as such, and now that the monotonous movements of moving and climbing were at an end and I wanted nothing else but to breathe, a great calm spread throughout my body. I breathed like someone who has run the race of his life and now knows that he can rest for ever. Often I looked around because the first time I did not see what I had expected of the panorama from Everest, nor did I notice how the wind chased the snow over the summit the whole time. In my absent-mindedness I was no longer my normal perceptive self, rather a single, tight, coughing lung, floating above mists and summits.

Only when I could breathe strongly a few times, did I notice my legs and arms, and my head, which was quite clear even if I was not completely aware of where I was. The instant Peter reached me and hugged me, we both burst into tears and lay there in the snow, wracked with emotion. I had thrown down my camera. The flood of tears, after this enormous outflow of will-power, suddenly released everything. We lay side by side on the summit like two people who had both lost their heads at the same moment. For a while we lay there thus, covered in drifting snow up to our necks, mouths wide open, and rested. When I stood up Peter stared at me as if he were trying to commit my face to memory, as if he did not recognize me.

Standing now in the diffuse light with my back to the wind, I suddenly had a feeling of fulfilment. Not a feeling of having achieved something and of being stronger than all who had been there before us; not a feeling of having arrived at a culmination; not a feeling of omnipotence – only a breath of happiness deep inside my mind and breast. The summit suddenly seemed to me a quiet place, as if up here I had not expected such. Looking at the steep, sharp ridges below us, I felt that had we arrived later, we would have been too late.

Everything we now said to each other we said out of embarrassment. I stopped thinking. As, trance-like, I was fetching the tape recorder out of my rucksack to record some rational sentences on it, tears filled my eyes.

'Now we are on the summit of Everest, it is so cold that we cannot photograph', I began a little later.

But once more I was shaken with sobs. I could neither talk nor think; however, I noticed how this deep spiritual emotion threw me into a new equilibrium. Only a few metres below the summit the exertion had been just as great, also the worry and the accompanying danger. An outburst of feeling such as this was, however, only possible on the summit.

Everything that is, that I am, was based on my knowledge that I had reached the top. The summit – at least temporarily – was my naïve, intuitive answer to the question of existence. I sensed no feeling of triumph or of omnipotence, only the feeling of being there and gratefulness to my partner. I had ceased to understand for a short time in my happiness. No longer was I thinking about things. Emotions dominated me, breaking out seemingly without any resistance. We didn't speak with each other, we just took pictures.

Peter noticed all at once how, just as under the Hillary Step, his fingers were tightening up. Was it cramp or a potential stroke? He thought of the Sherpa who had been carried off a few days before, paralysed down one side with cerebral apoplexy after overexertion at great height. Peter became restless and wanted to go down.

So he set off alone, without a rope. I saw him on the South Summit as I dictated a tape on the top. Then I unpacked a film cassette and threw the film on the ground instead of the paper. Only when he vanished from sight did I notice what I had done. I took a second cassette out of my rucksack and then loaded the film. After so much concentration suddenly my feelings overwhelmed me again. With relief, I drew a deep breath, then dropped everything into my rucksack, one after the other: tape recorder, ciné camera, still camera. I tied the batteries, which were now superfluous, to the Chinese tripod and squatted down again. My self-confidence was not greater than usual, although now I managed to think calmly about the forthcoming descent.

It was still early afternoon yet the light gave the impression that it was already evening and the notion came over me that I had been sitting up there a long time, for some hours in fact. Nonetheless, I sensed a definite lack of desire to descend, as if climbing down did not form part of my plans. Actually, during the time of preparation – which stretched back over several years – I had only ever occupied myself with the ascent, at most with the summit but never with the descent. Now I had to urge myself to stand up and leave this spot.

'Now you are going to climb slowly down the ridge', I said to myself. 'Take care on the Hillary Step! Careful, it's exposed! In a few hours you will be in oxygen-richer air, then things will go better.'

I concentrated only on looking at the way down. Then once more I fingered the bit of rope and the batteries out of my camera on the tripod and climbed after Peter, in the hope that he was waiting for me on the South Summit.

A few paces below the summit I turned around once more and was almost sorry not to be sitting up there any longer. I was sad that I had to descend now and could not stay up there where I seemed to be so certain.

Where Peter had descended, he had left behind fine scratches in the snow with his crampons. In contrast to the ascent, I could now think occasionally while moving downwards. During my rest stops there were moments in which I had the desire to stretch out in order to be able to breathe. Sometimes my thoughts consisted of spontaneous perceptions: at the sight of the Nuptse Ridge blurring in mist, it was the deep knowledge that this was a sad day for me. Something conclusive had happened and the mountain which I was descending was a shattered illusion.

The summit ridge of Everest looking back, these footprints in the snow, this axe in my right hand, all that belonged to me, was me.

After the South Summit it was downhill all the way. One foot in front of the other, facing outwards, treading down the snow with the greatest possible concentration, putting on my crampons – that was my salvation. Once more I saw the summit of Everest for the last time. At long last I had succeeded after years of day-dreaming!

Of Peter there was no trace anywhere, likewise almost no trace of our ascent, as if I were descending another mountain, or as if the person who had climbed up inside me had gone missing in the mist. Thus I had the sensation of being quite close to Peter, as if the mountain, Peter and I were one, the one unthinkable without the others. Looking for him was a measure of our friendship. I was not cross with him because he was not waiting. I was only concerned.

When I arrived on the South Summit half an hour after Peter, he was no longer there. Panic must have seized him. As I plodded slowly through the steep snow, letting myself flop from one step into another, all of a sudden I saw to the left of me a slide in the fifty-degree snow slope. It vanished somewhere in the mist. At this moment I realized – logic now ruled me again – that the east flank fell away 4,000m and was shot through with crevasses.

When I saw the track of the slide again just below the South Summit, losing itself on the Chinese side of Everest, I did not think of a catastrophe. I only thought that now I wanted to die.

I climbed down the ridge to the right of the slide, almost proud of the anxiety which forbade me to follow Peter's example and slide down on my bottom. I looked forward to meeting up with Peter and hearing him tell of his descent. Thus I had the very strong feeling of being on the move with the best possible partner. I didn't need to worry about

The completely snow-covered South Col (7,986m) and the two tents.

him; Peter didn't make mistakes!

At last I had discovered how alone I was. It was as if the fact of being alone spread out in my head, or as if the isolation expanded in my head, which seemed to be quite empty and big. The enormous sky above me was shapeless without any moving clouds.

Just above the place where Camp 5 stood on the ridge the slide ended. Apparently Peter had traversed right to the South-East Face and slid down this to the South Col. As I plodded past the tents, I winked to myself in confirmation: you were right.

Now I waited more frequently for the mist to pass. Then I could recognize the two yellow dots below, which were our tents, otherwise I saw nothing. But I was sure that Peter was already in camp or would soon arrive there.

When I was tired I simply sat down in the snow. At last I sensed how the joy of success was concentrated on a point in me. This point broadened gradually and soon filled my whole body while I remained seated, and I did not notice my tiredness.

At last a mountain on which I did not 'live ahead'; did only what I actually did. Even just before the summit I had thought ahead, I knew that I would soon be up. Now I no longer played things out, I did everything in the here and now, could carry on and didn't want to think.

I had no fear that I would not reach camp but I didn't think, as far as I still could think, about snuggling up in my warm sleeping bag.

I was so tired that I could no longer hurry on ahead in thought. Across the last snow slopes above the South Col I moved like a sleep-walker. Every time I squatted down to rest I looked at the time but, nevertheless, I never knew how late it was. Now, with my last steps to the tent, I had the feeling of having done something and of having nothing more to achieve. A feeling of security passed over me in front of the tents.

It was soon submerged, however, in the universal desolation of the South Col. Only inside the tent was there real security, there I felt it. Peter and Eric were there. As I crawled into the tent and saw Peter, this triumphal thought: 'We've done it!'

And we would do more eight-thousanders without oxygen. Now a state of joy arose in me so that I even forgot my breathing, and during the radio conversation with Base Camp I breathed deeply only occasionally.

Meanwhile I turned to Peter: 'Tell me again what you felt after the Hillary Step, about not being yourself.'

'After the Hillary Step it no longer felt like me who was climbing that steep wall.'

'Peter, if we left today between five and six o'clock, we must have been on the summit for one or two hours. So we must have taken eight hours for the ascent. You came down in an hour. That's fantastic, really fantastic! And I did it in one-and-a-half to one-and-three-quarters!'

'Are we sleeping in the same places as yesterday?'

'Yes, I suppose so.'

'I don't need to cook so much today.'

'Did you think early on that we would make it?'

'I wasn't 100 per cent sure.'

'When were you absolutely sure?'

'On the South Summit.'

'On the South Summit I began to shoot more and more film but for a long time I didn't know whether I had you or a crevasse in the view-finder, the wind was so strong. There was only a black dot and a wild storm that looked really terrific. Didn't you notice that at all?'

'No, I didn't notice.'

At last in camp were we both 'high', euphoric.

By the evening my eyes were hurting and Peter had banged his ankle which had swollen badly. My eyesight became dimmer by the minute, the pain unbearable and, at first, I was afraid I was going blind. At great height nerve damage is no rarity, and irreversible brain damage is possible. But then I noticed a feeling of sand in my eyes and knew that I was snow-blind.

A frightful night followed. I felt that where my eyes had been earlier, there were now two holes. Time and again I had to sit up, pressing my fists into my eyes, weeping and crying out. It helped as the tears soothed the pain and Peter looked after me as if I were a small child.

The descent the next day, 9 May, from the South Col to Camp 2 succeeded only because I – snow-blind as I was – was able to stumble along behind Peter, although I could see no more than a metre.

On 10 May we arrived in Base Camp like two invalids. But our brains had not suffered, or so our comrades confirmed. Could the venture have gone wrong? We didn't think about that at the time. In the death zone success and misfortune lay as close to one another as storm and stillness, as heat and cold.

Of the seven eight-thousanders which I had attempted up to that point, I had reached the top on only four occasions. And today I know that – on every real adventure – the path between grave and summit is a very narrow one. That one does not know beforehand where one will end up does not make life up there more meaningful but it does make it more intense.

The summit of Mount Everest: the circle indicates the Chinese marker.

# THE SUMMIT OF MY MOUNTAINEERING DREAMS

Some weeks after I had returned to Europe from Mount Everest, I was packing again for an expedition. I wanted to make a totally solo ascent of Nanga Parbat. Why was I in such haste? Firstly, I had received a permit for this solo climb Secondly, the ballyhoo after the much-discussed Everest ascent – television appearances, being introduced, being squeezed dry – was getting on my nerves. Thirdly, I wanted nothing more passionately than to climb one of the eight-thousanders alone, alone from the very bottom to the top. Now, on the high of my Everest success, conditions were ideal: I was in top form, acclimatized and had more self-confidence than ever. This time it must work!

This was my fourth run-up to an right-thousander solo. With Ursula Grether, who had visited me in Everest Base Camp, I travelled to Rawalpindi. There, our liaison officer, Terry, joined us. By jeep and then on foot, after many detours we reached Base Camp under the Diamir Face. The road through the Indus Valley was blocked at that time and the approach march was thus costly and long.

In Base Camp at 4,000m – an ideal spot on grass with spring water and two tents – I spent a good two weeks acclimatizing myself better and observing the face. Then I set off; it was 6 August 1978. I wanted to climb this eight-thousander by a new route, alone and without oxygen, naturally, without helpers and without having set up depots beforehand. For the time being I did not ask myself if I would get down again. All I wanted was to climb to the summit of my mountaineering dreams!

# Solo

## WITHOUT OUTSIDE HELP ON
## NANGA PARBAT

For two hours I had been climbing up steep ice. I was not moving especially quickly but I was moving steadily and without resting. It was shortly after seven o'clock in the morning.

I had to keep to my right in order to reach the narrow ice ramp which lies between the Great Ice-Fall and the Mazeno Wall. I already had one ice rise behind me: without any belay, just with crampons and ice axe I overcame an almost vertical ice wall about 15m high, which formed the right-hand border of the central avalanche channel in the ice hose. Once up, I asked myself how I was going to get down it again.

Again there was a bulge of ice in front of me. It was at least 100m long and overhung here and there, blocking off the face like the wall of an embankment. I could not see over it and to the right it became higher. I did not know what was above.

I had been alone for a few hours.

'Left side', I heard.

'Sure?' I was startled by my own answer. Was someone there? Yes, to the left it really did seem to be better. So I climbed to the left, as if I knew that this other person was right.

It was not easy there but I managed it. I was able to overcome the steep step by chimneying up a recess. With my legs straddling wide, pressing against the gaping walls, and my hands at the back of the steep, dièdre-like gully, I inched my way up. Was I afraid? The climbing required so much concentration that there was no place for fear. I had enough time to make the climb but not for reflecting on what I was doing or where I was.

Suddenly the ice field around me lit up in a strong, warm light. It lasted for a moment, then only the air above me shone as the first rays of the sun hit the face. I did not see where they fell but I sensed how the ground shone above the Great Ice-Fall. High above me the sunlight filled every corner of the Diamir Face. My body warmed up and relaxed. Everything in me was alive.

Sunrise! Those were magnificent, exciting moments. The air hung like quicksand under the sky and Nanga Parbat appeared in outline as a shadow on the clear horizon. I could still go on or go down. But I drove myself upwards into a world which seemed closed and simple to me, which had nothing confusing about it.

'Come back safely', Terry, our Pakistani liaison officer, had called as I left. 'We'll wait for you, whatever happens', Ursula had said. I gazed down at Base Camp and tried to make out the tents but could not recognize anything.

Suddenly there was someone there again, speaking to me. At first this world of silence was broken only by noises of a second presence, then I saw a man standing at the edge of my field of view. I felt a sense of my earlier home. My father was there and I was walking behind him. I felt his presence as if my feelings towards him had never altered since my childhood.

By the time the sun finally climbed over the horizon I was alone again. My father was exactly the same age as I am now when he took me climbing the first time, I thought, as I cramponed up a forty-five-degree ice slope. Alternately, I jabbed the front points of my crampons into the brittle surface beneath me. With my legs slightly straddled I took three short steps and only then took my eyes off my feet and gazed upwards. Next I inserted my short ice axe about 80cm above me and took three more short steps. I had found my rhythm.

I could scarcely remember my childhood, just a few events: that I had fallen into a ditch and had cracked open my forehead. I could remember myself in a small forest clearing. Only my elder brother and I were there and we were helpless. Our parents had left us behind there. We both cried. First my brother, then I too.

'How wilful you were then.

'Not only wilful, obstinate.

'You're the same as your father.

'Possibly.

'Same old-fashioned ideas.

'No, you believe that because usually I made the decisions.

'Not usually, always.

'As far back as I can remember, as a child I was always superior to my brothers. I'm not proud of it but not unhappy either. That's the way it was. In our family of two parents and nine children there were always age groups. There were the big 'uns and the little 'uns. Then more arrived and they became the little 'uns.

'Later we went to school where Father was teacher.

'On the whole, I'd rather forget about school.

Suddenly one of my crampons slipped. 'Look out!', I said aloud. Was I talking to myself?

I was already at the height of the Great Ice-Fall. The weather was not fine but it was not bad either.

Three hours ago I had set off from my first bivouac. Yesterday I had checked once more the first page of the Gutenberg Bible which a friend had presented to me as a sort of summit book. He had also made a small aluminium case. In this shell I had placed the precious parchment and now wanted to deposit it on the summit. I did not know whether my photographs would come out, even if I would be able to take any up there. Also I did not know whether I would get there but, in case I did, I had this document with me.

I must have slept really well – no fears – for I was rested. I was still confident. In a sudden, hard decision I continued.

I gazed up at the big wall of Mazeno Peak and then traversed left above the seracs.

The Diamir Face of Nanga Parbat with Messner's routes of ascent and descent.

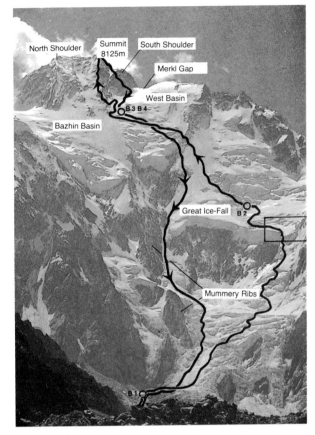

What tremendous dimensions! It was not an easy matter to orientate oneself on this face. To the right of the Mummery Rib, almost 1,500m high and bathed in warm morning light, there glittered bare ice. The big serac near me was more than 500m wide and up to 200m high. I was now fairly safe although one could never be wholly safe here. Today would be the deciding one for me, that I knew. I must reach a height of at least 6,000m. Lower than that there was nowhere for me to bivouac; it would have been too risky. The first relatively safe area was above the Great Ice-Fall. Somewhere there I must put up my tent.

Shortly after eight o'clock I was above the danger zone. I would have loved to shout out with joy. To start with today I had managed a height of 500m per hour. Because I was so fast, and because I had managed to overcome the ice bulges so well, I was in high spirits. I had taken only a few photographs on the way as it was not simple to snap oneself. I used an ice axe on which I had had a screw welded so that I could fasten my camera to it, then I stuck the axe in the snow, set the auto-release timer and took pictures of myself.

Was Ursula feeling alright? She didn't know how I was getting on. Perhaps she was watching my progress through binoculars. But just seeing and not knowing was so hard to bear. Before I left, I told the pair of them to wait in Base Camp for ten days.

'If I'm not back in ten days, twelve at the most, you can set off home.'

I didn't want anyone to search for me if I didn't come down again. That would have been futile. I didn't want anyone to risk his life fetching me off the face. I had made my will before the expedition.

The 'Bridge' below me, 600m high, was as big as one of the classic faces in the Eastern Alps. Far above me was the summit. Bathed in cold morning light, it seemed to be infinitely far above like a fairy-tale glass mountain. Nevertheless, I felt I could get up there and had only momentary flushes of fear of perhaps being stifled up there by loneliness, by myself. I had no sort of fear of never coming down again though.

Even on the steepest ice passages I photographed myself from eye-level for I had screwed a powerful wide-angle lens, a fish-eye, on my miniature camera and was thus able to take pictures of myself at close range.

The snow was still holding well and I left no footprints behind. I was at a height of 6,200m. Not once today had I had to belay myself — I had needed neither my one ice screw nor my rock piton. The glacier lay far beneath me but when somewhere on the Diamir Face something cracked, I did not jump. The danger zone had been overcome.

For a good hour I ascended over firm snow. The sunlight grew warm and yellow on the blue surface of the snow. In the angle under a vertically towering ice serac the blue was especially intense. I decided to stop there.

I sat down on my rucksack. Here was the ideal spot for my bivouac and here I felt well and strong. A sense of well-being, of sitting in the right place, ran through my whole body. I stretched myself and looked away over the clouds at the horizon. I felt that the weather would hold.

It was not that I was going against the rest of the world, nor that I had conspired with nature against everything else. I was sitting here as if I were a constituent part of this mountain. At each movement I was extremely careful, for I must not slip, set off any avalanches, or fall into a crevasse. I was like the snow which lay there and I had sensations of rock and snow and clouds. No more need for philosophy. I understood everything, death too.

I had not set out to conquer a mountain or to return as a hero. I wanted to get to know the world through my fear. I must be able to feel new again. The fear of being alone, however, did not once enter my head. The certainty of meeting no one up here was even comforting — loneliness was no longer a catastrophe. Apparently, in this peace, I had reached a new self-confidence.

How different it was being alone: once a frustrating separation, now a conscious freedom. For the first time in my life I experienced 'white' loneliness — loneliness no longer as fear but rather as strength.

Under the overhanging ice bulge I trod out the site for the tent. I had to bivouac right under a projection because the Diamir Face was so covered with seracs that one could not be entirely safe anywhere in the open.

The world below looked further away than the summit. Was I emotionally more inclined to go down or up? For the moment I was completely immersed in myself. And as thick clouds and mist spread out in the valley I remained calm. I twisted the ice screw

Ursula Grether photographed the lower part of Reinhold Messner's ascent with a telephoto lens from the foot of the face.

into the wall above and anchored the tent to it. As the sun reached its zenith, I lay down inside; there was just room for me, my rucksack and the cooker.

I melted snow in the tent bag which I had hung behind the tent wall in order that it could be warmed up by the sun. Out dripped water which I caught in a cup-sized cooking pot. Every time the pot was full, I warmed it up for tea or soup. I had to drink a lot.

A partner was not so important. At first I believed I would not manage without a human – without a partner as a mirror image, without another face. Often it was nothing to do with conversation, just someone to look at. I would say nothing and he would say nothing, but each would know what the other was thinking. Had I found that partner in myself now?

Time and again figures emerged before me, imaginary friends. I talked with someone who sat near me all the time. Was it a person? There was some other being present, that was all I knew. Not only were there voices around me, there was something physical nearby, not tangible, but it was there and it moved. I could almost see it although I didn't look for this being, did not stand aside for him. Sometimes I said to myself: 'You're a fool, there's no one there.' Then again I had the deep awareness that this intangible life around me was real. I was speaking with someone who answered my questions. There was something there that I could not explain rationally but which concerned me with its whole existence and which had the same life as I.

In small sips I drank the hot soup out of a cooking pot which was scarcely bigger than a cup. My throat felt as rough and sore as if someone were going over it with a rasp. I forced myself to swallow a bit of cold corned beef out of the tin. That was a mistake – I had to be sick in the snow outside the tent in which I squatted. In so doing I threw up half the fluid which I had absorbed laboriously during the course of the day. And without sufficient fluid in me, up here I was lost from the start.

I had been sitting in the tent for six hours now, 6,400m up, in the middle of the almost 4km high West Face of Nanga Parbat. It was wretchedly hot. However, I didn't want to cover the tent because inside I was melting snow with the sun's energy. Thus I could save on fuel and survive longer. The tent bag, 40cm long and as thick as my leg, still hung from the ridge. The whole thing looked like a sausage. It kept dripping and just before sunset the pot was full for the third time. Again I made soup. I had to take in a lot of fluids and forced myself to drain this potful too. For the time being I could eat no more.

I had used up a lot of energy on the climb today: 1,600m of height gained in six hours with 15kg on my back – that had been too much. And all without safeguards. Who was there to have held me? This time I was climbing without belt and braces. Three times I had been conscious of that fact during the morning's climb. Three times a vertical ice pitch had been in front of me and I had had to get up it. Each time I had hesitated. I was unsure, I could not afford a slip. With a partner the whole thing wouldn't have been easy but it would have been simpler. We would have been able to belay each other with the rope. But for me alone there was not this possibility. And so each time I had taken the plunge: 'I will not lose my balance'.

One only does the likes of this once in a lifetime. Nothing can compare with these endless vertical ice deserts, not only on account of the drudgery, but also the risky climbing without safeguards.

I didn't seem to be lost, but when I thought about the descent, I always saw the most difficult sections in front of me. That depressed me because I had not even reached the top yet. Perhaps I would not get right to the top. If it were as difficult tomorrow, I did not know whether my courage and my skill would suffice. With every metre that I gained in height, I would become heavier and weaker.

Would I get down? I didn't want to think about it any more. I didn't want to think as far as the end. I had to melt snow and rest. While meltwater dripped out of the tent bag into the cooking pot regularly, I massaged my legs and the cramp in the muscle under my right arm. The whole morning I had cut steps with my ice axe, scratched out holds, pulled myself over the edges of crevasses. Every movement had to be right. A single pull-up not made would have meant failure.

My socks were dry as were my double-layered boots which I had placed in the sun outside the tent. I fetched them in. The fireball in the west plunged between piles of clouds, lighting them up like atomic mushrooms, and then went down. At once it became cold. As long as it was warm – in the sun it was even stiflingly hot – water had dripped regularly out of the tent bag. Before the meltwater froze again in the sudden cold, I poured it carefully into the little cooking pot and balanced it on the gas flame. I had to keep drinking and make good my fluid loss so that my blood did not thicken; so as night fell and the temperature sank to −15°C, I drank. I must not be sick again. If I vomited once more I would have to go down if I wanted to survive.

Solo: only a few people before me had seriously tried to solo an eight-thousander. Maurice Wilson, who attempted Mount Everest in 1934, never came back. The following year his remains were found at a height of 6,400m. The Canadian Earl Denman reached a point just under the North Col on the same peak.

Solo: the nearest people were now 2,400m below me in a tiny base camp. Terry, who had voluntarily joined us as liaison officer out of sheer curiosity, had no mountain experience; nor could Ursula help me in emergency. They could perhaps fetch help if I announced by means of rockets or over the radio that I was in danger. However, I had neither radio nor rockets with me, or any sort of method for sending an SOS. It would have been pointless. The nearest place which had occasional connection with the outside world was Babusar, four days' march away. There they had a hand-cranked telephone that functioned occasionally. To cut down on weight, I had not even brought a torch. The gas flame was my sole source of light, until I had drunk enough and tucked myself up to sleep. Here nothing could happen to me during the night. My mini-tent was protected by an ice overhang and I had anchored it with a bit of rope to an ice screw. It would even withstand the suction of a nearby avalanche. It had to.

I was fairly exhausted and let my head sink back on my anorak which I had laid on the mat for a pillow. Now it occurred to me to look at the time; it was a few minutes after 6 p.m.

Suddenly I had the feeling that I was floating. It was as if I were completely weightless and had no fear of falling. No longer was I thinking and feeling in the customary way. Then I lay there exhausted again, switching between tiredness and self-resolution. I perceived everything, at first alternately and then at the same time. I see-sawed between customary perception and these extraordinary sensations. After a while the two feelings separated themselves and I noticed that I was suspended from the roof of the tent, looking down at myself. Then it was reversed again. It was more than just a sensation, I saw everything as in a picture in front of me – now from above, now from below. These feelings were much the same as I often have on waking up. Both I can neither remember nor express. The picture is so blurred, the perception of it so clear.

Again I was speaking with someone and not just with myself. I was convinced that I was talking with people, with beings who I thought I could see out of the corners of my eyes. No, it really wasn't hallucinations. Such I had experienced in 1970 when I had come down from Nanga Parbat. Then I had seen people who came towards me, and then who suddenly were no longer there. I had even recognized some of them. They were on horseback, riding towards me, moving. But then I identified them as blocks of stone, saw in place of a white horse a patch of snow on the dry glacier. Now I was certain that people were here but could not see them. I conversed with them, yet did not know whether I was speaking aloud. I did not want to find out anything specific, but

119

was just there, observing, was everything. Rationally I did not believe in these companions but if I thought about nothing, they were back again. For me it was clear that these voices came from outside of me. Occasionally I said to myself: 'There's no one speaking to me. I'm alone.' But this feeling too was dispelled by the presence of the voices. I didn't know whether I was making it up or not; I communicated thoughts in the strong conviction that these other people were there.

If I closed my eyes I could hear my friends better. Then I noticed them more distinctly out of the corners of my eyes. That people were there, helping me with the cooking, talking with me, I did not find it funny; I was glad about it and I conversed about everything possible with them: my childhood, my 'failed middle-class' life ...

The chains of hills to the west were bathed in a greeny-brown light when I looked out of the tent for the last time. The sun had set some time before and the rain clouds, which were now forming on the mountain slopes, grew quickly. I had to wait here until the weather became either good or bad. As long as clouds gathered around the mountain crests, it was much too dangerous to continue.

The silence on this face was splendid. Only the light breeze, which drove on the mists in the valley, whispered in the tent poles. I could smell in the air that it was going to snow.

'I suppose it will rain down below', I declared.

'It's raining already.' The person who said that had no definite form, he was just there.

The mist and the damp air made me drowsy and I was very cold. How heavy and thick these banks of mist were. Against the bright, starry sky they looked almost black.

In the bivouac my problems surfaced for the first time. If there had been just distance separating me from my supporters, I would have known that I could get back. But here, on such a dangerous and difficult face, I did not know that and thus was not sure of myself. That made the distance and the time, which lay between me and other people, grow immeasurably big.

The loneliness which one experiences when locked up, perhaps locked up voluntarily in a room, and the loneliness which I now experienced, were not the same. Here I was not waiting for something else. With each step I had taken upwards, I made two paces away from the nearest human habitation. And each step became more strenuous the higher I went. Ultimate solitude is a problem with which man cannot cope.

Presumably it is more simple to sail around the world single-handed, and to let oneself drift in the storm. Of course the sailor must battle against the forces of nature as well; but I would never get up an eight-thousander if I did not also fight against my body, which by itself would not even go downwards.

I hid myself deeper in my sleeping bag and put the half-filled cooking pot on the gas flame. The meltwater must not be allowed to become ice again, otherwise I would use too much fuel. It was difficult doing everything alone. With my left hand I held the grip of the cooking pot, so that it could not tip over, and with my right I poured the soup concentrate out of the aluminium foil into the steaming water. No one was there to stir it.

It occurred to me that my left crampon was broken. With a defective crampon I would neither get up nor down, so I must patch it up. With my pocket-knife I repaired

Ursula Grether.

the binding and calmed down when it worked properly on my boot.

What was wrong with me? My fingers had gone numb as soon as the sun went down; my arms and legs constantly went to sleep. Would I reach the summit in two days? If I had to be sick again, it was all over. Then I would have to descend as fast as possible and neither my psychological nor my physical powers were sufficient for a fresh attempt.

For safety's sake I took no sleeping pills.

On the morning of 8 August, there was great excitement in Base Camp. Ursula told me about it days later.

At 5.15 a.m. she heard Terry shout loudly. She was lying still half-asleep in her tent. Terry's excited, breathless voice tore her at once into the present: Nanga Parbat – Base Camp – Reinhold on the move for three days.

'Ursula, an earthquake and an avalanche right on the face!'

Avalanche! Earthquake! 'How? Where?'

She was now wide awake, no, really still asleep. Her eyes didn't want to stay open. She got tangled up in her sleeping bag, upset the bowl with the provisions and the cooker at the tent door, got caught up somewhere on the tent poles, couldn't find the knot. Never had she heard Terry so excited. While she was still fumbling with the tent fastening, she called out: 'Can you see him?' In the meantime Terry had arrived in front of Ursula's tent, our only binoculars in his hand. With her legs still in her sleeping bag, Ursula crawled far enough out of her tent to be able to see the Nanga face beyond the small canopy. The avalanche was already completely down. Quickly she pulled on her jeans, ran barefooted to Terry and took the binoculars. She searched for the 'dot' which she had been following for more than sixty hours. Suddenly a strong wind got up and it began to snow. Ursula's hair whirled around her head and snowflakes beat in her face. With her arm in front of her face, she turned around, bent over and huddled up. After a short look at the blue sky, she thought she had gone mad.

Ursula often had trouble distinguishing dreams from reality and thus needed substantial proof in order to be able to assess reality. So far she could not say for sure whether this was a dream or reality. As she looked up at the blue sky once more and at the same time was turned away by the air pressure, she knew all. The ice crystals hurt her eyes and face. She turned away from the face and the avalanche. For a short time she was relieved. Once more she thought it was a bad dream — with luck it was only a dream.

She was first conscious that this snowstorm was the result of an avalanche and therefore not a contradiction of the blue sky, when Terry enlightened her. His explanations robbed her of her illusions. It was no nightmare, no bad dream. This reality — dream-reality phase — lasted a few seconds at most and yet this time sufficed to frighten her with the idea of a falling body. 'He's there', Terry beamed. He had made out the 'dot' on the face, a dot which moved. Ursula breathed again, nevertheless she was not certain. Since yesterday she was already in doubt whether the dot was me. She could not imagine that I had got so high on the first day. To her way of thinking, the 'dot' was much too high. 'But supposing his bivouac site had been far below, the avalanche must have swept him away for sure', she thought to herself. Happy to push her fears aside, like a straw she clutched at Terry's assertion that the avalanche had gone down below my bivouac site. He could see me sitting up there, cheerfully looking at the clouds of snow and dust. But at the thought that I might have postponed — as I had done once already — my start by a day and then inevitably would have been in the path of the avalanche, cold shivers ran up and down Ursula's spine. Most of all she wanted to fall on Terry's neck when she herself saw through the binoculars that from just that spot where yesterday the tent was standing a dot moved away towards the summit.

Terry told Ursula about an earthquake more than 100 years before that had caused such great ice and earth slides that an unforeseeable catastrophe followed. Around the end of 1840 and beginning of 1841, the west side of the Lichar Ridge on the Nanga Parbat massif, opposite Gor, had fallen in an earthquake and had filled in the Indus Valley to a depth of some 300m at the narrows where later the Rakhiot Bridge was built. The river bed was completely blocked. In April 1841 Jabbar Khan, the headman in Astor, warned the government of Kashmir and told them that the river would perhaps remain dammed up for a month. The reservoir was already 60km long. At the same time, Rajah Karim Khan of Gilgit also sent warning, which he had had written on birch bark, down the main Indus Valley. But little notice was taken.

Then the dam broke. All the dry channels filled with water. With a wall of mud the flood burst asunder. It bore not the slightest resemblance to the colour of water. It was a terrifying torrent of churned up water, corpses, camels, tents, mules, donkeys, trees and household objects. Anyone who didn't see it in time was inevitably overwhelmed. Many clambered on rocks which, however, also became quickly inundated. Only those who had immediately run to the bordering heights escaped.

The havoc was enormous. The water had torn up and flushed away hundreds of hectares of arable land. All the trees which had lined the banks, the men in the trees, the horses and mules which were tethered to the trees, all was sunk in the swirl and vanished for ever. As a woman with a wet cloth wipes away a host of ants, so had the river washed away a whole army.

While Ursula and Terry were preparing breakfast in Base Camp, up above I was already on the move. A Pakistani farmer brought them news of the earthquake; he had heard it on the radio. The epicentre lay exactly in the region of the Great Bend of the Indus. Strength 8 on the Richter Scale. I knew nothing of all that.

This Tuesday, 8 August, I awoke at 5 a.m. My altimeter showed 50m more than the evening before. No, I had not been wafted aloft in sleep — the air pressure had fallen, which was not a good sign.

Again I melted hard, frozen snow in my cooking pot, heated the water and hung a tea bag in it. After the tea, I cooked soup made from water and concentrate from an aluminium foil packet. In the icy silence of day-break there was suddenly a noise like a mighty, distant waterfall.

I tore open the iced-up tent door and stuck my head out. Below me half the ice face must have broken off. Everything seemed to be moving. To the left ice avalanches thundered like torrents valleywards. Below me a broad avalanche rolled like a foaming tidal wave down to the foot of the mountain. It consisted of ice which I had ascended. It rolled over the bivouac site from which I had set out yesterday at this hour. Spellbound, I gazed at the fate that would have overtaken me had I started twenty-four hours later.

I didn't panic although my temples were pounding. I just said to myself, 'There goes your way down. You won't get back that way. You'll have to think of something else for the return route.'

In the cold, blue shadow of the face I folded up my tent and stowed my things in my rucksack. I took along with me all the rations for the ensuing days: two tins of corned beef, a tin of liver sausage, a 1lb tin of cheese-spread, two hard South Tyrol flat loaves, soups, tea and coffee.

I felt that I could not get warm. The snow was uneven in parts, then bare ice, then breakable crust, then powdery. My feet only felt secure when firm ground grated under my crampons. A cold wind was blowing in my face from the summit. My rucksack weighted heavily. Originally I had intended to leave a small depot at the campsite as provisions for the descent, but now that there was no way down below me, I had to carry everything further, higher. Perhaps I would climb down the south side.

I climbed obliquely up to the left, towards a broken serac on which I spotted a weak point. Once over that I would be in the flatter summit region, and would be safe for the time being. The weather disquieted me, and I suspected snow. Cirrus clouds were evident to the west, and over the summit of Nanga Parbat a rainbow-coloured cloud lay like a hat.

The first 100m of height took me longer than 500m had done the day before. At this speed I would never get to the summit.

As avalanches came down in all corners of the Diamir Face — below me, to the left of me and to the right of me — my first thought was: 'Avalanches at this early hour, that is outside my experience'. But then I resigned myself to it. The frightful scene stuck in my mind. As I saw the masses of ice swimming out towards Base Camp, I was afraid they might wash over it.

Otherwise, I only felt the certainty of having survived. Not that I thought I had been lucky. I had been high enough. I didn't know what power had led me through the dangerous lower face zone at the right time. It was the same power which another time might have compelled me to start a day later and thus be directly under the avalanche.

When, whilst climbing, I looked down between my legs to the bottom of the face, it struck me that yesterday's dirty glacier looked as if it were covered with fresh snow, otherwise little had altered. I was now as high as the highest summit of Mazeno Peak and could see away over the mountain ranges left and right of the Diamir Valley. From this height I felt I could trace the lines of the world. I could have gazed thus for hours but I had to get on. I climbed upwards, compelled by something that I did not understand, only sensed.

This ice face was a wondrous world. I felt at one with it. When I looked up at the summit, a wave of positive feeling took hold of me. It gave me strength. Now, stretched between this summit and the questionable descent, I could divine what I really was. When I looked at the clouds or mountains around me, I knew that I belonged here.

Between nine and ten o'clock in the morning the sun reached me. It became warm and later unpleasantly hot. I had passed the 7,000m mark and was approaching that rocky trapezium-shaped summit block, at the foot of which I hoped to find a safe campsite. At times wallowing up to my hips in snow, I moved myself step by step towards the rocks. Five paces, breather, five more paces. In the glittering light and with my very strong sunglasses, it was difficult to make out a protected spot for the tent, and the heat and heavy rucksack had worn me out. Nowhere could I spot an overhanging rock, under which I could have pitched my tent. And this bottomless powder snow. If only I had a partner to help with breaking trail! But I had to do it all alone: lead, look, lug. No one to help me, no one to encourage me.

The rock strata were downward sloping; nowhere a square metre of flat ground for sleeping. I dragged myself back to the right in the snow. There, between two crevasses, I found a usable campsite. I was completely dehydrated, had no strength left and let myself drop on the snow. I simply couldn't even put up the tent.

Again I had climbed some steep sections but had taken very few pictures. The fact that the weather had improved again scarcely interested me for the time being, although I knew that no one could get me out of here if I could no longer do it myself. Not even a helicopter could save me. I hoped only that Terry and Ursula were not worrying unduly in the circumstances.

I could not contemplate what had brought me up here into this misery. The ascent of Mount Everest without oxygen in May earlier in the year had been quite revolutionary enough.

I lay in the snow, sucking in the thin air and exhaling so that shortly before breathing out it accumulated once more in my lungs. The afternoon sun glowed. I must drink and melt snow again in the tent bag.

In this burned-out state, in this suffering, thoughts which I had not completely thought through were suddenly extinguished. Perhaps my limitless lonely position was still bearable only for that reason.

As I lay there thus in my tiredness, pumped out, unthinking, I suddenly had the feeling that a girl was sitting near me. I said to myself: 'Why should I put the tent up by myself, we can do it together.' My tent was a simple construction: an igloo-shaped bag suspended from two semi-circular, criss-crossed Duraluminium poles. It was only difficult to put up in as much as one had to tension the poles.

The girl looked at me as I trod down the snow and I thought it would be too hot for her to get up. Although I had to continue to do everything myself, it was nice that she was there. After half an hour the tent was up. I laid my sleeping bag over the top to keep out the heat of the sun and I put the mats and rucksack in their places, hung the snow bag in the tent. It only began to drip after two hours.

I was now more confident than I had been the day before, although a sea of mist lay below me enveloping all the valleys and peaks up to a height of 6,500m. To the west, however, I saw a reddish streak of vapour on the horizon which promised fine weather. It looked as if the world stopped there. Temporarily I was not interested in what lay beyond. Around me, however, I observed children, men and women. I knew them not and wanted nothing from them. They were just there, on and off. And I conversed with them. We discussed all that I was doing, for example, when I looked at the altimeter and counted the points it had fallen.

Through the mist the heat of the sun burned particularly fiercely on the tent. I lay there almost naked. I ate a mouthful from a half-opened tin of corned beef occasionally. On the tent wall I saw the silhouette of my ice axe which I had stuck in the snow outside. Now and then I opened the entrance of the tent to fetch in snow or to check on the weather. The huge cumulus clouds on the horizon formed their own mountain range. What fascinating forms, vague like objects under water!

As I cooked and drank, and occasionally accumulated air in my lungs, my confidence gradually returned. I was now embedded and sheltered in this forlorn situation.

Only occasionally did I have the feeling of absolute loneliness. Awkwardly I crawled out of the tent. The girl was still there. 'We are already a lovely way up', I said.

'Tomorrow you'll get to the top', she thought.

'Only if the weather holds.'

'It will.'

I stood for a while outside the tent and looked westwards. There was nothing but cumulus clouds all around, the glaring light in the snow, the still, warm air, and occasionally stars in the sky. The girl only laughed when I told her. Out of the corner of my right eye I believed I saw her get up and move away.

Again I gazed through a gap in the mist up at the afternoon sky and again I noticed stars. 'I've never seen that before', I said.

'Have you not?', she asked.

In the clouds above me more windows appeared, and the sky above was blue-black.

'Fetch plenty of snow inside', said the girl and I noticed how she stooped. I liked her voice, it stayed in my memory a long time. She told me no stories, we just talked. Purely banal stuff but we talked.

'Sure', she said, 'the weather will hold ... until you're down again.'

That must be right: it was almost windless and, despite the mist, still warm.

Four o'clock in the afternoon. 'I'm glad I'm alone', I said.

'Glad?', asked the girl.

'Yes, glad, I feel better than on previous expeditions. I'm not getting on anyone's nerves and no one is disturbing me. I climb as fast as I like and camp when I like. I feel much freer, up here on my own.'

With the sunbeams which broke through the grey, everything around me came alive. The mists were no longer as peaceful as before, I heard strange noises around me, a hissing and then again a whispering. Hallucinations? I was quite aware that I was speaking to myself, or to my shadow, that everything else was an apparition. But then my friends were there again and we carried on talking. How strange these meetings were; these opposite numbers which I only sensed, did not grasp, could not see! Sometimes the girl was so close that she almost touched me. But when I looked I did not see her.

It was a crazy feeling, simply being there, alone yet able to talk to friends all the time. How often had I previously held an inner dialogue and unconsciously established to myself that I was not alone? I was not alone here either.

In the evening I went outside one last time. My gaze fell on my own shadow. I watched how the light changed from a warm yellow to a cool red. Later it became greenish and then violet-black. Up above on the summit of Nanga, the last glimmer was extinguished. Lying in the tent, I peered out of my lair like an animal for a while. I squinted at the sparkling snow and the setting sun and knew, this world apart, that I was still thinking rationally.

When I awoke on the morning of 9 August, something was weighing me down. It was as if my eyes would not open. My condition was a waking state without me wanting to wake up. I experienced an oppressive transition stage out of half-sleep into terrifying reality: fear of being there, fear of being myself, generally of being a person. In sleep I had forgotten that I was alone. The sudden confrontation with such an absolute loneliness triggered off depression in me at once.

During the months after my separation from Uschi, it had often been similar on awakening. This sudden pressure, which threatened to blast me to pieces, was like a despair which came from deep down and seized my whole being so strongly that I had to weep.

I opened the tent and looked out. At once I felt better. I had the feeling that this was a good place for me. My ordeal was over. My fear of loneliness and longing for loneliness had reconciled themselves; it was possible to be friends with myself.

It was not quite dawn. It got lighter but then all night it had not been completely dark. It was very cold. The sensation of being left all alone had made way for a strong feeling of identity. My dreams and I were one.

The play of the gloomy clouds below alarmed and fascinated me simultaneously. Between the rising clouds now and then I saw a mountain summit. It was as if I were at the Creation, as if I could see from without.

In my initial amazement at the threatening weather my mind went blank. I just looked around. The situation was peculiar. 'Tike', I said – it was just a word that came to mind. I would have been able to blow soap bubbles and hang the tent on them. I thought to myself. For a brief moment something warm went through my dog-tired body.

Once more I slept and only emerged from the tent at seven o'clock. The weather was dull but I could see the summit. If firm snow or ice had lain between me and it, I would have been up in two or three hours at the most but the snow through which I burrowed was bottomless and as insidious as quicksand.

Infinitely and laboriously I forced myself onwards. My invisible companions were not there and I was alone again. I seemed rooted to the spot and had the feeling of being paralysed. The hip-deep snow was hard to push aside. I had to tread it down and burrow my way forwards, leaving a deep, wallowing track behind. At ten o'clock, after three hours' absolute drudgery, I knew that it was impossible to reach the summit in this manner. I also knew that I would never get back down if I went on using up my strength in this way.

As soon as it became a matter of life or death, the summit ceased to matter – the summit whose drawing power yesterday was so great, as if only there lay an explanation of this last alpinistic adventure. Either turn round on the spot . . . or? Or risk the last possibility which remained to me: to climb up the steep rock barrier on the shortest line to the summit.

This helplessness! This being separated from everything living that drives each person in time to madness! No possibility of comparison; no other face as a mirror image; no comrades to cling to and lean on. I was not fully conscious of it but it was there subliminally and with it an impeding fear of going on.

The gap between giving up and going on had already become very narrow. I wanted to have one more try. If the rocks above me were climbable and if the snow there was not too avalanche prone, I had a small chance. Rock climbing had been my forte since childhood. I climbed carefully but to my limit, as one has to on a vertical Dolomite wall in order to get up. But Dolomite walls are harmless, cheerful outcrops compared with Nanga Parbat. How I did not come to slip, at a height of 8,000 metres, with clumsy double boots on my feet and bad visibility through my goggles, I could not explain. Apparently my natural instincts helped me. Perhaps, as the summit was palpably close, I was already up there in spirit. I balanced up ledges the width of a hand and wallowed up a snow gully. All my senses were wide awake, and my inner reserves, of which I had thought there were no more left, were mobilized.

Sometimes I was in the sunlight, then again in shade. Clouds moved across the sun and everything was indistinct; now and then it snowed. The valley was still in darkness; only sometimes a view of an infinitely small mountain pasture rose out of the mists beneath me. Everything was unintelligible, beyond all description. Sometimes it was as if everything were clear, then again as if madness were spreading. I would never belong to it more wholly.

The horizon to the west seemed unreal to me and endlessly far off. I could no longer imagine people down there. I sensed no sort of compassion with myself, also no pride. The terrors of the early morning and the wonderful fact of being there had made peace in me. I felt nothing more of the proud satisfaction with exposure as I had on earlier expeditions. I didn't want to escape from the industrial age into primitive times. I was also not fleeing from people, I was only on the move. It was as if climbing senselessly up the vertical ice desert, I wanted to remove myself into this loneliness which for months was my custom. Already I found myself completely outside the well-ordered world. For days I lived in the ice, in this chaotic emptiness. And everything that streamed through my body became recognizable. Thus I discovered the world anew.

The images around me were unreal. The emptiness called to me louder than advertising hoardings or boulevards lined with publicity signs. The more desolate the ice slopes, the better I could see, and the more images could grow in me. In this climbing my humanity was awakened and at the same time deadened. Then again my exhaustion was so great that there were no more thoughts. And yet in my tiredness everything was crystal-clear to me. In my moods sublimity and banality lay very close together. My simplest physiological needs were just as important as the most high-sounding philosophical argument.

Slowly I made progress up the summit block. Here and there I was able to make use of rock barriers; often I had to labour up snow ledges and gullies. While resting, I now saw big, arid stretches of countryside to the west. They lay beneath a transparent veil of mist and clouds. Empty and ghostly as the world around me appeared, it was yet liberating and beautiful to gaze at. I had already climbed so high! One might have thought there was something arrogant in feeling that I had penetrated into regions scarcely accessible to anyone, but I experienced only a feeling of floating above everything that I had left behind and that perhaps was not there.

The climbing progressed without incident. Only where the snow lay crusted in narrow clefts, did I have trouble finding secure holds for my feet. I drove no pitons into the rock to belay myself. Yet I had no fear of falling; only now and then I had thoughts that my strength could give out.

Now I liked the contact with the ice, the rocks, the snow; above all I liked it when I took off my gloves on steep pitches and felt the rough rock under my finger tips. Despite a slight numbness in my fingers, I could feel the rock's firmness. It was rough like emery paper and my boots could not slip.

I had to stop and wait as soon as I tried to progress faster than my strength allowed. I consciously breathed faster and hyperventilated to pump more oxygen into my blood. Because I knew how much exertion lay between me and the summit, it was anguish to look up; its silhouette touched the sky.

Time and again my eyes spotted small cracks into which I could have driven pitons but didn't. The only piton which I had with me, was in my anorak; it was only for an emergency. When the cracks were wide enough for me to push the fingers of one hand in, to hold myself firm, I felt safer. I tried to place my boots so that the leverage was not too great and my calf muscles not overstrained. The grating noise that my crampons made on the rock was, next to my heavy breathing, often the only noise that surrounded me.

When I had about 80m of the steep rise behind me, I came to small snow fields across which I had to wallow deeply. It dawned on me that the exertion was not over yet. I much preferred the rocks to the flatter snow sections. From here I could have pendulumed into the almost vertical wall to the right of the summit fall line and there ascended on dry rocks, but without a rope this traverse was unthinkable. For that reason, despite the more strenuous trail-breaking, I climbed directly on.

I had always distinguished between a solo ascent with self-belaying, and a solo ascent without any artificial aids and self-belaying equipment. To conquer such a face by means of pitons or bolts, to nail one's way up, had never attracted me.

My progress was no longer so smooth. Sometimes I had the feeling that my legs were no longer properly co-ordinated. I forced myself each time as far as I could, then crouched in the snow and rested. Only when I had recovered a little did I look upwards. Then I continued. Even on the final snow fields I still had the feeling that it would

The Braldo Gorge represents the most dangerous part of the approach march to K2; the porters were constantly threatened by stone-falls.
*Overleaf*: The route led over flat snow slopes and a step in the Godwin Austen Glacier between Broad Peak and K2, almost to the foot of the steep Abruzzi Rïdge. This approach climb was threatened by avalanches from both sides.

After over fifty hours alone in the death zone, Reinhold Messner lay in his third bivouac at about 7,400m and photographed the sunset from his tent.

View from the summit of Nanga Parbat; on the right is the South Shoulder (8,042m).

Reinhold Messner on the highest point (8,125m).

Descending to the last bivouac, just 800m below the summit.

Laboriously loads were hoisted up the steep House Chimney between Camp 1 (6,100m) and Camp 2 (6,700m).

Camp 2 at 6,700m; below is the ice stream of the Godwin Austen Glacier.

*Above*: Ascent to Camp 3 (7,350m).
*Left*: In the dangerous 'Bottle-neck'.
*Below*: The final ascent to the summit.

The last bivouac at just 8,000m under the summit of K2. To the left are the Gasherbrums, Broad Peak and Chogolisa.

Reinhold Messner on the summit of K2 (8,611m), looking eastwards to the brown-grey mountain ranges of Sinkiang.

*Above*: The Potala in Lhasa, once the palace of the god-king Dalai Lama.
*Below*: In a few monasteries a large part of the statues and wall paintings were spared by the Cultural Revolution. Since 1980 the Tibetans have been able to practise their religion freely again.

*Above*: The heavily snow-covered backdrop of Everest at the end of the upper Rongbuk Valley.

Reinhold Messner's tiny Base Camp in the upper Rongbuk Valley. It was sited at the spot where the 1922 and 1924 British pioneers put up their tents.

*Above*: The long-haired yak is the Tibetan mountain dwellers' most important domesticated animal.

The Tibetan yak nomads also carry on migratory sheep herding.

Reinhold Messner on his Everest solo ascent (telephoto from Base Camp).

Above the North Col with a view of Cho Oyu, Gyachung Kang and Pumori.

perhaps be impossible. At the same time, however, I had the conviction that I would make it: every metre demanded self-conquest.

For my oxygen-starved, worn-out body it meant a torment to have to continue to battle against the force of gravity, yet at each step my whole body responded. This team-work, although already familiar from many ascents, I experienced very intensely. This time it was clearer and stronger than usual. I was certainly conscious of the danger of the climb, but this consciousness did not cramp my muscles or movements.

A heavy tiredness made me slower and slower. Yet when I looked around again after some minutes' rest I felt good. The rocks were icy-cold but every time the sun shone on them they seemed warm and less exposed. In the shade it proved more difficult to get a grip.

The air above the summit ridge was still clear, the sky deep blue to black. Did the world come to an end up there? Although I was not sweating, a salty taste lay on my tongue. When I ran it over my lips everything stuck together. After another half-hour I reached a rock projection on which I could place my whole foot. Briefly, I considered whether I should bang in a piton and belay myself for quarter of an hour. But I rejected the idea and simply squatted down, let my legs dangle over the precipice and tried to relax, while leaning my body against the rock wall which rose almost vertically behind me. I felt its pressure in my back and the damp cold from underneath through the seat of my pants as it crept high into me.

I rested for a shorter period than was necessary, then stood up awkwardly and looked upwards again. It seemed as if this rest had altered the distance to the summit. Also the face below me seemed steeper and more exposed. I would have plunged into the depths had I let go. I struggled for a while with photography and after two pictures, which I had taken of myself from eye-level, I fetched a small piece of hard bread out of my trouser pocket and chewed it slowly.

Once more I nestled up against the rock which bellied out above me. With both feet on the stool-sized pedestal and with my body leaning against the wall, I could stand there without holding on. I stuck my gloved hands between my left cheek and the wall so that I could sleep standing and could rest. Highly satisfied, I pushed the bread around in my mouth and thought that now there could be only 50m to the top at most; the last 50m of this 400m rock pillar on the summit trapezium.

'It'll go', I said to myself.

'Sure', said someone else. 'You're climbing slowly but it'll be faster going down.'

'Yes, I know, I've still got to get down.' I did not fool myself for I knew that these last 50m were the most strenuous, and I also knew that I should dawdle no longer.

I stood up straight first of all, then leaned out a bit and looked down the face. I had no desire to think about the descent now, I had to press on. I was suffering from thirst but I would not be able to drink again until evening. When my gaze slid down past my clumsy plastic boots to the great shimmering glacier tongue at the foot of the face, I felt an uneasiness in my stomach. Instinctively I clung fast to the wall. When I looked down into the seemingly endless depths an uncertainty factor came into it which was never there in climbing. As long as I was climbing and weighing each step, this tingling did not arise, nor did it when I looked down between my legs. Only when I was not concentrating on the rocks, as I stood there unbelayed, did it take hold of me. It was not

On the summit of Nanga Parbat. Reinhold Messner photographed himself with the highest point in sight and in all directions.

an unpleasant feeling, it was as if something shifted my point of gravity, which returned to normal when I was fully alert. Even when I had climbed in the Dolomites as a child I had experienced this feeling on very narrow ridges, on stances and on exposed ledges.

This ample rest had done me good, and now I was climbing easier and more confidently. I had myself under control and yet let myself go. It was nothing to do with my decision and the final spurt; I was climbing more self-confidently than before. There was no longer any question of failure, even if my strength was nearly exhausted. For a moment I thought that I would not have enough time for the descent, but this thought evaporated quickly. I relaxed again.

I was no longer battling against gravity; I floated in a tiredness which absorbed everything. The spittle which ran out of the corners of my mouth, through breathing dog-like, froze on my beard. My forehead, propped on my ice axe, was hot. With a contorted face I crouched there, oblivious. How my lungs gasped in my ears! How my heart was hammering. It was painful when the two noises superimposed themselves in my head.

I bridged up a small dièdre. Suddenly a soft jingle: the lens cap on my camera had fallen off and was lying 10m below. I could not go back for it. I had not the strength to do it and anyway it was the wrong direction. I could only climb upwards and wanted only to climb upwards.

I photographed myself more seldom and on the difficult pitches I could not take pictures of myself in any case. I needed both hands for climbing and I didn't want to use the self-timer because then I had to do the climbing three times. I had not the strength for that and I was glad when I had done it once without falling off.

It was about 4 p.m. when I arrived on top. I stuck my axe in the highest point of the snow and looked around: the Silver Saddle, below which Willo Welzenbach and Willy Merkl died between the wars, seemed near at hand below me. To the right of that the Rupal Valley. In between a sky-high precipice. Eight years before I had stood here once before at the same time of day; that time with my brother Günther who then was killed by an avalanche.

I circled around, looked about me once more as if I did not believe that I was actually on top. I experienced no such emotional outburst as on Mount Everest, and was quite

146

calm, calm as never before on an eight-thousander. Since then I have often wondered why these emotional outbursts, which had shaken me on Mount Everest with tears and sobs, were wanting on the summit of Nanga Parbat. I have come to the conclusion that as I was alone on Nanga Parbat I could not have afforded such violently passionate outbursts. If so, I would have remained up there. Our body knows more than our head.

I looked back at the snow ridge and after making a complete revolution had taken in everything. Nevertheless, I could not say what. I felt neither marvellous nor depressed, yet not indifferent; only relieved and a bit proud. I shook myself at first then sat down, facing westwards, on the rocks which rose out of the snow only a few metres below the sharp snow pyramid of the summit. It was 4.30 p.m.

As I sat there, I remembered my document, and I fetched the aluminium case out of my anorak along with the piton and banged it into the first crack which I could reach from my seat. I attached the case, fished out the parchment once more and scrawled name, route and date on it.

When I looked at the cornices through which Günther and I had climbed out of the Rupal Face in 1970, I was calm.

I photographed myself over ten minutes, first in colour, then in black and white and once more in colour. I photographed myself looking eastwards to the Silver Saddle, southwards, westwards and then eastwards again. The Karakoram peaks were scarcely recognizable, for a cloud cover which had pushed up from the Indus Valley across the countryside covered them all. To the south the tiny Rupal Peak was clear. I could hardly believe that it was a 5,000m peak. The Mazeno Wall was steep but small and also from here Ganalo Peak made no particular impression.

My concept and I were one and the world stood still. How far removed it was up here! Below me, to the south, immensely far down I saw through a window in the mist a pool and green meadows. Already the first clouds were beating up over the ridge. It was a short game that opened up even more mysteriously the view of the Diamir Valley. I pointed north-eastwards along the Silver Plateau as if there were something to see there. The wind had got stronger and was whirling snow in my footprints.

The summit on which I was standing cast its blue-grey shadow on the deep Rupal Valley until the sun disappeared behind the clouds: it was five o'clock.

I would not get back down the rocks, they were too steep and the detour via the western basin was strenuous.

'It'll get late if you don't start down.'

'The moon will come up.'

I was still fascinated by the massive banks of clouds which filled the valleys some 1,000m below me and sailed over the mountain ridges. Slowly night spread out across the valley bottoms. It was like a vague, dew-cool layer of vapour which blurred all the details. Only in the higher clouds was there still warm sunlight.

Still I could not tear myself away from the summit. In the sun's bright rays ice crystals suddenly flickered in the air. 'Now you really must go down', I said to myself. Would I find the tent again in the dark? How strange many decisions are concerning survival. The summit seemed so peaceful to me and the descent so unimportant, as if I meant nothing to myself; as if I had climbed out of a sea of loneliness into the safety of the universe. As far as the eye could see were clouds and snow peaks but no trace of life. This mountain, symbol of hostility to life, of cold and seclusion, conveyed to me a strong feeling of the universe. The horizon around me was like a circle. My footprints in the snow provided the only visible change far and wide.

I suffered in that I could not say anything, could not tell anyone about these sensations; yet what I felt I could not have put into words. I had arrived at a point where at last I could stop thinking. The blurred horizon, the veiled sky – all that was beyond language. I did not perceive these sensations with my understanding. I simply sat there and let myself dissolve in feelings. I knew everything at once, without doubt. I wanted to lose myself for ever in this twilight above the horizon.

'I', I said; but already this single sound from my innermost self threatened to tear me apart. As I sat there I too became cloud and mist. This infinite calm released contentment in me. And the silence urged me to touch the summit very gently. 'I am it and yet I am not it.' When I tried to speak again, it silenced me. My personal story spread out before me like the wind with the clear consciousness that it would not continue endlessly. I was not sad about that. The world enveloped me and spat me out, I experienced it seething and whirling.

When I had stood here eight years ago, my feelings were more intense, or different; perhaps the same. Then Günther had come over the last snow edge towards the summit. For a moment I had the feeling of floating on one of these clouds and of seeing us as we embraced. Then I saw the despair come over us, as it became clear that it was

impossible to climb back down our ascent route. Like a reproach it remained between us. I could recollect the very same course of events as if I had two separate remembrances.

Today I was not so excited. Nanga Parbat had been my first eight-thousander when I was still inexperienced.

After an hour I descended from the summit. At first I went down the South Ridge and then over the snow of the Western Basin. The shadows were long and the track behind me stood out darkly against the rose-coloured snow. Step by step I slithered down the uneven snow.

It became clear to me how knocked up and how tired I was. Often exertion consisted solely of dragging my boots out of the deep track behind me. By the time I noticed that the ramp-like ledge on which I was moving merged into the steep rock wall it was too late. Go back I could not, I was much too tired for that. There was no question of a direct descent because vertical steps lay between me and the Western Basin. Trusting to my instinct I searched for a new route amongst the drops and isolated snow fields. Sometimes I had to concentrate all my powers on a single point so as not to slip.

Arriving at the bivouac site, this world had a meaning for me. The tent was small and iced up, all its walls sloping, the entrance so narrow that I could only force myself in with difficulty. Sitting in the tent, I pulled off my boots outside, then banged them together so that the snow fell off and then fetched them inside. It was still light. I lay down on my sleeping bag and tried to sort myself out. I closed my eyes the better to be able to rest. I thought of the descent. Cut off — how familiar to me that was!

Before falling asleep I knew the weather would turn bad. At first I only thought it, then it really did. In the night I sensed the mist pressing against the tent. I was overly still and I had a hunch that the storm would pin me down. From all the cols and ridges a whistling and rustling suddenly resounded.

In the morning I cooked and looked out of the tent. I could not see how heavily it was snowing because it was still rather dark. Everything was overcast. The new flakes merged immediately with the dirty snow in front of the tent. Only to the left above the tent gleamed a remnant of bright sky, perhaps it was a delusion.

Towards six o'clock I crawled out of my lodgings and stared into the mist. The snow trickled from the roof of the tent. My hands were immediately moist. It was snowing and blowing a gale. Near me a woman was talking again but I did not understand her. With a handful of snow I rubbed my face awake. The altimeter had risen twenty-seven points: visibility was nil and a descent was impossible. I must wait. It was all about survival.

I still had food for five days but when the weather turned bad on Nanga Parbat it could stay bad for ten days. Therefore, I had to ration fuel and provisions; I didn't want to die.

Were I to set out now, unquestionably I would lose my way as had Franz Jäger and Andi Schlick, my two companions who went missing in the snowstorm on our descent from Manaslu in 1972. So I bided my time, squatting in the tent, parched and very, very tired. I became clumsy too. Twice the full cooking pot fell over, burning a part of my down sleeping bag. Still my will to survive was undiminished. 'If I save gas', I said to myself, 'I can hold out here for five days. However, I must drink a little every day.'

Already the first avalanches were rushing down the face, blown on by the wind. For a while I watched the drops of water which ran down the inside of the tent walls. I was lucky to have discovered something. Then I conversed again with my invisible companions and spoke of a country in which one can talk with everybody one meets, just as we talked with each other; in which one is taken seriously by everyone and also takes everyone seriously.

It was still snowing. In vain I tried to tidy up some more in the tent. Time and again I envisaged the way back, now cut off: gigantic seracs over which I could not abseil because I had no rope with me; bare ice over which avalanches were now thundering.

I had not reckoned that the bad weather would break over me without warning and had no idea how long it would last. I knew the Diamir Face well, but nevertheless in mist it would have been a trap for me.

I spent the next few hours until it got light day-dreaming. It was strange that I could occupy myself with them in this hopelessness. In clear images I saw my tent become snowed up in the hollow: the future which became life before death in my imagination. Later I was thirsty and I saw myself as a young lad walking towards a spring with an empty bottle, in order to fetch water for my grandfather who was harvesting hay on a mountain meadow. I had often done that and I knew that cress grew around the water that sprang gurgling out of the ground. I made a puddle and let the sand sink before I laid the bottle flat in the water-hole, then waited until the bottle was full.

If my shoulders were not covered by the sleeping bag most of the time, I felt chilly. Although I kept moving with small gymnastic exercises to fight off the cold, I could not warm myself up. Absent-mindedly, I sipped the first of the hot water and summed up the situation again and again: the traverse out to the Mazeno Col on the Rupal Face was out of the question in fresh snow, for the avalanche danger was too great. Descent via the 'Bridge' had become impossible through the earthquake. The upper Mummery Rib was now iced up. The only way which remained was the steep ice runnel to the right of the Mummery Ribs. If I couldn't climb down there I was lost. Doubtless the lower part of this runnel was covered in water ice but there were no big drops and my crampons were still holding well.

The cloud cover over Nanga Parbat sank lower and lower. Terry could not see me the whole day. Nevertheless, he scanned down the face with the binoculars through every window in the mist. In between he stood up to stretch his strained back. Obstinately he tried to get a bit of the summit wall in his sights.

Up above on the mountain, storm, new snow and icy cold dominated. All the rocks below me must be covered with a thick layer of ice. If every chimney, every crack, every cleft were iced up, there was no way back for me alone. Of course, I knew that there was no bivouac site where I wanted to descend. If I broke down half-way there was no salvation.

When I stuck my head out of the tent again, the first star was showing in the dark sky. It was evening already; or did I see between the clouds the stars at midday? To the west and below me in the valleys lay gloomy mist banks. I had no idea of the weather forecast, no idea that new monsoon outrunners were approaching from the south.

On my small gas cooker, in its rickety position between the tent wall and my sleeping bag, I brewed another beaker of tea. Then I tried to sleep. Sometimes I half sat up, my right arm propped on the sleeping bag to drink another gulp. I drank not with pleasure, rather because I had to. My blood must not be allowed to thicken. Food — a bit of cheese, then hard bread — tasted sticky and stale on my dried-out palate.

Despite the doubts which plagued me, I forced myself to relax. But as long as I was not warm, I had no control over myself. This day of inactivity gnawed at my nerves. To just lie doing nothing also took energy. At this height and seclusion everything was strenuous.

On the steep ice face below me there were no resting places, so I would not be able to recover on the descent.

While dozing I remembered how shreds of clouds were racing across the sky outside. 'It'll be over soon', I said, repeating a favourite expression of my mother's. In saying something I broke the silence, perhaps just to encourage myself. From the small differences in brightness I could recognize through the tent wall that it was night-time. The moon alternately revealed and concealed itself and there was an uncanny atmosphere outside.

The stars were suddenly extinguished as the weather worsened again. The drama of this changing light was strengthened by the fact that on the face it was now completely windless. For the first time since I had been on the move alone the air stood still. Not once a whispering in the snow crystals. And what promised still worse, it was now warm! Or did it only feel so because I had been snuggling inside my sleeping bag to warm myself up? For a long time I lay there like that and listened to the silence. Nothing and no one interrupted it.

The softness and warmth in the air reminded me of bad weather, of snowstorms; reminded me also of the dramatic days in 1934 when Merkl and Welzenbach died. How often I had read that story! Now I was at exactly the same height as the expedition had been then — and in a snowstorm as well. They had already been far above the Silver Saddle with the summit near at hand. In the night, however, as they prepared themselves for the final assault, the storm overtook them. It was scarcely endurable even in the tent. The cold gave them a hard time. Their clothes were icy and began to thaw in their sleeping bags with their body-heat. The storm blew enormous snow plumes from the ridge over the camp. Merkl and Welzenbach had survived numerous dangers in the Alps without harm. They and their comrades also knew the difference between a storm in the Alps at 3,000—4,000m and a Himalayan hurricane at 8,000m.

It was a stormy day on 7 July 1934 with the sunlight smothered in the whirl of the snow squalls. Merkl, Schneider, Welzenbach and Wieland deliberated in the main tent. What to do? Wait it out. Sahibs and porters lay apathetically in their sleeping bags. The hurricane frustrated all their attempts at cooking. So came the second night, a night of sinking hope. Tent poles bent and snow-dust spurted through all the crevices and seams. The storm raged on ever more frantically.

On the morning of 8 July all were convinced of the necessity of an immediate retreat to the lower camps. The lives of five climbers and a dozen porters were at stake. Merkl ordered Aschenbrenner and Schneider to go on ahead with three porters. The others also got ready for the descent. The advance party fought their way down grimly. When they came to the Silver Saddle, the storm increased to such a degree that they were able to make the descent of the steep face only with the greatest caution.

About 100m below the saddle Sherpa Nima Dorje was plucked off his feet by the storm but they managed to hold him. In the raging snowstorm the men could barely see 10m. Only once, as the storm tore the clouds apart for a moment, did they see the second party coming down from the Silver Saddle. At seven o'clock in the evening Aschenbrenner and Schneider were in Camp 4, covered in ice. They waited in vain for the others the whole evening and night.

Willy Merkl and his men did not come. Below the Silver Saddle they set up an intermediate camp. Welzenbach slept in the snow without a sleeping bag. Again they had nothing to eat. One Sherpa died. Merkl's right hand and both of Wieland's froze. Continuing the descent, three Sherpas collapsed. They remained hanging on the ropes or lying in the tent dead.

On 9 July the heavy snow clouds tore apart once more and for a few minutes one could see up the ridge. Below the Silver Saddle they spotted a bigger party descending. Why weren't they further on? Behind the group wandered a single dot at some distance. This was Uli Wieland who a little later fell asleep in his exhaustion and died. During that night a further half-metre of snow fell. From the Silver Saddle, 100m snow plumes whipped horizontally over the Rakhiot side. Four men waded down from above, leaving open behind them a man-sized trench. They were four Sherpas, totally exhausted, simply at the end. Their hands were frozen and one was snow-blind.

Welzenbach wrote his last message:

Camp 7, 10 July. To the Sahibs between Camps 6 and 4. We have been lying here since yesterday after we lost Uli on the way down. We are both sick. An attempt to get through to Camp 6 failed on account of general weakness. I, Willo, have probably got bronchitis, angina and influenza. Bara Sahib is generally exhausted and has frostbitten hands and feet. We haven't eaten anything warm for six days and have drunk almost nothing. Please send help soon to us here in Camp 7. Willo and Willy.

In the night of 12 July Welzenbach died in camp. Next morning Merkl pulled himself together. Propped on two ice axes he moved downwards along the ridge. When the mists parted he saw the tents of the camp standing below. Rescue from there was out of the question for the snow was too deep. Merkl did not manage the climb up to the

Moor's Head again. He tried again and again but collapsed. Two Sherpas were still with him and the three of them dug themselves a small ice cave. With his Sherpa Gay Lay Merkl rolled himself up in a blanket, and as an underlay they had a foam-rubber mat. But it was only big enough for two and Angtsering had to make do with a blanket. Thus they spent the night in the inexorable bluster of the storm.

On 13 July three people were seen descending from Camp 7. Half-way to Camp 6, in the col before the climb back up to the Moor's Head, a man stepped forward and waved. Again all three pulled themselves together to continue. But Merkl and Gay Lay got only 3m further then could not go on. Laboriously they dragged themselves back to the cave. Angtsering still had the strength to overcome the climb.

Only on the next evening did he reach Camp 4 completely exhausted and with severe frostbite. On 15 and 16 July Schneider and Aschenbrenner tried once more to reach Camp 5. In vain. In the enormous masses of fresh snow they were thrown back. The next morning they distinctly heard shouting on the wind but the waving man on the saddle was no more to be seen.

When they found Merkl and Gay Lay four years later, their bodies lay fully preserved in the snow. From Merkl's position it was concluded that he still had not given up on life. He lay there like one who just wanted to take a rest, had his gloves off and spread out on his thighs. Yet everything pointed to the fact that Willy died before Gay Lay ...

I had the feeling of having been there. The thought of death made me conscious that nothing is really important. The question as to what would come after death did not concern me. For me both things were feasible: a life after death as well as total extinction.

I had no mirror with me, nevertheless now and then I ran my fingers through my hair. Did I still look like a human being, generally speaking?

Later, lightly at first, then gradually becoming stronger in stages, a buzzing and hissing arose around the tent. I didn't know whether I had slept or had just lain there. Also I didn't know how much time had elapsed while being lost in contemplation of the silence. Now it was windy again outside. The air had something tense and tingling about it.

I wanted to open the tent but I didn't. I caught myself staring through the tent wall trying to make out the ice axe and crampons which were stuck in the snow not half a metre away, but I could not see their outlines. If the storm made off with them I was lost, for a descent without crampons and ice axe was impossible. Although I knew without any doubt that a fresh bout of bad weather was imminent, I didn't want to think about it any more. I would not perish so quickly.

I fell asleep. Just at that moment, however, the first of the thunder rumbled. This rumbling stifled my last hope of better weather.

At night I sat right up in my sleeping bag gasping for air. I felt constrained like someone who is suffocating in his own unconsciousness. It was still snowing but only lightly. I could not distinguish from the noises outside whether the snow slides were coming down near the tent, from the tent roof or over the face. The noise of unseen avalanches formed a bridge between my restless sleep and the ice desert outside.

I opened my eyes so as to orientate myself in the tent. If I had seen correctly, it was three o'clock in the morning. My shoulders and back were cramped, perhaps because the cold had bored through my sleeping mat and bag into my joints. Time and again I heard a thundering in the distance and the sinister rustling outside. Again Merkl's fate came to mind. At night I awoke often quite senseless, moments in which despair and astonishment at still being there merged into one another.

The tent wall was stiff, covered inside and out with a brittle layer of ice. An ice crust had also formed on my sleeping bag. Day was already dawning. Only in the east, where the summit of Nanga Parbat towered up, the black of the night had not completely dispersed. Indistinctly I could see my ice-encrusted axe and crampons through the slightly transparent tent surfaces. Everything was still there. Instinctively I groped for my boots and stuck them, half-frozen though they were, in my sleeping bag.

I must have slept for a few hours; but perhaps I had only lain there without noticing anything. Now the wind was dropping.

Despite the biting cold, which had set in over the mountain, I had warm feet. The icy tent was apparently a perfect igloo. During the next half-hour I tried to brew up, a cupful only, before I opened up the tent. I could not eat. I knew now exactly what I wanted to do. If it was clear and only the sky cloudy, I would descend, throw the tent in a crevasse and simply go down in one day to Base Camp. Only if there was mist or snow so that I couldn't orientate myself would I stay put.

How lovely it was to be able to decide everything alone! Here I bore the responsibility for no one except myself. Nevertheless, my thoughts strayed and I directed my attention on something outside of me, often I knew not on what.

The descent would be treacherous, strenuous. Thought of the seracs alone already made me shiver.

It was a mistake to drink so little. My blood was already thickening, as I noticed with every manipulation.

I was anxious about Ursula and Terry who were waiting for me down below. Probably they thought I had disappeared. I had no idea what they were doing but I hoped they were not worrying too much.

On the morning of 11 August Ursula wrote in her diary:

Occasionally I try to imagine what would happen if Nanga Parbat were to see its chance — perhaps its last chance, after Reinhold has already slipped through its fingers once. Several times I catch myself thinking that perhaps once briefly the world would turn to me, were I to report on the last hours of the 'great Reinhold Messner'. I could produce this scene theatrically and pathetically with impunity because no one else is here.

But otherwise I feel rotten. For the first time for twenty-seven years I'm taking Valium without success. Have stuffed myself full of cheese and honey (should be good for me, especially for my nerves), read, written, reflected, stared my eyes red through the binoculars; thrown the bloody things away because they made me still crazier, only to fetch them after a short time to stare again. And then once I flew into a rage: what justification has he for climbing up there. Pursuing his 'natural high', seeking satisfaction through the mountain and probably also getting it, while I, Terry too perhaps, are going crazy here at the bottom of Nanga

Parbat, not sleeping, keeping our fingers crossed and praying. Have you ever prayed for anyone? I mean prayed in the widest sense?

I have been crying too. Actually not on his account, solely because it helps me to endure emotional stress. Most of all I would love to fetch him down by the ears off this rubbish heap.

Later on the Austrians arrived. They are attempting another route and were very nice to me, really nice. They offered me all too many explanations for the disappearance of the 'dot'. One gives me a mountain crystal. My pleasure at that is great, still greater my astonishment. I say to myself: the mountaineering world has closed ranks – this was the last straw!

Then a great rage seized me again. Just think, I said to myself, not a bit of it, now more than ever: Reinhold's made it! There is no other possibility. And generally I am afraid no longer, am firmly convinced that he is undergoing up there a good, strong and intense experience. He will come down tired, certainly, but safe. I envy him and am glad for him. How could I doubt for a minute in his safe return? What can happen? I have boundless faith in his mountaineer's skills and what has he to lose? So what if he returns without having done it. At least he will still have his dream! And if he remains sitting up there on Nanga Parbat or somewhere down below? Who else can experience such a high shortly before death? My God, when I think of our German intensive care units! Actually I must pray that he be granted the one and spared the other. Anyway, he is a lucky person. So why this fear, this silly fear? Madly I envy him his situation, without grudging him it. I am happy for him. And I can well imagine that even I as an anti-mountaineer would accept considerable hardships for such an experience.

On the morning of 11 August I noticed that the weather was better, if not good. Without thinking too much, I made the only correct decision: leave everything, go down. I threw my equipment – tent, sleeping bag, cooker – into a crevasse. In my rucksack I had only some film, cameras and odds and ends like an altimeter and some goggles.

Nothing held me back now. At 5 a.m. I was out of the tent, having made my decision, staking everything on one throw of the dice. I left behind also all my provisions – soups, cooker, everything. I had to try to reach Base Camp in a single mighty stage this day. Down 3,000m in the steepest, most direct line. If I didn't make it, I would not survive the coming night.

With this knowledge I set off. It was the last powerful incentive. I moved obliquely to the slope, slipped suddenly and lost my balance. Already I seemed to be falling, yet I was still standing on my crampons. I made some flying leaps, trying to get them to grip again. If only I could get into balance again! After springing down the steep face for ten or fifteen metres I was standing firmly once more, trembling from head to foot, and the blood had drained from my head. This carelessness could have ended in a fall! With my ice axe I chopped a big step for a rest.

Things had turned out well once again. A sprained ankle, a fractured shin bone would have meant the end. The shock made me concentrate all my powers; I was all attention.

The ice hose down which I wanted to climb was the most dangerous place on Nanga Parbat. But I said to myself, if I can go nowhere else, then needs must.

I knew I would die if I did not ration my strength or did not get through this day, but I had not actually written myself off yet. After the bivouac I was certainly dehydrated and therefore clumsy, but I was still mobile. I knew exactly what it was like to climb down through bad snow. The face here was not steep, so that the snow was still lying – a wretched, breakable crust. I had to summon up all my skills and could make no more errors. The crust was fairly hard so that I only broke through with my crampons. At each step one foot went in. Each time I risked losing my balance. Lower down sometimes I came to bare ice.

Climbing down ice is more difficult than climbing up. At first I tried to go down facing outwards, bending forwards, hacking steps. However, I could not cut steps down the entire face. There was only one method that was feasible: to climb down facing inwards, with my axe in my right hand and my gloved left fist as support. That way it went better, so just as I had climbed up, I climbed down. I couldn't cut steps as I couldn't lean outwards or twist my body.

This sort of descent was the most dangerous. One slip and I would have been away down the face which fell 3,000m below me. When I looked down I could not adjust myself to this face. After every 100 paces – or was it only ninety? – I was coughing from exhaustion. I leaned my body against the ice wall as the air went stabbing into my lungs. My arms were leaden from the constant use of the ice axe, and when I rested I exchanged one torment for another. Everything was strenuous here.

In the rest stops, small snow slides banked up over my boots and arms. The wind drove drift snow towards me and soon I was covered with an armour of ice. The valley bottom still lay so discouragingly far off that it did not pay to look down. Therefore I concentrated again on what I had to do.

At the next rest stop I chopped a step in the ice so as to get a better foot-hold. Slowly I progressed with many pauses. Once, when I sat down, it was especially difficult to stand up again. Only by deceiving myself with falsehoods did I succeed in getting to my feet. One more step, just one more step, then it was easier again. It had to be!

The fine cracks, where the front points of my crampons had gripped a few seconds before, glittered in front of my eyes. I could not rest between the enormous seracs and every minute I won here was a gift of life.

On this day I took no more photographs. But now more than ever I talked with someone; even in French. And this although I had never learned French.

Time and again Terry peered upwards with the glasses into the dark ice hose. Embedded between the seracs and the Mummery Rib, this runnel constituted the steepest part of the Diamir Face. For the whole afternoon Terry watched. His eyes burned and in between he made himself stand up and walk around a bit. The glasses, however, were like a drug. He had to have it, he had to look.

The further I descended, the slower I became. The face was no longer as steep and sometimes I moved facing outwards again. The ice here was so hard that I could no longer kick steps.

For a good hour I climbed down without registering where I was and where I was going. When I arrived in the vicinity of my first bivouac, I knew that I was safe. The feeling of security and the first water that I sucked out of a melt gully, drove away my tiredness.

Gloomy cloud banks were moving up the Diamir Valley. I realized that I could endure a night in the open but I had to continue. Each time I breathed out there came a sigh of relief: a sign that I was on the brink of complete collapse?

I was not sure whether I would still make it down to the greenery. My calves, the muscles in my arms, everything in my body was knotted up and hard. I held my ice axe in my hand as if it were welded to it. Still a good two hours to go to Base Camp! To my invisible companions I said little. I heard them no more either. Once I had to leap over a crevasse. The jump, a big step, required concentration. It was already warm, almost hot. Everywhere little streams ran across the ice. I clenched my teeth and determined not to think of it. Drinking made me still more tired.

Step by step I came down the mountain across the ice, which shimmered green-blue under me in the crevasses. The world around was interspersed with seracs, avalanche slopes to the left and right. At least there was no longer an endless chasm below me. The nape of my neck hurt. Every time I placed my crampons on the bare ice I looked fleetingly to the left, then right, left, right. Bewildered by my slow movements and the size of the glacier, the distances seemed to me eternal. And yet, to be alone and trusting only to my own abilities gave me a strong feeling of identity.

I performed the rest of the descent in a trance-like state. Often I saw myself tottering over the mirror-smooth ice surface. Sometimes, when my crampons slipped a few millimetres, it was difficult to get a hold. But before I catapulted out of balance, they gripped again every time, as if they did the right thing of themselves.

In Base Camp they had long since seen me. Ursula came towards me across the scree of the enormous cirque. She had my trainers in her hand.

We reached one another. I pulled off my club-foot boots, threw them away and wanted never to see them again.

After his solo ascent, Reinhold Messner presented his liaison officer, Terry, with the ice axe with which he had climbed for five days.

Reinhold Messner at the foot of the Nanga Parbat face after his solo summit climb.

158

# RENUNCIATION OF THE MAGIC LINE

In 1979, the year after my successful solo ascent of Nanga Parbat, I set off to the Karakoram on an expedition to K2. During the winter I had given many lectures and written a book, besides organizing and financing the new trip.

The team I put together was to be international and young. I invited Friedl Mutschlechner, a guide from South Tyrol whose style and character was especially dear to me, someone I would most like to climb with. I gladly took along Michl Dacher, at that time the most successful high-altitude climber in West Germany. Robert Schauer had proved himself on Mount Everest in 1978; he was also fast. Alessandro Gogna had for many years been among the mountaineers whom I liked and respected way and above all competitive considerations. Renato Casarotto was at this time the leading Italian mountaineer and I was sure that he would be the strongest man in the group.

We lost three weeks' time on the approach march. There was no road connection to Skardu and we were dependent on aircraft and good weather. Meanwhile we had learned that, three weeks after us, a mammoth-sized French expedition would start to climb the South-South-West Pillar, the 'Magic Line' I had thought out. An attempt on our part would have been nothing less than a reconnaissance for the French.

After ascending to the middle of the South Face, we decided that we would switch over to the Abruzzi Ridge. There and only there we had a small chance of reaching the summit, mainly because there were only five of us.

Renato showed himself to be too weak for the summit zone. We set up three camps and secured the route with fixed ropes to a position above the Black Pyramid. Then it fell to me and Michl Dacher to make the first attempt. Sadly, Friedl Mutschlechner had gone sick.

# The Shadow of K2

## COMPROMISE ON THE MOUNTAIN OF MOUNTAINS

It was afternoon and still pleasantly warm as I emptied out my rucksack in front of the tent. Some ravens, which squatted around Base Camp like highway robbers, came a few hops nearer. I crawled into the tent. The items of equipment which I needed for the summit lay in orderly confusion on my sleeping mat. Only I could recognize a logic in the chaos of clothes, boots and laces. Bit by bit I stacked them away in my blue sack, weighed it and went on packing.

When I crawled outside again, the big black birds flew off with hoarse croaks. A gust of wind scattered them and they sailed off into the sky in different directions. One climbed so high that, for a brief moment, it came between me and the summit of K2 but not, I thought, close to it; as I was gazing up he came back down. That was my way, pushing beyond my own horizon.

Once more I opened my rucksack to see if I had forgotten anything. It was our first summit assault. As I held the items of equipment in my hand, I saw as in a kind of lantern-slide lecture ever-new, self-blending images: when touching my crampons, I saw a piece of bare, blue-green ice; when touching my gloves, I saw the cold at night; and when touching the tiny tent, I saw the chilly air of the death zone.

Back in the tent, I listened as someone made a noise outside. Stones rattled. Then Michl peeped in and asked whether by chance I had a second pair of gloves for him. As I handed them to him, I saw how happy he was. He only nodded and went back to his tent where his rucksack was standing. I listened as he busied himself with it.

For all his calmness and steadiness, Michl was ambitious and aggressive. The two of us had secured most of the route and had learned to appreciate each other. Already during the weeks of preparation and happy to be with one another, it was tacitly agreed that we would go to the summit together. We were well matched but not sworn partners.

Half an hour later my rucksack was packed and I placed it outside my tent. Twice I weighed it in my hand. 'So', I said to myself, simply 'so', as if this meant something.

During the day the dull haze, which had hung in the air since dawn and brought this heaviness, disappeared and the mist moved away eastwards. In the sky there appeared blue windows as clear as glass. The first days of high summer had arrived.

By four o'clock in the morning it was already light. As I crawled out of my tent in the dawn, I felt light-hearted. At this time of day the air was refreshing and encouraging. I saw the mountains, the glacier streams, heard the snow creak under my boot soles, and forgot what I actually wanted here and where I was going.

Michl and I had got up somewhat later than planned. Despite the forthcoming summit assault, we felt no special excitement. Would we succeed? Perhaps a snowstorm would turn us back that same day.

Breakfast in Base Camp was the same as usual. Ros Ali served steaming tea and we helped ourselves to linseed biscuits out of an open tin. It was cold and only a hint of brightness came through the red tent walls.

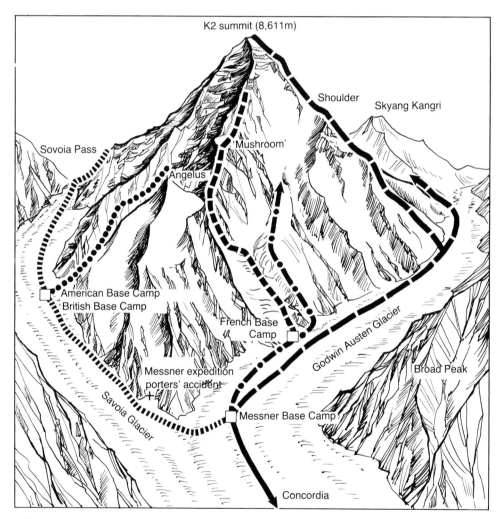

The routes on K2: ⅢⅢ = Abortive 1975 American attempt from Savoia Pass up the West Face. . . . . = Similarly abortive attempt by 1978 British expedition. ---- = In 1979 the French had to give up between the 'Mushroom' and the summit. —·—·— = Messner's reconnaissance on the South Face. —————— = Ascent route of Messner expedition via the Abruzzi Ridge.

On the flat glacier immediately behind Base Camp and after about a kilometre I stopped for the first time by a big rock. The sun struck the top of K2, probing it and bringing the snow and ice slopes to life. The caress lasted some minutes. I noticed how a wave of hope rose in me, while at the same time I experienced a definite loss of sense of scale. I had not the slightest notion how high this peak towered above me. My eyes fastened on the summit – now I knew where it was.

Michl was behind me; like a small black line he came across the dirty glacier.

'The light', I said to him when he stood beside me, 'will be especially clear today.'

Was that a good sign? This sun! Like a high summer morning in the Western Alps.

As I climbed on, I stared occasionally at the sunlit slopes, losing my rhythm in so doing.

Above the mountain ranges which bordered Base Camp to the west, and whose aspect was so familiar to me, streamed the first sunbeams. Bright and distinct, they contrasted in all their transparency with the still-glassy background. The sky too was the texture of space. Tattered wind plumes fluttered from the summits.

How harmonious it was here where everything rhymed. I did not think about myself or about this scenery. I just moved and gazed. We wanted to be up there! That was my sole, dominating thought.

Slowly, and in a great right-handed arc, we approached the start of the climb. Michl and I climbed the snow slope to the right of the Abruzzi Ridge as was our custom. We had never discussed why we took this route rather than the usual one. We had always done it: a good two weeks ago we set up the first and second camps; and then again when it was necessary to secure the route to Camp 3.

And now for the last time we continued on our accustomed course as, in sharp zigzags, we moved across the sun-roughened snow. I supported my body lightly on my ice axe, so that my whole weight was on the inside edges of my boot soles as I kicked steps in the snow. Each went at his own speed, unhurried by the other.

There was no sense of urgency in Camp 1 as we lay, dozed and slept, occasionally making tea. We had to drink a lot.

Such elation in the morning at the sight of the sun! The valleys beneath us were filled with vapour and the slopes seemed to steam. To the west it was quite clear. The landscape was so extensive that I did not try to count the summits. Every time I gazed skywards, I involuntarily did a hop, skip and a jump despite my morning clumsiness.

I kept to the centre of the Great Tower. Half-way between Camps 1 and 2, I stopped to rest and look around. I sat there for a while quite alone, looking down at the glaciers and moraines which grew ever broader the longer I stared. In enormous meanders they wound their way to Base Camp and on down to Concordia, where they joined the Baltoro Glacier in a sharp, right-hand bend. From above, these glaciers looked like motorways. The mountain ranges beyond were icy, with winding moraine ridges in between and following the exact line of the horizon from whence we came.

Above the Baltoro Glacier the air seemed to sway and float like an amorphous mass. We were already high up – it was strange how transparent the air was here. I saw myself strolling about down there with K2, the great unknown, before me. What wonderful madness this ascent was and being able to look down on myself! It was a happy memory when I thought of the view from below.

The wind whistled amongst the rocks but time and again my thoughts went down to the valleys, to the glaciers. Once again I saw myself seduced into reflections which were all too familiar to me: going home with the mountain behind me. I knew that the beautiful thing about climbing was that it wasn't all uphill. At that I came back to the present, looked up and wanted to get on.

With a jerk I stood up, put on my rucksack and took a few steps. Climbing was strenuous at this height. The steepness of the face and the smooth rocks, on which my crampons often found no hold, forced an irregular rhythm on me. I climbed around an edge and rested. The sun shone hot on my back like a second load. Only after several minutes did I feel strength again in my arms and legs.

Always when I was moving, climbing, or scrambling, I felt physically and mentally good. Even the first part of a rest when my lungs still heaved and my heart pounded in my neck was fine!

In camp I began to think back over my day-dreams, but I did not succeed. In the tent — the floor was just bed-sized — we sat for a while, sorting our things. It was all so confined and yet comfortable. Michl agreed and in that I was not disappointed. Security? The feeling that such a 'nest' promotes is something else, another sort of safety. We were not embedded here, only encapsulated and hidden in the mountain. Soon I forgot where I was, forgot everything except the self-imposed constriction and domesticity. I covered myself up with the world.

My thoughts were concentrated not on the dangers which surrounded us, not on the exertions which awaited us, nor on the distances which separated us from humanity. I was just there. At least that was easy for me. I opened the tent door and leaned out to fetch snow. A pair of crampons lay on the stones, together with an ice axe. Far below in the valley the air quivered; or did it only seem so?

In the tent were the buzzing cooker and Michl rolling over in his sleeping bag. The narrow snugness — and then again, on looking outside, the almost endless profundity. Stones, on which ice crystals glittered; the most subtle breath of wind brought goose-pimples to my face. What was real now?

In the afternoon we slept a little. Suddenly we both sat up in alarm, a falling stone

Panorama of the Baltoro, Abruzzi and Godwin Austen glaciers; K2 is on the left.

rumbling through our consciousness. There was no time to tear open the door. We could only hope that the tent would not be hit.

On this third day of climbing the weather seemed to change. Certainly the sun was still shining but its light was livid and in the morning it was even ghostly. Vapour lay in the valleys, grey or blue-green, and the lack of wind depressed us.

That we continued climbing nevertheless was due more to something instinctive, rather than experience or intelligence. Easily we overcame the Black Pyramid on the fixed ropes, much the most difficult part of the Abruzzi Ridge; this time it was a stroll in comparison to the ascent of a week before. Camp 3, erected by Friedl and Robert, was still standing. The snow slopes above looked sinister to me; as sinister as the veiled sky and the many cirrus clouds over Sinkiang and Tibet.

Now, in the afternoon, all the weather signs were bad. In the valleys there was transparent mist like milky glass. In the west, clouds towered up with gloomy streaks above. The mountains looked too near and yet too far.

In the evening these bad weather signs were still increasing. Nevertheless a sharp north wind overnight drove away all the clouds and broke up the mist. Had it not been so, we would have had to give up our summit assault.

The whole night long the storm raged over our tent. Michl and I, united by the worry that our plans might go awry, were for hours the only hope for one another. It was as if I were experiencing the dissolution of the world and as if we were floating, shaken by the wind, in a spaceless, timeless universe. How it howled and whistled around the tent. Every stick, every thread bawled its own tune.

Shortly before waking up I dreamed that K2 had vanished with us for all time, dissolved, as if it had never existed. When I then looked out, it was already light and the sky was as clear and as peaceful as I had experienced it while suspended over nothingness during my dream.

An immaculately clear, cool morning. Only in the far distant valleys was there any mist, seeming to suffocate the world beneath. Broad Peak stood opposite us in all its hugeness and the mist moving high up in between us made it change in form and size. The moon, wholly visible on the western edge of the horizon, was almost full.

Today we had to be off very early and we wanted to cook before the sun came up. So that we would have hot tea at the right time, Michl had placed a bagful of snow at the bottom of our sleeping bags the evening before.

As we set off, the sunlight on the wavy snow surface above us was so strongly reflected that the crevasses hardly stood out. Carefully I poked my axe into the white, wind-stirred surface. Step by step I groped my way to the edge of the blunt ridge between the South and East Faces. Here the snow was hard in places. Michl caught up with me. Often we broke through the crusted snow cover up to our waists. Like moles we burrowed in the floury whiteness, leaving an open grave behind us. We made a right-hand bend around a big serac. Alternating the lead, we toiled cross a steep snow field pregnant with avalanches. I broke through the cornices and stood up on the Shoulder. Done it!

We rested for a while. The extent of the gently ascending snow slopes above us was alarming. It seemed to me that an eternity lay between us and the summit.

The heat was not oppressive. We pulled ourselves together. Loose and composed of blue-white crystals, the snow lay ankle-deep on a hard underlay. At each step it creaked under our crampons and this noise soothed me. Now, with the slow climbing, I had the feeling of having become lighter, and of moving without clear form over this broad snow ridge. Tiredness. Nothing solemn in me any more, only lungs and heart which expanded my chest ever wider. I was no longer body, rather floating surfaces, moving like the surface on which I stood.

On a flatter part between the Shoulder and the 'Bottle-neck', I threw off my rucksack. Then it occurred to me to check how high we were already. The altimeter showed 7,950m; that might be right but then it seemed to me too much and I rejected it because of my old fear of deceiving myself at this height. The wind blew snow across the ridge, the sun was still high and the sky was so black that one could imagine darkness behind it. All fine weather days at high altitude are similar.

'Beautiful spot', said Michl.

'Um, yes', I replied.

'It's sheltered over there, to the left.'

'Yeah.'

'We must dig the tent in', observed Michl.

'Do you think that's necessary?', I said.

Our tent was red and blue. The tents far below were green and yellow or just blue; the tents at Base Camp were red.

At this altitude campsites were only safe if the tents stood under an overhang; whether of ice or rock made no difference. However, here there were no overhangs and for that reason there was no ideal bivouac site. We looked for the most suitable spot – it was a niche which we kicked out of ice and firm snow on a 30-degree slope. We anchored the tent with ice axes and pitons. It lay embedded between hip-high snow drifts and a flattened ridge on the right side, and would have offered protection in the case of a storm out of Sinkiang. Our lodging gave the impression of being placed like a dormer window in a ski jump that fell 3,000 metres to the Godwin Austen Glacier at the foot of K2.

Actually it had been my plan to climb as far as the last Italian bivouac site but in the

Michl Dacher.

meantime I had realized that that would have been too far. Michl, too, said: 'It's better here'. Nonetheless, I knew that it wasn't right. The higher we could get that day, the less we would have to climb the next. Who knew what the snow was like up there?

Michl seemed optimistic: 'We'll knock off this top in six hours', he declared, convinced of making the summit during the next day. But a whole night still lay ahead of us, a night in the death zone. And it was these nights of which I was frightened, as a child is of a dark cellar.

Dusk came slowly as if the night were still somewhat delayed for us. From underneath, through the pencil-thick foam mat, cold and torment crept into us. I felt as if isolated, sharply separated perceptions were tearing me from the mountain, dragging doubts into my unity again. It was not the exertion, the heat or the cold which often drove me to despair, it was this terror of being there, which had no counterbalance to being able to do nothing. I knew that Michl underestimated the route to the summit. I could not share his optimism. My mood was born of considerations which condensed themselves to fear with the increasing blackness of night. Not confused, whipped-up fear, but much more the light gnawing, nourished by a thousand doubts, which enveloped, tormented and disquieted me in half-sleep.

For the last time Michl fetched in some snow from outside — snow which only began to melt after minutes in hands warmed up inside a sleeping bag. Carefully he closed the zip on the tent entrance and stuck the cover of his sleeping bag in the small hole which was still open in the right-hand corner where the two zips ran together. Thus we could be safe from the force of the storm to some extent.

Cooking at this height was an exhausting and lengthy business. We took it in turns. Now one held the pot, now the other. It was an hour before the meal was ready: soup, warm tuna, a slice of bread, then tea.

In the light of the gas flame, Michl's face looked strained, as if he were constantly trying to improve something or to understand it more exactly. His voice had got fainter, his movements cautious. We talked little. Occasionally Michl murmured something as if he wanted only to talk with himself.

For a while we lay there, groaning, waiting, without knowing for what we waited. Although we were both thirsty, still we could not decide to prepare something to drink.

I tried to think of nothing, yet meaningless thoughts went through my mind. Occasionally I fell asleep. Awareness that we must drink made me start up.

Michl was awake too. Our breath settled on the inside of the tent roof, changed into hoar frost and trickled in crystals back on our faces.

I woke up at two o'clock in the morning. I poked Michl through his down sleeping bag, down suit, pile suit and silk underwear: 'Michl, we must cook!'

First a groan, then his: 'Right.'

Even as Michl crawled half-way out of the gap in the tent door into the −30°C temperature outside to fetch snow in a Perlon bag, I had already fallen asleep again. And as soon as I turned my back on him and melted snow, Michl was slumbering again. It was hours before we could have a drink.

We came awake only after tea and hot, strong soup. And still the high storm swept in from China until morning, pressing the tent walls into our backs. We wanted to set off before light, yet the storm pinned us firmly in the tent.

'Bit of bad luck', I said.

'We'll be up in six hours.' Michl was confident.

Shortly after 5 a.m. the sun rose; bright and warm, it shone through the blue synthetic walls. We still could not go outside, although we had to be off in order to make the summit assault, so that we could reach the tent again before the onset of night.

At 7 a.m. the wind finally died away. Glaringly the sunlight hit us as we crawled out into the open. We were both wearing blue down-filled suits, standing opposite each other like two moon men. That's what I look like, I thought to myself, as I gazed at the muffled Michl. His movements were slow, very slow, and his face was small and pointed.

As I put on my crampons, he ducked inside the tent once more. Then he went half around it. Again he dived inside, as if there was something important he still hadn't found. Then he began to fiddle with his crampons. Meanwhile I picked up my ice axe, took a couple of steps, stopped, took two more steps. Over my shoulder I smiled at Michl.

'Everything OK?', I asked.

'Fine, no problem'.

'Right', I called, 'Shut the tent up'.

Resolutely I set off. Shortly above, on the ridge, I stopped and asked Michl with a wag of the head whether I should wait for him. But he waved me on. He stuck something in the tent and closed the zip.

Soon he was just a dark dot. The snow under my feet was still so hard that only the tips of my crampons left a track. We did not find the terrain – a steep, exposed snow slope – difficult. For that reason I carried my axe casually in my right hand, although I was always ready to maintain my balance.

I moved obliquely upwards to the left. Where the wall fell steep and holdless below me to Base Camp I rested, before traversing in a zigzag back to the ridge again.

Somewhere here Walter Bonatti must have camped with the Hunza porters as they carried oxygen bottles up to the summit team of Compagnoni and Lacedelli on the first ascent in 1954.

Zigzagging all the time, I made for the fracture where, as though cut by a knife, a section above me cut across the whole width of the face. An avalanche must have come down there some days before; a snow slab – 80cm thick and 0.5km sq. This fracture would be decisive, that I knew. If the snow above it was hard, it would go well. If, however, snow lay there as deep as the fracture indicated, we had no chance.

This thought occupied me as I climbed up to the rocks, then again to the left on the open slope through the enormous basin which narrowed higher up into the 'Bottle-neck'. Occasionally I forbade myself to look up for, subconsciously, I knew that one goes better when one doesn't know how far there is to go.

As I stuck my axe in the snow, which was banked up like quicksand above the fracture line, I stopped instantly as if paralysed. Done for! I gasped, head spinning and my body slumped. Why didn't I turn around at once. Not once did I look back at Michl. In an attack of defiance I lifted my axe high and rummaged around in the snow. I could not and would not believe that it was like it was: waist-deep drifted snow!

I trod it down and wallowed leftwards to the rocks but found no saving there. Bottomless powder snow was everywhere. I weighed up whether it were more sensible to climb up directly above me on the rocks. In this way I would have avoided the exertion and would have been able to eliminate the danger, which with every step became greater in this avalanche channel. But the rocks were too steep, as well as being icy, and anyway we had no rope.

Michl caught up quickly, as the trail-breaking interfered with my climbing rhythm and I progressed more in rushes. A few steps – rest – a few more steps.

The 'Bottle-neck', the narrow snow couloir between two rock ridges under the Giant Serac, was steeper than I had thought looking at it from below. Here, too, was deep, bottomless snow.

It was not will-power that drove me on, it was habit. As if high-altitude mountaineering were a part of my fortune. This need for harmony and synthesis; this hunger for perfection and completion as the driving force against all rational insight!

Above the 'Bottle-neck', where the snow changed into the vertical ice of the summit seracs, I began to traverse to the left. I suspected the weakest place to be in the crack between the rocks and the overhanging ice. Far from it. The ice was brittle and flew out in lumps with every blow of the axe. My axe would not hold and I was too weak to cut holds. So I went back to the snow again.

Meanwhile Michl was below me, trying to climb the rocks to the left. Skilfully he balanced up over two small rock projections until that also became too dangerous and he had to pull himself up by my axe shaft which I reached down to him. We deliberated, then Michl began the traverse. Feet on the rocks, hands in the snow, he burrowed a dozen paces to the left. There the ice was bare but only two paces wide, then again bottomless powder snow. We alternated the trail-breaking.

After this section we came to a slope with bottomless soft snow – a part of the enormous mass of fresh snow which had fallen this spring in the mountains of northern Pakistan. Like two dachshunds in deep snow, we had to burrow up the slope. For a

169

K2 (8,611m) from the
south.

while we were afraid that the snow masses would flush us down to the Godwin Austen Glacier. In the Alps we would have turned back.

It was already midday when we reached the rock which lay in the snow field like a foundling, left of the Giant Serac. Snow, snow, snow as far as I could see; above it the blue-black sky.

Our movement had become an irregular crawling. The snow slope in front of us grew endlessly. I didn't want to believe it: it extended with every metre we pushed ourselves upwards. This untouched emptiness took away my sense of distance. On the slope below us I saw no sign of our tracks which had been swallowed up. Endlessly and eternally we moved through the snow. Why did I climb on even though I thought that we would never get to the summit?

The sun had left us and it became icily cold. We still had time, although to me it seemed much too late for the summit. I always had the same feeling of helplessness as I lifted my head after a rest and gazed upwards. It didn't occur to me that at great height dimensions can be distorted.

The snow slope in front of me did not seem desolate, only unendingly big in a strange way. There, by the sastrugi, the shadows were darker. Round about was the same colour – the colour of the shadows – and the air above us was grey-blue. The snow, too, had the colour of the sky. Only high above did the world still gleam. Somehow there lay a mood of deliverance. Sometimes the edges of the sastrugi were so thin and transparent that I dared not touch them; I did not want to disturb their harmony. But when once my gloved hand had broken through them, I ignored my crampons which followed the plodding of my fists. When I moved, an animal moved; when I lay down, a rock lay there.

I no longer bore alone the responsibility for our survival. Michl would indicate when he wanted to turn back, I thought. I was worried only about his hands. So long as Michl said nothing, I wanted to go on. Thus I thought as I looked across at him. His movements were those of a drunken man and yet with a single purpose, clear and upwardly directed.

Still the snow slope above us was endless. I became anxious. Since we had been climbing in shadow, it had been impossible to guess the position of the sun.

Silently we tunnelled through the snow: Michl ahead, I behind, or the other way around; proud of each metre we gained. Our track was perfect and yet it was not without danger, what we were doing. It was in parts as steep as a church roof and lower down the face fell away vertically. I knew that we had no chance of surviving if one of us slipped.

Then the slope became flatter and less dangerous. Our mittens were encrusted with an armour of snow, our feet stuck in a lump of boots, gaiters and ice. We looked like lost polar travellers. We worked steadily and thoughtlessly. The one resting did not look at the other.

'Put your down gloves on', I said to Michl as he closed ranks.

The air was now cuttingly cold. Michl gave me to understand that he had no down gloves. He had left them behind in a safe place. Our burrowing forward was like marathon runners who exert themselves when they are at the end of their strength but do not know how far it is to the goal.

I had progressed a good bit again. When I looked back, I could not say for sure where I had rested last. It seemed a long way. Michl moved ahead a bit and led, trampling snow, burrowing. Far below in the open snow field was a sort of crevasse, otherwise there was no shelter far and wide. I rested by a sastrugi, leaning on my axe. Out of tiredness I crouched down without previously having trodden out a stance in the snow.

From the innards of the snow I heard a rustle. It was so near that I wanted to burrow inside in order to know whence it came. Then the noise of crampons above me; Michl crawling on all fours. One can swim in snow — swim upwards that is. When I became cold from resting I had to continue. Michl waited for me to take over the trail-breaking. Going past him, his face seemed unknown to me. We would not make the rest of the ascent by crawling.

The stretches which we put behind us between rest stops became ever shorter. I did not know how long they were. As I moved I could not count the paces, and when resting nothing passed through my mind. When I got going again, everything moved in me, not only my body.

It didn't have much to do with mountaineering. It was only about enduring, seeing through a torture beyond pain and exhaustion. We went on because each hoped that the other would give up first. Our partnership became a suppressed wrestling match with each other that drove us on. And Michl, the forty-five-year-old, was, as far as giving up was concerned, just as stubborn as I.

On the summit block the snow gradually diminished. The ridge before me ran to the left in a half-moon, gently climbing all the while, endlessly far. I could not estimate its distance.

'My strength won't last out!'

The snow was now hard in places. Thus I progressed faster without actually being distinctly conscious of it.

Suddenly I was standing in the sun and simultaneously I knew that we had reached the summit.

'We're there. We're on top.'

This statement of mine apparently jolted Michl out of a sort of trance. Thus startled, he looked at me.

Standing between light and shade I was able to orientate myself. The ridge had shortened. To the right and below, a rock. In front of me, a cornice which billowed out to the left and southwards. Therefore, I must get over there where the sun was. In no time I was warm.

'We're on top!' I shouted once more to Michl.

I wanted to take his hand although he was still ten paces away from me. I waited as he approached, then threw off my rucksack. For a while we just stood there, could not believe it. We wondered and meanwhile forgot the reason for our being here. It was beautiful to stand there at the heart of things looking at each other.

Michl's face once more wore the expression of the young scamp which he had been on setting out. We conversed without speaking. I was silent, just listening, paying attention to his movements and what his eyes were saying. Like Michl I continued to share my happiness. At last I remembered the radio, fetched it out of my rucksack, pressed the transmit button.

'Kappa Due calling Base Camp, Kappa Due calling Base Camp, do you read. Over.'

Reception was bad but it sufficed to explain where we were. Also to understand the joy and congratulations of Jochen Hoelzgen in Base Camp.

When I gave Michl the radio, he squatted down and, as I plodded up to the highest point on the ridge, I heard him ordering flowers for his wife.

Only on the summit itself did I sense my exhaustion, which a few minutes before I scarcely believed myself still able to overcome, as a calm inside me. A calm embedded in strength and self-control. Despite my many doubts while climbing, it could not have turned out otherwise. If I had not been up there, I would have disintegrated like a mountain, into many stones.

The panorama was clear in all directions for a distance of 300km. Over everything lay a breath of cheerfulness: the most beautiful panorama I had ever seen! To the east, only the shadow of K2 fell on the Sinkiang highlands like a black wedge. Like a vault, the clear design lay on the ground.

Briefly I took off my gloves, the better to fiddle with my camera and the radio. Every time I touched the snow my fingers went white and I rubbed them on my trouser legs. Occasionally I stuck them in my pockets.

In the shadow of K2 I looked for a sign and recognized this in a pencil-thick stroke on the summit lying far below. That must be me then. I had to laugh at this notion. This odd feeling at the sight of my own shadow thrown miles across the face of the earth reminded me of death. Now I knew where I came from and where I was going.

I turned around and gazed at the sun sinking into the western horizon. How fine things must have been many thousands of years ago! One saw that in the colours. Where there were no settlements, the blue above the valleys was more peaceful and calmer. To the north, over Sinkiang, the world seemed gloomy and agitated. Mountains and valleys blurred in shadow with one another.

As my gaze roamed across the steep granite towers of the Ogre and Latok to Concordia, into which glaciers flowed like a motorway interchange, and held briefly on Broad Peak, these summits soared above their shadows, the valleys became invisible and the horizon shivered. It seemed as if the world came to an end behind it.

Looking away from the western horizon, my gaze again concentrated on the summits, and I recognized in this round of peaks and valleys the most peaceful stretch of land in the whole world.

A little later I stowed the radio and camera gear away in my rucksack. Michl and I climbed eastwards down along the ridge. We were still in the sun. Then we quitted the ridge on the south-east side. The night absorbed us and in no time it became bitterly cold. When we called a halt in front of a narrow crevasse, I pointed to Michl's nose. It was almost white, his beard a single crust of ice.

'You look like a polar explorer', I said to him.

'I look rather like you then', he replied and in doing so cracked the ice on his face.

With long, heavy strides we descended the middle section of the snow field. There was danger of avalanche but I paid no particular attention to that. Sometimes I recognized a crevasse; the snow glimmered there somewhat darker. In jumping across I warned Michl. The long ranks of 2m high drifts which we passed, taking care not to vanish suddenly into bottomless snow, were also darker than the gently waved regular snow surface. Precisely where it looked most harmless, I moved especially carefully.

I could hear Michl's footsteps although he was a long way behind me. I could see his cheerful face although I was descending facing the valley. When I turned around sometimes to make sure that I was seeing correctly, there behind me was a young man who moved like a dancing drunk. How beautiful, how cheerful he was. And he had ordered flowers for his wife from the summit.

The air around me rustled. The first star emerged in the sky. I looked down at the overshadowed ridges which stretched out from the foot of K2 over hundreds of kilometres, northwards and eastwards. The world below charmed me and repulsed me at the same time with its coolness; even more so the shadow of K2 which grew longer and on which I seemed to stand. I looked again at my feet wallowing through the snow. Slowly I descended into the world to which I no longer belonged.

When I flopped on the snow outside the tent, my face was numb with cold. My bones were aching. There was nothing to drink. I sat there for a long time and then tried to take off my gaiters. Nothing doing, although I did manage to wrench my crampons off my boots. My gloves were in shreds, down mixed in with snow. I looked around and saw that Michl was not too far away, coming along the ridge between the South and East Faces like a tottering black line, directly towards the tent.

We had taken only two hours to get down. How had that been possible?

'The traverse to the "Bottle-neck" was not so difficult', said Michl.

'I thought so too', I answered, as I carefully pulled the icicles out of my beard.

There was only a foot-wide path around the tent. There I deposited my crampons. Michl stood in front of me, grinning. He was covered in ice as well.

At this moment the shadow of K2 reached its furthest point. On its highest point still stood that small dot. And again I had the notion that this elevation was my intangible self. I had not deceived myself. That, therefore, was the direction in which I had to go. This vision lasted for a moment. Then I crawled into the tent.

There were fist-sized lumps between the two mats. Crawling in, I almost tripped over them. I twisted and turned on the mat; everything was uneven and hard. I wondered whether there was something underneath but found nothing. I also pondered what we could cook in the evening, but nothing occurred to me about that either.

My sleeping bag lay in the middle of the tent where I had left it that morning before setting out. Irresolutely, I pushed the mat and items of clothing to and fro. Then I began to unpack my rucksack, but gave up half-way. Later I played around with the knobs on the radio without being able to decide whether to switch it on. Finally, I spread my sleeping bag over the mat and crawled inside.

We were both too tired to sleep and too tired to cook. The blue of the tent wall shut out the light of the starry sky a little and in the half-dark of the night, ice crystals gleamed on the tent surface. How strange everything became to me at night! How strange I myself was now in my battered state! As I half got up in order to lie down afresh, I looked over at Michl. I saw how he lay there despairing.

During this night of complete exhaustion we tossed and turned, thickly wrapped up in our sleeping bags, groaning by turns. All our bones ached. Soon the cold penetrated through both tent and down. Out of tender habit I moved as if to warm myself on my partner, yet this caress was just a reflex action. In sleep, something is often awake in me waiting for someone, for something, which makes me real and makes life bearable.

I woke up at three o'clock in the morning. It was still stormy outside. In thought I moved around the tent and faced the wind. My thoughts were whirling around the tent with the snow-dust, until it stopped through total lack of wind. In the face of distinct loneliness I hid myself completely in the mountain. That was for me the only haven in these hours of waking and falling asleep again, in these hours of perception. Only in the arms of the world did I feel myself salvaged and safe.

'We have to cook', I said at last.

'Yes', answered Michl and closed his eyes again.

Later he fetched snow from outside and we made two cups of tea. We were too tired to cook and rolled to and fro sleeplessly on our hard, thin underlays until morning.

We set out only when it was warm in the tent. The ski stick which I had stuck in the snow two days before was still there and I hung my icy gaiters on it, so that they fluttered in the wind like a flag. They should show the next group the way.

Swathes of mist and snow-dust spilled over the ridge from the west, past the tent. A thin curtain of vapour seemed to stand in front of the sun and only to the north-east was the air still clear and calm.

The tent threw a colossal shadow on the snow. To me everything now seemed so simple, so self-evident. Only the expected had come to pass.

We had plenty of time for the descent and could afford to rest as often as we liked. Out of my tiredness came a sort of drowsiness, so that many places seemed new to me, as if not only had I never been there, but rather no one at all.

All at once there came swathes of mist, darkness, driving snow and storm. Everything filled in completely around us, so fast that we lost our sense of direction. Sitting on the ice, supporting ourselves with our crampons, we let the worst of it pass. But we were not getting anywhere. Only for seconds did it let up. For the blink of an eye the sun came out. Sleety hailstones danced amusingly over the ice surface nearby, then again the hurrying wall of mist came down.

From ice bulge to ice bulge we groped our way down, not entirely lost after all! To have been on top and then perished! Too late now to reflect on so much senselessness. In a hollow, sheltered for a few minutes, I continued to reflect: to climb K2, where was the sense in that?

Beyond the South Shoulder the atrocious showers continued and the mist became thicker with hail and driving snow. The black clouds foreshadowed nothing good for the morrow, but so what! It was desolate. Enveloped in the darkness of the clouds, we sought refuge under the big serac, sat down and waited until it left off somewhat.

A bit further down we crouched again. If I stared for a few moments into the seething cauldron of the clouds, it made me dizzy. Ever-darker shreds of clouds rushed past us, enveloping us, so that we sometimes could no longer see each other. Between this moving and looking, this resting and doubting, I seemed to myself like a piece of mist.

Suddenly we saw three silhouettes far below us, and all at once all our confidence was restored: it was Alessandro Gogna, Friedl Mutschlechner and Robert Schauer climbing up to the top camp. So we were still on the right track: it could not be far to Camp 3.

'We mustn't pass by them', I said to Michl.

'Yes, we'll wait here for them.'

'No', I said, 'We'll go down steadily, only not too far.'

Half an hour later we were all standing together. The greeting was sincere. In Camp 3 we had a short rest. Sandro made tea. Michl drank and became cheerful. He held the mug with the hot drink like a bowl in both hands. Between sips he tugged at his icy beard.

Then there was a discussion: Friedl thought the three of them should wait in Camp 3 for better weather. Robert, on the other hand, felt it would be decidedly more sensible to descend to Base Camp again to wait out the weather there.

'Staying in Camp 3 for days we shall deteriorate bodily. Besides we shall consume the provisions which we urgently need in case we are pinned down on the mountain by the storm.'

'You're responsible for yourselves, you must decide', I said.

Robert, although only twenty-five years old, had already climbed three eight-thousanders. His experience made the others doubt. Friedl had never been to the Himalaya. That gave Alessandro the casting vote. He came down on the side of experience.

While descending the Black Pyramid the wind howled. There was no place to squat down on the precipitous rocks. Wherever there was a narrow ledge, snow lay on it. Grey clouds chased past above me. The ropes were coated with a fluff of new snow, the rocks covered in part with verglas. When the mist tore apart briefly, the face below me seemed endless.

I was climbing in the middle of the group. In front of me moved someone whom I could only sometimes recognize as a shadow in the mist. Behind me another must be following; I heard the scraping of his crampons. Now and then scraps of snow hit me, now and then a shadowy figure emerged.

The tents, the glaciers, the ropes – everything was now different from the ascent. The people, too, who were climbing with me. Michl was happy. Sandro and Friedl were hugely pleased about our success. I read it in their eyes. Robert was grimacing since he knew that Michl and I had been to the summit. I was sorry – envy is a corroding affliction.

Just above Camp 2 it brightened up abruptly. The sun was not shining but one could now see as far as Base Camp. When I looked up at the grey sky as I walked, I dragged my feet with heavy steps.

The countryside below me with its truncated, grey mountains looked desolate, as wasted as a skeleton. Between the grey-white slopes of the mountain ranges, the river of ice flowed broad and heavy, shot through with the white bones of a giant prehistoric creature.

'K2', I said, just to myself.

On the evening march across the glacier to Base Camp the sun broke through. Terry and Jochen came towards me out of the camp and, as I looked upwards along the slopes of K2, I saw only big, empty snow fields, nothing above that. Some ravens flew away over me.

Friedl Mutschlechner.

*Below left*: Alessandro Gogna.

Robert Schauer.

# THE DOT ON THE i

In 1979 the first mountaineers and scientists from the West and from Japan went to Tibet via China. This news occupied me more than all my other mountaineering plans at that time. In the spring of 1980 I flew to Beijing and received from the Chinese Mountaineering Association a permit to travel to Rongbuk via Lhasa in the summer in order to climb Mount Everest.

With that, two new worlds opened up for me: Tibet, the mysterious land north of the Himalaya, and a solo ascent to the highest point on earth. I had already climbed Mount Everest from the south, without oxygen and within the framework of a classic expedition. Solo, it was to be the dot on the 'i' of the reality of my mountaineering philosophy: one man alone and without technological aid on the highest mountain in the world. With that, classic mountaineering would reach a high point and new objectives would have to be found.

For six months I lived almost exclusively for this idea. Nena Holguin, a Canadian girl hungry for adventure, agreed to accompany me to Base Camp and to act as doctor in emergency.

On my first attempt to reach the summit from Advanced Base Camp, at the end of June, I foundered in sodden, waist-deep snow. For six weeks Nena and I travelled around Tibet. This was the best way for me to acclimatize and get fit.

During the first break in the monsoon, in the middle of August, I got ready for my second attempt. The weather was fine and it had got colder. To test the snow, and to save time on the actual climb to the summit, I carried my rucksack up to just under the North Col the day before the final ascent. All my senses were directed towards one goal — the summit of Everest.

# The Crystal Horizon

## THROUGH TIBET TO MOUNT EVEREST – SOLO ASCENT

The ascent to the North Col was the most dangerous part of my solo ascent. The Chang La Face, almost 500m high, is, like the ice-fall on Mount Everest's south side, broken up and threatened by seracs. But above all it is prone to avalanches. In 1922, during the first assault on Everest, a whole party was swept away there by an avalanche and seven Sherpas died. Miraculously, Mallory and his comrades were able to save themselves. As a solo climber, not only did I have to pay attention to the recurrent avalanche paths, but I also had to get safely over the crevasses without a rope.

To find a safe route of ascent between ice towers and crevasses requires many years of experience; there is a marked instinct for it. I had no radio with me, as I quite consciously wanted no contact with 'below'. Apart from the fact that Nena would not have been able to help me, I refused to let other people risk their lives because I undertook a self-imposed risk and thereby endangered myself. A solo ascent of Everest is really only a solo ascent when there is no connection between 'above' and 'below', no security link through vigilant ground personnel.

How quickly I climbed this time! In high trainers, really light-footedly, I ascended 400m. I kept far to the right, in the blunt corner where the faces of the Chang La and Mount Everest meet. The snow was so hard that only the burls of my soles penetrated, leaving behind a dainty pattern on the snow surface. This was not climbing with hands and feet – I climbed at a regular pace, placing my ski sticks for balance like a second pair of feet.

An enormous quantity of snow had fallen during the past weeks but now it was packed together and firm. For the first time, where the slope became steeper after a left-hand bend, I rested after every fifty paces. Now I shortened the adjustable ski sticks. How precisely programmed my body was! Always the same number of paces plus or minus one without having to rest. It did not lessen higher up, a proof that I had completely acclimatized myself to the altitude. A pause for rest sufficed to compensate for the oxygen deficit in my blood; freshly topped up reserves exhausted themselves in around fifty paces. Between whiles a feeling of energy, security and almost high spirits flowed through me. While resting, a comfortable tiredness of mind enveloped me and only my lungs heaved.

The sun was not yet hot. Although it stood high above the cloud streaks in the east and beat down almost vertically on the 45-degree snow slope, the air remained fresh. If

Routes to Mount
Everest

- – – –   Normal route (Hillary) 1953
━━━━━   South Buttress (Poles) 1980
━ ━ ━ ━   South-West Face (Bonington) 1975
━━━━━━   West Ridge (Americans) 1963
•••••••••   West Ridge Direct (Yugoslavians)
            1979
—×—×—   North-West Face (Japanese) 1980
—•—•—   Chinese route (Mallory) 1975
▼▼▼▼▼▼▼   Messner variation 1980

Changtse

North Col

North Ridge

Rongbuk Glacier

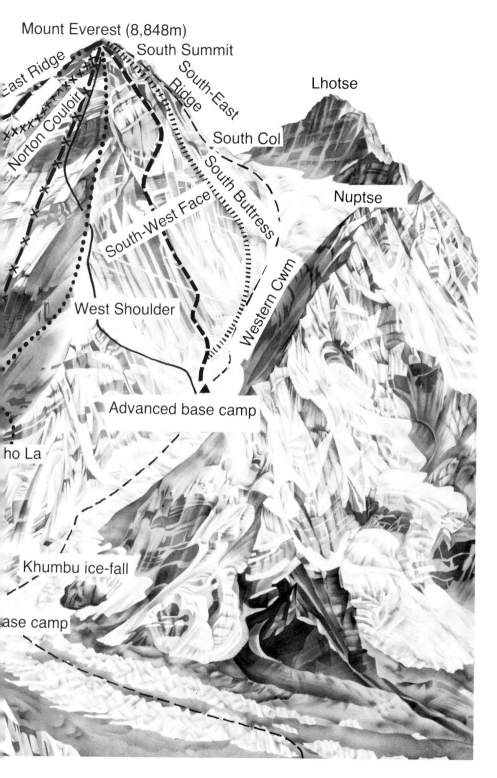

Mount Everest (8,848m)

East Ridge

South Summit

South-East Ridge

Lhotse

Norton Couloir

South Col

South Buttress

Nuptse

South-West Face

Western Cwm

West Shoulder

Advanced base camp

ho La

Khumbu ice-fall

ase camp

the weather held like this, I would make it.

Just underneath the North Col, about 80m below the edge of the ridge, I concealed my rucksack in a tiny ice cave and fastened it to an ice screw. I cast a glance back, then turned around and marked the spot in my mind. I had to find it again in the early morning, perhaps even in darkness.

I wanted to descend quickly to my Advanced Base Camp. I had to recover, sleep, drink a lot. I had to prepare myself spiritually for the decisive days. Nena had watched me the whole time through the telephoto lens of her camera. She wrote in her diary:

17 August 1980. I am surprised how fast Reinhold climbs in his hiking boots towards the North Col. When he left with his rucksack at 8.15 a.m. to test the snow and deposit the equipment, I didn't realize that he was not just testing the route. In spirit he is already on the way to the summit. I had the impression he would go up only a little way and immediately come back again. I turned over and tried to go back to sleep. But an hour later when I peeped through the tent flap I saw that he was already half-way to the col and was going on. Suddenly I was wide awake. When he goes up to this col I always feel cold shivers up and down my spine. Each time it is a great risk and I marvel to myself how he finds the way between the gaping crevasses.

Half an hour later I was back in the tent with Nena. In spirit already absent, I prepared my body for the days of utmost exertion. I drank and ate, slept in between. In the tent the temperature was pleasant with both the ventilator and entrance open.

This time I had myself under control. From the first I did not allow fear to arise. The most dangerous part of the route, the ascent to the North Col, I knew already and so I knew that here I could only get stuck in the snow or lose myself in mist; I would not perish.

The weather was beautiful – there would be no mist. My self-control cost energy as I detected how tense my whole being was. Even during the night, I forced myself to lie there quietly. Only twice did I check the weather. It was fine, yet the air was too warm. In the blue of the night Mount Everest stood over me like a magic mountain. No brooding, no asking why; I prepared myself with every fibre of my being for my big effort.

When the time came to get up, I picked up socks, boots, breeches and top clothes like a sleep-walker. Each action was as quick and sure as if I had practised it 100 times. There were no wasted movements.

I stretched myself in front of the tent and sniffed the night air. Then I continued my ascent of the previous day. Soon I was far above the campsite. I reached the ice cave and picked up my rucksack. Nena had remained far below and wrote in her diary:

18 August 1980. Yes, he has gone! A tender kiss on the lips was all. Just once. When Reinhold kisses me it is full of meaning. I call after him: 'I shall be thinking of you!' He didn't hear me properly or didn't want to hear me. His voice sounded absent-minded, as he asked back: 'What?' He was a bit disturbed because the night had been warmer than usual. He was much afraid that the snow would have

The 8,848m high Mount Everest or Chomolungma — up above there is the top of the world.

become too soft. So what I called after him in the still morning must for him have been irrelevant. So as not to hold him up any more I said simply: 'Bye, bye!' And back comes his answer: 'Bye, bye!' Empty words hanging in the air. What experiences will he have? What sort of change will take place in him, in me?

Suddenly the snow gave way under me and my headlamp went out. Despairingly I tried to cling to the snow but in vain. After the first seconds of panic, and although it was pitch-dark, I seemed to see everything: snow crystals at first, then blue-green ice.

'I'm not wearing crampons!' I thought. I knew what was happening but nevertheless remained quite calm. I was falling, experiencing the plunge in slow-motion, striking the walls of the widening crevasse once with my chest, once with my back. My sense of time was disrupted, as was my perception of the depth of my fall. Had I been falling only split seconds or was it minutes? I felt completely weightless and a torrent of warmth surged through my body.

Suddenly there was support under my feet again. At the same time I knew that I was trapped, stuck forever perhaps in this crevasse. Cold sweat broke out on my forehead. Now I was afraid. My first thought was: 'If only I had a radio with me.' I could have called Nena. Perhaps she would have heard me. But whether she would have been able to climb the 500m up here to me, in order to drop me a rope, was more than questionable. I had quite consciously committed myself to this solo ascent without a radio and discussed it many times before starting.

I fiddled with my headlamp and suddenly all was bright. It was working! I breathed deeply but scarcely dared move, for the snow on which I was standing was not sound. Like a thin, transparent bridge, it hung precariously between the walls of the crevasse. I put my head back and saw, some 8m above, the tree-trunk-sized hole through which I had fallen. From the bit of black sky above a few far, far distant stars twinkled down at me. Sweat broke out all over me and covered my body with a touch as icy as the iridescent blue-green walls between which I was imprisoned. Because they converged obliquely above me, I had no chance of climbing up them. With my headlamp I tried to illuminate the bottom of the crevasse but it appeared to have none. Black holes were to the left and right of me. The snow bridge which had broken my fall was only a square metre in size.

I had goose-pimples and was shivering all over. My bodily reactions, however, were in stark contrast to the calm in my mind: there was no fear of a renewed plunge into the bottomless depths, only a presentiment of dissolving, of evaporation. At the same time my mind was saying: 'That was lucky!' For the first time I experienced fear as a bodily reflex, without psychological pain in my chest.

My only problem was how to get out again. Mount Everest had become irrelevant. To myself I seemed an innocent prisoner. I didn't reproach myself or curse. This pure, innocent feeling was inexplicable. What determined my life at this moment I knew not. I promised myself to go down, to give up, if I came out of it safely. No more solo eight-thousanders!

The sweat froze in my hair and beard, but the anxiety in my bones disappeared the moment I started moving, as I tried to get my crampons out of my rucksack. At each movement, however, the feeling of falling again came over me, a feeling of plunging into an abyss, as if the ground were slowly giving way.

I then discovered a ramp running along the wall of the crevasse on the valley side, a ledge 2ft wide in the ice, which led obliquely upwards and which was full of snow. There was the way out! Arms outstretched, carefully I let myself fall forward to the adjacent wall. For a moment my body made an arc between the jammed snow block and the slightly overhanging wall above me. Carefully I straddled across with my right foot and made a step in the frozen snow on the valleyside wall of the crevasse. I put my weight on it and it held, thus relieving the insecure spot on which I had been standing.

Instinctively, I made each of these movements as precisely as in a rehearsed ballet. I tried to make myself lighter. My whole body identified itself with the new position, I was for a moment, a life-determining moment, weightless. I had pushed myself off from the snow bridge with my left foot, my arms keeping me in balance and my right leg supporting my body. My left foot found a hold and I breathed deeply with relief. Very carefully I traversed, face to the wall, to the right. My right foot groped for a fresh hold in the snow, then my left boot was placed to the millimetre in the footstep which the right one had relinquished a few seconds before. The ledge broadened and led upwards to the open air. Saved!

In a few minutes I had regained the upper surface – still on the valley side to be sure but safe. I was a different man. I stood there, rucksack on my back, ice axe in hand, as if nothing had happened. For a moment I hesitated and considered what error I had made. How did this fall happen? Perhaps my left foot, placed a couple of centimetres over the lip of the crevasse, had gone through as I sought for a hold for the right one on the opposite snow wall.

While in the crevasse I had decided to turn around, to give up, if I got out safe and sound. Now, standing up there, I continued my climb without thinking, without consciously willing it, as if I were computer-programmed.

The first glimmer of dawn illuminated Everest's North Col. I looked at the time: just before seven o'clock. How long had I been down there? I didn't know. The fall into the crevasse was already expunged from my mind. My vow to descend could not have been basically serious. I didn't ask how I had managed to deceive myself so. Determinedly I went along the lower edge of the crevasse, concentrating entirely on the summit, as if this perilous incident had only shaken my body and not that identification which, for weeks, had constituted my being: my identification with Everest.

The fall into the crevasse had jerked me into a far greater state of alertness than normal. I knew there was only this one spot where I could cross this crevasse which ran right across the 500m high face. During my reconnaissance ascent four weeks ago I had discovered the snow bridge, just 2m wide, which now had almost proved my undoing. That time it had taken my weight. It might hold up now as well if I kept well away from the middle.

On my solo climb I had no aluminium ladder or rope with me, aids which large expeditions would use to overcome such hindrances. Two ski sticks and my titanium ice axe were my only tools. Trance-like, I turned back to the hole I had fallen through and shone my torch in. It was as black as night. This time I must be hellishly careful so as not to make any mistake.

On the other side of the crevasse was a steep wall of snow. I made up my mind quickly, bent forward and thrust the ski sticks – handles foremost – into the snow up to the discs. High on the wall above me they made two firm anchor points, or artificial holds. Now I had to cross the gap with one big stride and, on the other side, find a hold with my ice axe near the ski sticks. Even though I knew that I would have to find another route on my way down, I was as immersed in my climb as if there were nothing more afterwards. With a power move I swung myself over and up, made a few quick steps and felt safe again. All these movements were quick but not hurried.

Slowly day broke. Far to the east soared the great massif of Kangchenjunga, otherwise there was not much of the world to be seen. Above a grey-blue sea of mist, the firmament spread out, imperceptibly changing from blue to red.

The weather was fine and the air cuttingly cold. What a good thing I had broken off my July attempt! The snow, softened by the monsoon, had been bottomless then and the avalanche danger had been great. It was not without danger now – more than once I had lost my way on the slopes to the North Col – but now, on this eighteenth day of August, the snow was so firmly frozen that I left behind only a faint track.

The highest slope was steep indeed but the bad snow of earlier days had consolidated. What I was climbing on was not iron-hard névé as it was lower down, for shallow crust predominated here. Time and again I broke through the splintering surface and sank in up to my ankles.

As I stepped on the top of the col, quite suddenly I felt a strong westerly wind in my face. It took my breath away and made my eyes water. Briefly I stood still, looked around, and breathed more quickly and intermittently. Then a regular rhythm returned again. The wind did not penetrate my thick clothing, but occasionally it made me stagger. Instinctively I hunched over my supporting ski sticks.

I followed the old route along the North Ridge, the British route. For the first 500m this ridge looked like a steep ski slope. Its rises were slightly undulating and perhaps inclined to 30 degrees, with endless masses of firm snow overhanging to the east. An intense dawn seemed to enliven the cornices. The snow was blue in the shadows and the contours blurred in the soft light of the rising sun. In between, on the blunt knife-edge, snow crystals sparkled like diamonds.

The sun touched the summit of Pumori and the broad flank of Cho Oyu. The nearby North Peak stood like a gigantic edge between night and day. Above the summit of Mount Everest, too, lay a rosy dawn. It showed so clearly against the deep blue sky that I could recognize each free-standing rock tower on the North-East Ridge. Up there in 1924 George Mallory and Andrew Irvine were seen for the last time on their bold summit push . . .

The distance as the crow flies from me to the 'First Step' was now perhaps 2km – a distance at which one would not be able to recognize a person's shape. Odell, who had stood much higher, said that he had been able to see the two climbers for five minutes. He had not spotted them through moving swathes of mist, rather through a sudden clearing of the air, such an air as now lay above me. He had seen them on the 'First Step' and did not mistake rocks for men, as has often been put to him. I excluded the possibility of an optical illusion, although I myself, as I stared at the 'First Step', for moments succumbed to the illusion of seeing black dots in motion. Mallory did not surmount the 'Second Step' – he attempted it but gave up. That I knew now for certain as I stood there and stared.

Where did the ability to look back nearly sixty years come from? Or could I no longer distinguish between reality and fantasy because I had read so much? Did this attempt of 8 June 1924 continue to play itself out up there, visible only in a heightened state of consciousness? This was no optical illusion, for a sensation of human energy surrounded my body like the wind and sunbeams.

As I climbed higher, the tiny figures vanished. I placed one foot at a time so firmly in the snow that my whole person became this step. Propped on my ski sticks, I climbed as rhythmically as possible; fifty paces – rest – fifty more paces. When I was sufficiently rested I cast a glance upwards to orientate myself approximately. Thus, time and again, the feeling came over me that I was not alone on this slope. As intensely as I now gazed upwards, I was observed from below by Nena:

> I carry on with the daily tasks which have to be done in camp at 6,500m and watch him as he climbs higher and higher. In many respects I envy him. I would love to look down here from up there, to see the summit from up there. But more than anything else I would like to climb with him. 'One day perhaps', I tell myself . . . He gets smaller and smaller in my field of vision and the further he is from me, the stronger becomes my love.

Nena did not know that the most dangerous moment of my expedition already lay behind me. She had not seen the fall into the crevasse, as it was still dark then. She followed my track and photographed it. The sun flooded the slopes to the North Col and, through the telephoto lens, Nena could make out my track which looked like a pearl necklace. She would not notice the hole I had fallen through because the chain of pearls

Rest stop on the East
Rongbuk Glacier.

continued on over the crevasse.

I was climbing smoothly now and was at a height of more than 7,200m. The air warmed up quickly. The sun beat full on Cho Oyu to the west and on the North Peak of Mount Everest. Only its shadow spread like a gigantic black hole across the glistening valleys. I could take my time.

I had climbed a height of 700m already this morning. Never before in my life had I climbed so easily at over 7,000m. It was not only the ideal snow conditions which urged me on, it was also my mood.

Nevertheless, I must not overstrain myself. I inserted a rest stop before total tiredness became a numbing pain in my legs. I had to allow myself time and apportion my strength.

Often, whilst sitting, I traced the route along the North-East Ridge. I wanted to get to just under the shoulder and then cross the flat ridge to the 'Second Step'. The views during my rests imprinted themselves like pictures in my mind's eye. As I sat on my tightly packed rucksack, with my back to the slope and facing the valley, I photo-graphed, as it were, with my brain. Only rarely did I fetch my camera out of my rucksack, and then I took more snaps than I really meant to.

Photographing myself – camera screwed to the ice axe with the shaft stuck in the snow, delayed-action release set, walk away a dozen paces, stop, go back and dismantle everything – I always found comical and an unnecessary waste of strength. Once I discovered my shadow in the view-finder of the reflex camera. I had to laugh, just as one laughs at something clownish in a friend.

Yet I found the climbing soothing, like the rhythm of my very being, almost musical. Leaning on my ski sticks, I could thus rest while standing. On the move and on uneven snow they helped me to balance.

With pitiful equipment by today's standards – normally I would not even climb the Matterhorn with it – Mallory and his friends Norton and Somervell crossed the 8,000m barrier nearly sixty years ago for the first time in the history of mountaineering. George Leigh Mallory, that fiery spirit, recognized then that, even after thorough preparation and a six-week acclimatization, Mount Everest would have to be stormed in six days from Rongbuk Base Camp. This early realization seemed to me like a vision. Since I had arrived in Base Camp via Lhasa and Shigatse, more than seven weeks had elapsed. I had been on the move for four days and I needed two more to reach the summit – if all went well and if the weather held.

By now I had reached a height of 7,220 metres. Again I squatted down to rest. Haste at this altitude produced exhaustion and I had my day's quota behind me already. However, I wanted to go on for as long as I had the strength to do so. Far below was the valley head of the Rongbuk Glacier. The view to the west was still clear. To the left lay Nepal, and in front of me lay a tip of the west shoulder of Everest. In the distance great mountain ranges faded away. The bright morning light dissolved mountains and valleys.

The rock bastion of Changtse – also known as the North Peak – fell abruptly to the Rongbuk Glacier and was now the most impressive picture for me. The beautiful pyramid of Pumori looked supernatural and uncanny. To my right the Tibetan Plateau lost itself in infinity. The few clouds there, distributed like spiders' webs, were motionless. Up here, too, there was no wind. Only far below on the North Col was snow whirling through the air. It seemed to me as if this col were a funnel for all the winds in Tibet.

Orographically speaking, looking downwards the broad northern flank of Mount Everest was slightly sunken and protected from the wind on the left. Likewise, the north-east flank to the right was hollowed out and the ground plunged steeply on each side. There, however, the rock slopes on the North Face were deeply snowed up, and everything looked more gentle and flatter than it really was. From above everything seemed peaceful.

I had to rest now at shorter intervals, but each time my breathing quickly returned to its original rhythm and I felt myself revived. This change between climbing and stopping, between exhaustion and returning energy, determined my speed. With each metre of ascent this rhythm became shorter phased and more constrained. Far above, I knew from experience, it would be only will-power which would tear my body from its total lethargy to make another step. This sort of snail's pace now compelled me to rest for some minutes every thirty paces, with longer rests after two hours. As the air at this height contains only a third of the usual quantity of oxygen, I climbed like the Sherpas: I climbed and rested, rested and climbed. I knew that I would feel comparatively well as soon as I sat down, and put off this compelling feeling minute by minute.

The approach march shortly before reaching Advanced Base Camp.

I had to be careful to avoid any harsh irritation of my respiratory tracts. My bronchial tubes and throat were my weakest points – I knew it. And already I sensed some hoarseness. So I was doubly glad that on this windy mountain scarcely a breeze was blowing that day.

A steep rise cost me more energy than I had thought. From below, going over it by eye, I had surmised it would require five rest stops. Meanwhile it had become eight or nine and I still wasn't on top. There, where it became flatter, something like deliverance awaited me. I didn't want to sit down until I was over the rounded top.

Now and then small snow crystals swirled in the air above me. A glittering and glistening enlivened the space. A whistling and singing came and went. Still another eighty paces?

Whilst climbing I concentrated on my foot making the step, nothing else. The air tasted empty, not stale, just empty and rough. My throat hurt. While resting I let myself droop, ski sticks and legs taking the weight of my body and lungs pumping. For a while I forgot everything. Breathing was so strenuous that no strength to think remained. Noises from within me drowned out all external sounds. Slowly, with my pulse throbbing in my throat, my will-power returned.

On again and thirty more paces. How this ridge was fooling me! Or was it my eyes? Everything seemed so near, yet was so far away. One more standing rest stop and I was over the top.

I turned around and gazed, then I let myself flop on the snow. I looked again and again at the countryside, at the almost endless distance. In the pastel shades of the hills there lay something mystical. They strengthened the impression of distance, of the unattainable; as if I had only dreamed of this Tibet, as if I had never been there.

I stared at the plateau and thought I recognized a village. Tingri perhaps? In spirit I saw before me the whitewashed mud houses with the black window holes. Red scarves waved beside Tibetan prayer flags. I saw blunt-featured faces. The people of Tibet no longer laughed as merrily as those in the mountains of Nepal. All this I experienced as I stood at the edge of the village. It wasn't a memory, it was the present.

The altimeter showed 7,360m. It was 9 a.m. and I had done the stretch to the North Col in two hours. By this ploy I had spared myself a bivouac. Now I climbed slowly quite consciously.

Now and then I went in up to my ankles – snow-drifts cost energy. Mostly though, I was able to detour around the patches of crusted snow. Each successful avoidance felt like a personal triumph. I could not afford to waste my energy. This impulse determined my thoughts more and more, and also my feelings. Tomorrow and the day after things would become much more strenuous. The two adjustable ski sticks were really a great help. I was able to distribute my weight over my arms and legs, thus balancing myself from above, instead of with my legs.

To the right of me the North Face was an enormous snow slope. Only a few rock islands lay scattered darkly across this vertical ice desert. Avalanche paths were distinctly recognizable. I remained for the time being on the blunt North Ridge. Not only was it the safest route, but the wind had also blown away much of the snow. Nevertheless, there was no trace of any previous climbers. Everything was buried under a thick mantle of snow. Only once, at about 7,500m, did I see a red rope in the snow. I went over and touched it. It seemed to be fairly new and was anchored to a rock island. It must have been one of the Japanese ones, I thought. In usual expedition-style and team-work they had erected a string of high camps last May. On steep sections they had anchored fixed ropes, on which to descend to Base Camp when the weather turned bad and up which they pulled themselves to prepare the route further. Step by step they had pushed on with the support of Chinese porters to just below the summit.

With just these tactics I had climbed Mount Everest myself in 1978 by its south side. Then there were eleven climbers, employing two dozen Sherpas as porters and taking turns at camp building. Only for the last 900m did Peter Habeler and I climb on without support – right to the top.

This time there was no one to help carry, no one to prepare my bivouac, no comrade to share trail-breaking in deep snow and no Sherpa to carry my equipment. Nobody. How much easier it was to climb as a pair. The knowledge that someone stood behind me brought comfort. Not only was solo climbing far more strenuous and dangerous, above all the psychological burden was more than doubled. Everything that lay ahead of me, including the descent, weighed me down and, while resting, often this was blown up out of all proportion.

Like a snail which carries its home on its back, I carried my tent in my rucksack. I would erect it, sleep in it and take it with me for the next night. I was equipped like a nomad and could survive for a week. Nevertheless, I had scarcely any reserves – I had to be back within seven days. Nothing could be allowed to go wrong; a second tent would have been too heavy to carry, to say nothing of oxygen apparatus, which would have doubled my load again. The 18kg I was already carrying weighed so heavily at this altitude, that now I stopped every two dozen paces to struggle for breath, and was oblivious to all around me.

The stretches between rest stops became shorter and shorter. Often – very often in fact – I sat down for a breather. Each time it took great will-power to stand up again. Knowing that I had completed my self-imposed stint for the day helped me, and it was as if the thought of this released new energy.

'Still a bit more, you can do it', I said to myself softly by way of encouragement. 'What you put behind you today, you don't have to climb tomorrow.'

Being alone no longer seemed like isolation. Only occasionally did a feeling of impotence overwhelm me at the thought of the awful, endless exertion still to come. If a friend, a partner, had been there, we could have changed the lead. Physically I was carrying the exertion alone. Psychologically, helpers appeared sporadically. There was someone behind me again. Was it my *alter ego* or some other form of human energy which was compensating for the lack of a partner? Thus, in this way, I was accompanied up to a height of 7,800m.

The first campsite which I trod out on the snow didn't please me. I had to camp on rock in order to anchor the tent securely, as the wind was getting up. A few metres above me, I saw the ideal campsite. Once more I hesitated. Perhaps it would be better a few metres lower. At last, here, I felt right.

At first I lacked the strength to unpack my rucksack and put up the tent. I stood there and gazed down at Advanced Base Camp. It must have been warm down there, as there was much less snow on the hills.

It was gone three o'clock and I had to cook. Down below I recognized a tiny red speck. Nena had placed the sleeping bag on the tent roof to protect herself from the heat. Or was it a signal for me? I hoped she could see me too. No longing, only the knowledge that she was down there, waiting.

Down below the heat was generally harder to bear than the cold, even though the temperature there at night dropped below −10°C and up here it dropped to perhaps −20°C. I was parched by the sun and dry air, and remembered I had a capsule of Japanese medicinal herb oil, so I put a couple of drops on my tongue. For a while that brought relief and opened my air passages. Apart from aspirin, this herbal remedy was the only medication I took with me up the mountain.

The oxygen-starved air worked like a grater. Every breath pained my throat and left a sticky feeling in my mouth. I took my time setting up the bivouac.

I was tired and glad that I had finally decided to stop. Already the awareness that no further effort would be required of me was working wonders. Was it not myself but rather a power from without which drove me on? It felt like it. Then my mind returned to its normal state and I began to think clearly again. I could perceive, not merely see.

I had a magnificent view of the glacier below and the snowy world to the east. Far below stood the gloomy form of the North Peak which looked as if it had turned its head around. Behind it, mountain ranges swam soft and wavy, and behind the Tibetan Plateau were people. For a long time I searched in vain for the ice pyramid of Pumori, over 7,000m high, in the western sea of summits. It had shrunk to an unimportant hump of snow beside the Rongbuk Glacier.

Meanwhile I had unpacked the tent and placed the rucksack higher up in the snow so that it wouldn't get disturbed and roll away. Between the only hand-holds I stood upright and peered upwards. Another short rise, then the big dip before the ridge proper. The conviction, a hunch condensed almost to certainty, that I would reach the summit in two more days, made me light-hearted. There didn't seem to be any serious obstacles. The 'Second Step', the only section which could have scared me, had been secured with ropes and pitons for years. Good thing I knew that. Above me I thought I could see a band of yellow rock under the snow. Some rock islands indicated the mountain's horizontal stratification.

Before starting I had already reckoned that there should be no problem if I made 1,200m in height on the first day — I had actually climbed at least 1,300m. On my solo ascent of Nanga Parbat in 1978 which had given me the psychological support for this solo attempt on Everest, I was actually able to climb 1,600m during the first day, but that time I started from a height of 4,800m. And there is a vast difference between climbing at 6,000m and 7,000m above sea-level. Here, just under 8,000m, every hand-hold becomes a triumph and an ordeal.

My tiny tent, less than 2kg in weight, and constructed so that it could withstand storms up to 100kmph, did not take up much space. It was just big enough for me to lie in with knees bent. Even so, it took me a long time to level out a spot for it. I pushed the snow backwards and forwards with my boots and made it firm, for I had no shovel. The

Reinhold Messner concealed his rucksack in an ice cave the day before his final ascent.

tent had to be level. I had difficulty putting it up as, time and again, a gust of wind got in and lifted it up. Once I had the cover stretched over the light metal tubes I felt good. With my ski sticks, ice axe and my only piton, I anchored the bivouac shell. Then I laid a finger-thick, foam-rubber mat on the floor and, pushing the full rucksack before me, I crept into the tent.

For a while I just lay there and listened to the wind hurling ice crystals against the side of the tent. It came in waves, ebbed and flowed, its rhythm keeping me awake. It was blowing out of the north-west which was a good sign.

I ought to cook; I had to. Again, this was a command that absorbed everything in me and around me. But I was even more tired after the many small jobs and erection of the bivouac, and I could barely bring myself to it. For the last time I went outside, fetched snow in my little aluminium pot and peered down into the valley – anything to put off the all-too-important work of cooking.

It became decidedly cold as I sat on the knob of rock which I had selected from below as the 'ideal resting place'. Far to the north I saw the Tibetan hills; still further northwards I could make out the grey-brown stone cone of Shekar and further in the distance I could see a chain of white mountains. Clouds filled the valleys to the south and the wind increased in force.

If Maurice Wilson had got as far as this, I thought suddenly, he would have reached the summit. Wilson, the fanatical Englishman who died in 1934 below the North Col on his solo attempt, was tougher than me, uncompromising and capable of enduring loneliness. The terrain above me looked really easy, so Wilson would have been able to climb it, at least as far as the North-East Ridge. Did I understand this madman so well because I too was crazy? Or was I taking comfort from the constancy of this man in my delusion to prove something? I didn't know exactly what it was, at least not rationally. I was still able to observe myself objectively but I was behaving like one possessed who stakes his life to express himself.

I knew of no other mountain, no other region from which there was such an infinite view as from Mount Everest across the Tibetan Plateau. Thus impressed, I crept back into the narrow confines of my tent. The space around me shrank to a cubic metre and I quickly forgot where the tent stood.

With my feet in my sleeping bag, I started to cook on my little gas burner. Taking off my rucksack, levelling the campsite and fixing the tent had all been hard work after more than ten hours' climbing. Now followed six hours of chores which were as strenuous as the climb beforehand. I devoured small crumbs of cheese and nibbled a piece of coarse South Tyrolean brown bread. Off and on I fell asleep. When I woke again, the first potful of water was warm. The soup tasted insipid and the snow had taken ages to melt.

I was surrounded by so much peace and at the same time so powerfully aroused that I wanted to embrace someone. Although I had not eaten since morning, I wasn't hungry and also had to force myself to drink. The feeling of thirst was less than my body's fluid requirement. I had to drink at least 4 litres, a basic standard which I had set myself, like the line of my route and my weather studies.

Again I thought of Wilson who had dared to make a solo ascent of Everest even though he was no mountaineer. He knew little about altitude. Nonetheless, he had not given up even after the worst snowstorms and several falls.

I lacked nothing, the forthcoming climbing difficulties lay well within my capabilities, and yet I had to force myself to believe in success. I knew I could do it. Nevertheless, I was trying to convince myself not to give up. For as long as Wilson could still stand, he had climbed on up like one possessed, borne up by faith and by God. I required so much energy just to fight fear and lethargy. Thereby I sought a goal which not even climbers understood. When would I finally be able to live without goals? Why did I stand in my own way with my ambition and my fanaticism?

'Fai la cucina', said someone near me, 'Get on with the cooking.' I thought again of the cooking. Half-aloud, I talked to myself. The strong feeling, of being with an invisible companion for the past few hours, had apparently allowed me to hope that the other person was doing the cooking. I asked myself, too, how we were both going to sleep in this tiny tent. I divided the piece of dried meat which I had fetched out of my rucksack into two equal portions. Only when I turned around did I realize that I was alone. Now I was speaking Italian, although for me, as a South Tyroler, German is my mother tongue and for three months I had been speaking only English with my Canadian friend Nena.

I knew I could prepare warm water from snow in a simple manner using the sun's energy. Basically it worked on the hothouse principle. I had brought a flat, black plastic bag especially for this purpose, and this was filled with snow and connected by a tube to a transparent bag. But it was too windy and the afternoon sun was veiled. So I cooked in the tent over the tiny gas flame. Half-outstretched and changing position occasionally, I lay there, my mat as hard as stone. The wind had grown so strong that the tent flapped. Every time I opened the tent door a few inches to shovel in snow with the lid of the cooking pot, it blew out the flame of the gas burner. It would be a nasty night, I thought. But at the same time the wind was a sign of good weather, so it also comforted me.

It required a lot of melted snow to get a litre of water. Once more I made tomato soup, then two pots of Tibetan salt tea, which I had learned how to prepare from the nomads. A handful of herbs to a litre of water, then two pinches of salt. I would have to drink a lot if I were not to become dehydrated and if my blood was not to thicken up. So I forced myself to melt more snow and to drink.

The cooking lasted several hours. I just lay there, holding the cooking pot and occasionally pushing a bit of dried meat or Parmesan cheese into my mouth. I had no desire to leave the tent. The storm got worse as ice crystals beat against the tent wall like hail. The tent poles were singing. That was good, for the wind would whirl away snow from the ridge and drive off the monsoon clouds which had been advancing in the late afternoon.

Sleep was out of the question. Frightful gusts tore at the tent. Or did my overwakeful senses deceive me? Time and again the tent and sleeping bag were lifted high. If the storm got any stronger, it would hurl me and everything else into the depths. I had to hold the tent down as powder snow forced itself through the chinks.

Cooking had now become impossible. I lay down with my arms in my sleeping bag and waited. I wanted to keep my eyes shut but every time a stronger gust of wind came I opened them again involuntarily. Was I still there? Just lying there tensely cost energy.

The tent walls fluttered, and the storm whistled, howled and pressed. Whirled-up snow beat on the surfaces like spray on a ship's bow. Once, as I peered out of the door, a torrent of ice crystals beat against me, but I didn't panic. My surroundings were blanked out although the black rock islands above me showed up like ghosts. This storm was really threatening to catapult me and my lodgings over the edge.

The fine ice dust in the tent and the fact that my fingers were sticking to metal, all made me shiver. However, I succeeded in remaining fairly warm. Time and again, when the wind permitted, I stuck my arms inside my sleeping bag and held it down from within, with only my face outside. Once I fell asleep briefly.

The night was tolerable and the storm died down. In the sleepless intervals endless thought chains circled in my mind. This thinking seemed to be something tangible. From the back of my mind sprang one fragment of thought after another, to and fro, like points of condensed energy, finding no exit and with a life of their own. It was as if there was an energy in my field of force which was independent of me. Certainly it belonged to me, but existed without action on my part and without impulse – even in sleep.

It came and went against my will. So I spent the night with this almost tangible power around me. There breathed constantly in and out a spirit which came out of nothing and condensed to nothing. Only somewhere between these extreme forms did I perceive it, even with my senses.

There was also my plan for the morrow. Was it possible to climb 'x' metres in 'y' hours? Over and over again I asked this question. I didn't answer it rationally, rather emotionally; a game like counting petals – she loves me, she loves me not. Perhaps 600m? Perhaps 700m? Below the 'Second Step'?

Then the weather penetrated into my half-conscious state once more, for the wind had not dropped completely. Nevertheless, its decrease felt something like peacefulness. The calm before the storm? The moon was shining, yet the night was warm and I no longer felt frozen. Was the monsoon break coming to an end? Were these still ice crystals that the wind was throwing against the tent, or was it snowing already? If it suddenly snowed heavily, I would not be able to go up or down and would be trapped. In my apathy I knew not which I preferred, fine weather or snow. What ought I to do in the case of avalanche danger? How long could I survive here?

These questions, to which my imagination neither knew nor wanted to give an answer, pursued me into my dreams. Again chains of thought without conclusion, and independent streams of energy flowed through my mind. Certainly higher up the avalanche danger was slight, but grainy new snow was like a bog which not only held one up but also sapped one. Once exhausted, I was lost for ever.

As morning dawned slowly, I noticed that the wind was dropping more. That lent me wings and I manoeuvred the gas stove into my sleeping bag to warm it up. An hour later I was drinking lukewarm coffee and chewing some more of the hard, coarse, brown bread from South Tyrol. In the constriction and cold of the tent, all the small chores added up to a physical ordeal. As I worked away with numbed fingers, hoar-frost trickled constantly from the canvas. To stretch out fully or to stand up to adjust my clothing was a luxury I could not perform in there. A tent of such a size as to allow this would have weighed at least three times as much as my special construction.

Once more I forced myself to cook. The lumps of dry snow made an unpleasant noise

View westwards over the Lho La.

between my fingers. It was ages before my fist-sized pot was full of water.

For another hour I lay in the sleeping bag with my clothes, drinking and dozing. I didn't want to look at the time. When I opened my eyes, often I didn't know whether it was morning or evening.

In my innermost being sat a driving unrest. It was not fear which suddenly seized me like an all-embracing hand, it was all the experiences of my mountaineering life, which spread out in me and pressed for activity. The exertions of thirty years' climbing, avalanches which I had experienced and states of exhaustion, which over decades had condensed to a feeling of deep helplessness. 'You must go on!' Time gained was energy saved. I knew what could happen to me during the ensuing days and I knew, too, how great the grind would be below the summit. This knowledge was now only bearable whilst I was moving.

I had to go and yet every smallest hand movement was an effort. Up here life was brutally racked between exhaustion and will-power; self-conquest became compulsive. Why didn't I descend? But there was no reason to and I could not simply give up. I had wanted to do the climb and I still wanted to. Curiosity (where was Mallory?), the game (man versus Mount Everest), ambition (I want to be the first) – all these superficial incentives had vanished. That which drove me now was much deeper than I or the probings of psychologists could detect.

Day after day, hour after hour, minute by minute, step by step, I was forcing myself to do something against which my body rebelled. At the same time this condition was only bearable in activity. Only a bad omen or the slightest illness would have been a strong enough excuse for going down.

As the sun reached the tent and slowly absorbed the hoar-frost on the inner walls, I packed up everything again, bit by bit and in the reverse order to which I must unpack it again in the evening. To make my sack lighter, I left behind a tiny depot consisting of two tins of sardines and a gas cartridge, as well as half the soup and tea. I would have to make do with what remained. It was coming up to nine o'clock, the weather was fine and tomorrow I would be on top! The moment I crawled out of the tent, my confidence returned, as if I were breathing cosmic energy. Or was it only the summit I was identifying with?

The air above seemed thin, the colour of that soft blue which appears transparent. I saw the mountains below me only as wavy surfaces, a relief in black and white.

'Take down the tent, fold it up!', I commanded myself. But now these impulses no longer came from my mind, they were once more gut reactions. Every breath filled my lungs with the air and my being with self-understanding. There could be no doubt and I continued on my way.

For the first 50m I went very slowly, then I found my rhythm again and made good progress. At an avalanche fracture I hesitated. Climbing somewhat to the right of the North Ridge, the ground steepened. There was more snow here than there had been lower down. Suddenly the weather worsened. Like massive wedges, grey-white cloud formations pushed themselves over the passes from the south into Tibet and already the valley bottom was full of monsoon mist. Instinctively I kept further to the right. The weather on Everest was often different from what it seemed – was it the monsoon or a sudden weather change? A storm?

You have to have experienced the wind in the vicinity of the summit to know that it can easily blow people away. Now there were streaks of cloud, signs of struggle high in the sky, which made me nervous. Rest stops between climbing became longer. Hesitation. Uncertainty. The slopes were not steep, with an average inclination of about 40 degrees, but at altitudes over 7,900m, all ground is strenuous.

The air around me was clear, but over the Rongbuk Valley strands of cloud formed constantly, shunted as far as the eastern horizon and then evaporated. As always at great altitude, I needed a long time this morning to get the life-giving energy flowing again, as if my harmony were disturbed. But through movement – right foot placed, weighted, released, dragged; left foot . . . – a field of energy developed in my body and, after the initial thrust, the sluices opened and the bracing stays slackened. With the reduction of anxiety, currents concentrated throughout my body – immeasurable, intangible forms of energy.

I climbed for a long time, and much longer than normal with this power dammed up. It was like a blockage, nothing to do with the altitude, rather something in me, so that I made hardly any headway.

The day before it had been so easy. Now each step became an ordeal. Why was I so slow? My rucksack weighed me down even though it was lighter. I felt lost, vulnerable. I could not make myself believe that there was a governing God of this world who concerned himself with each single one of us. There was no creator outside of me, outside of the cosmos. I don't know when I lost my faith, I only know that after I did, it was more difficult not to feel that I was alone and forsaken in this world.

The snow was deeper now and there was a noise when my boots sank in, as if someone were behind me. At last I had to accept that I was alone, inevitably alone. During the long pauses for breathing, a feeling similar to homesickness came over me. My need for security overwhelmed me and with that I knew that all hopes that someone was waiting for me down below were, like the anxiety before my solo climb, impeding and paralysing. Only in the activities of moving, seeking and gazing was it possible for me to accept this loneliness.

Thinking quickly used up the energy at my disposal; I could get no further on will-power alone. But when I released my mind, I was open to a power from without. I was like a hollow hand and experienced a regeneration. A clenched fist or stiff fingers led with exhaustion to helplessness. Only when I was like a hollow hand did an invisible part of my being regenerate itself, not only in sleep but also in climbing.

The rhythm of climbing — rest became determined by energy and energy determined by rhythm. The halts between climbing already took longer than the fifteen paces which I made each time. That was my measure of time, step by step; time and space became one.

It was so difficult to cope, to take upon oneself all responsibility, not only for one's actions but also for being there at all, especially when my whole body became desperate through exertion. Despite the risk I had freely entered into, I could not, like Wilson, now entrust myself wholly to a God. To what then? Whilst climbing I was like a walking corpse. What kept me upright was the world around me: the air, sky, earth, and the clouds which pressed in from the west. I gained a sense of progress with my first steps and a sense of my will as something tangible for the last two paces.

The ground was easy, yet it demanded my whole attention. That I could stand and make headway gave me the energy to think ahead, to want to get further. At least as important as experiencing success was the pleasure in my own skill. It was astonishing how often I had overlooked this part of the pleasure of climbing and written only of loads carried to the summit. High-altitude climbing requires a whole range of proficiencies, knowledge and inventiveness. The higher you go, the more you yourself become the problem. The ability to solve problems of this sort is what makes a good mountaineer. I see the usefulness of climbing not in the further development of technique, rather in the development of man's instincts and his ability to extend himself. Knowledge of his limitations is just as important as his claim to be able to do anything.

With my snail-like advance, I had lost my ability to estimate distance and also my sense of time. Was I on the point of breaking down? As I once said, development of the self is part of my motive, but what constitutes development when comparisons cannot be made?

If I am said frequently to have a compulsion to succeed, this is characteristic of the people of today, for whom experience of effort and not the learning process itself is what counts. Anyone who only perceives his body as a vehicle for success cannot understand me and cannot follow my thoughts.

I went on, without calculating or anticipating how far I had got. This climbing, resting and breathing process had become a condition which completely absorbed me. It was merely movement along a fixed line. The forward-thrusting impulse in climbing is often referred to as aggression; I prefer to call it curiosity or passion. Now all that was no

Traversing the North Face.

more. My progress had its own dynamism: fifteen paces, then a breather, propped up by my ski sticks, concentrating both inwards and upwards, and with the knowledge that God was the solution.

I confess that in moments of real danger, something acts as a defence mechanism; it aids survival but evaporates as soon as the threat is past. I was not threatened now. It was all so peaceful around me and I was not hurrying. I couldn't go any faster and I accepted this realization as a law of nature.

My altimeter showed 7,900m but altimeters can become inaccurate high up and generally show less than the actual height. It was also conceivable that the air pressure had altered during the night, so I no longer took the altimeter seriously.

The weather was still fine and I wanted to get on. There was no more thought of retreat. About 100m above my campsite I decided that the ascent of the ridge would be too dangerous and too strenuous. There the snow lay knee-deep in places. All the hollows were filled in and above me I could see a single giant-sized basin. It was not only the avalanche danger but above all the exertion which put me off this route.

I felt hopeless as I poked my right ski stick into the floury mess. Snow-slab danger! The topmost layer was firm but gave way with a crack when I stepped on it. There was grainy snow underneath. On my own, under these conditions, I would have quickly tired myself out. Alone I could not have trodden down the snow.

Then I noticed that on the North Face the snow slabs had gone. What luck! There the ground was firm. Yes, over there! Without giving it much thought, I began to traverse the North Face. Instinctively, as if I were programmed, I wanted to reach the Norton Couloir and ascend this next day to the summit. I made this decision as suddenly as the snow had become bad.

The traverse of the North Face extended a long way, and gained little height, but it provided good going in the firm monsoon snow and I had no need for my ice axe. Supported by my ski sticks, I traversed the slope. My rucksack, which had the tent tied on the outside so that it could dry out, was still heavy. At a height of almost 8,000m, even rest with this on my back was an exertion in itself. Without the ski sticks I would have staggered and collapsed. I rested like a four-legged creature and, in this way, the weight of the rucksack did not constrict my breathing. When I moved off again, I did so by bending well forward, having also shortened the uphill ski stick in my left hand.

I had given up counting paces and I had neither the inclination nor the strength to take any pictures. Moving rhythmically and resting, I progressed like a snail. And out of my progress, energy accrued to me which was just sufficient to maintain this rhythm.

The terrain was inclined and rolling. The stretch as far as the great snow couloir seemed short. Without asking myself how many dips lay between me and my planned bivouac site, I climbed unhesitatingly upwards. My confidence grew. I no longer felt loneliness as isolation but much more as detachment. The bridge of wife and friends, the embodiment in a community – supports which I need – I experienced now for what they were: aids to endure the awareness of loneliness.

I was now directly under the 'First Step'. Above me projected a stubby, flat pillar like a sickle. It was covered in snow and to the right of it stood a dark, unfriendly and steep wall. Snow lay on only some of its ledges. The rock islands in the monsoon snow increased, as did my sense of having been here before.

What disturbed me was the weather. There was scarcely any wind, hot sun and clouds pressed in from the south. Like wedges, they pushed their grey-white masses northwards. Yes, there was no doubt, the monsoon storms were sending out their scouts.

Nevertheless, I climbed on determinedly, always keeping up to the right, in a bee-line for the summit. The summit of Mount Everest or what I took to be the summit – the final point presumably was not visible – made no overpowering impression on me. I was standing close under the North-East Ridge and the route appeared flattened.

The view, too, was restricted – on one side by the mass of the mountain and on the other by the rising cloud ceiling. The North Peak now appeared flat and small; it separated the mist welling up from the valley.

Only after longer rest stops was I capable of such observations. Between the North Ridge and the Norton Couloir I was standing on a mountainside which has no equal in the Alps – a slanting trapezium, 2.5km high and almost 1km wide.

I was making such slow progress! How long my breathers were I did not know. I managed, with the ski sticks, to go fifteen paces, then I had to rest for some minutes. All my strength seemed to depend on my lungs and, when these were pumped out, I had to stop. I was breathing in through my mouth and out through mouth and nose. And while standing I had to use all my will-power to force my lungs to work. Only when they were pumping regularly did the pain disappear. Then I experienced something like a surge of energy and there was strength in my legs again.

I had decided spontaneously to traverse the North Face of Mount Everest, even though I wanted to be on the look-out for signs of Mallory and Irvine. Yet I had no resentment, not only because there was too much snow but also because I knew their fate. I was on the only right route to the summit.

The going was tiring, almost a torment; it all depended on the snow conditions. Luckily, the downward sloping slabs were buried beneath a layer of firn snow and so far I had been able to go around all the rock islands. I could see the North-East Ridge above me, but I knew that just now there would be no trace there of the pioneers. Mallory and Irvine climbed along this ridge, exactly on its edge in fact. I was convinced that Odell had seen the pair on the 'First Step', on that knob which rises above the line of the ridge. I knew now that they had foundered on the 'Second Step' and lay buried in the monsoon snow in the deep basin above me. This notion absorbed me like an old fairy-tale and I was able to contemplate it without anxiety.

It was as if I saw now the origin of that legend, as if I had perceived the truth. The observations of the Chinese climber Wang in 1974, who told the Japanese, Hasegawa, of his discovery five years later before an avalanche killed him below the North Col, appeared now just as stricken from my memory as the contradictory descriptions of the two steps.

The 'First Step' and 'Second Step' now stood above me. There Mallory and Irvine lived on. The fate of the pair was now free of all speculation and hope. It was alive in me. I could not tell whether I was seeing it as on a stage or in my mind's eye. At all events, it was happening in my life. It was as if I belonged to it.

Seen close to, the 'Second Step' seemed to overhang. Only a little snow was sticking to it. No, without pitons and ladders, like the Chinese had installed, it was unclimbable. A few months before, the Japanese climber Kato had also used the climbing aids left behind by the Chinese.

Between the two steps, therefore, Mallory and Irvine presumably died without having reached the summit. I didn't ask myself how they died, I only saw them turn back. Mallory and Irvine, legends for decades, still lived for me up there and not just in Odell's words.

Disappointed and exhausted, they turned round below the 'Second Step'. In failing daylight, the difficulties increased. The two forced themselves to make the laborious descent. They got slower and slower. Night fell. Only energy derived from success could have saved them. The vision faded. How the pair died can only be answered when someone finds Mallory's body or the camera which Somervell had lent him. Perhaps it can never be answered conclusively. That the two of them did not reach the summit is for me, however, beyond doubt.

After a longer rest stop my breathing was quiet and regular. Was there someone speaking nearby? Was somebody there? Again I heard only my heart and breathing. And yet, there they were again! In this silence every sound, everything heard over the sound of the mind, seemed like a spoken word. Frequently I jumped because I thought I could hear voices. Perhaps it was Mallory and Irvine? With my knowledge of the circumstances surrounding their disappearance, which had occupied me for many years, each noise now came to life in me as a vision. At any rate, I believed sometimes that it was their calls which a breath of wind carried to me. But I didn't know what their voices sounded like. I had never tried to imagine them. Were Mallory and Irvine really still alive? Yes, their spirit was still there. I sensed it distinctly.

I gazed up at the 'Second Step' and already two people occupied my imagination, releasing phantoms. In the driving mist everything seemed so near, yet ghostly. Despite my tiredness I stared time and again at the edge of the ridge above me. The 'Second Step' reared up nearer. A relatively easy snow gully led to a steep dièdre. Quite distinctly I recognized a barrier at the top. At this moment I did not know that the Japanese climbers Yasuo Kato and Susumi Makamura had taken forty minutes over the 'Second Step'. I now see this as the real proof that Mallory and Irvine, with their comparatively primitive equipment, failed there in 1924.

Because the swelling mist enveloped everything and because I was exhausted by the climbing, everything around me disappeared. My eyes hurried on ahead a few metres, looking for the route. Brightness streamed through me when the sun broke through the clouds. Sparkling snow crystals flashed past me like water from a spring.

Despite the gloomy snow desert around me, which ebbed and flowed with the pulsating clouds, I felt no panic. I knew the route and my track behind me was still there. It was snowing lightly of course but it was warm.

Across gigantic, gentle waves – I had already crossed two – I approached the Norton Couloir. I didn't see it, only sensed it. However, not for a moment was I afraid that I was too high. Was it tiredness which was making me indifferent, or was it this feeling I had that I already knew the way which gave me the assurance of a sleep-walker? I was convinced that all was well.

Every time I crossed a rib, more lumps of rock lay there. In a row above and below me, they made a sort of border. Far above and far below they disappeared in the mist. These rock islands were to show me the way – like cairns, each had a definite form and every dark speck had a meaning. Each provided something for my eyes and for me to hold on to.

Meanwhile the mists around me had become so thick that the sun broke through only now and then. Route-finding became more difficult. Sometimes the breathless silence after resting filled me with terror for moments. Had I gone too far already? When the silence became unbearable, I had to continue climbing, always obliquely upwards. The pounding in my body and the gasping for breath after ten paces now let me forget the emptiness around me once more. For a pain-filled eternity there was nothing more. I existed only as a mind above a body. While resting, I literally let myself flop, with my body supported on the ski sticks, rucksack on the nape of my neck. For a while I just breathed in and out. Then I perked up again and, with the first step, experienced the exertion of the next section. Carry on!

Sometimes I felt as if I were stuck in the snow. However, I didn't let myself get discouraged and continued traversing the North Face up to the right. The whole slope was like a single avalanche path. Fresh snow trickled down from above and it was sleeting. I told myself it was only temporary and that the snow would consolidate. 'It'll hold for another two days', I said to myself.

The rising traverse was endless with many, regular pauses. Because of the exertion and concentration, I did not notice that the weather had become so bad that I ought to turn back. Everything around me was covered in mist. I squatted down for a rest. Perhaps I should put up the tent? The spot seemed too insecure – I had to bivouac on a ridge. If it kept on snowing, there was a danger of avalanche. All this was not thought out rationally but came to me as instincts which lay buried deep inside me.

For at least another hour, I forced myself to keep going. On a blunt elevation, which ran across the face like a gigantic rib, I squatted down again. For a while I felt only heaviness, indifference, numbness. Then the clouds parted. The valley appeared, grey, lightly covered in snow and then was soon veiled in mist again.

Not only did the mountains seem flattened but so did the slopes beneath me and the snow shield in the great couloir. I saw all of this with the feeling that I no longer belonged to the world below.

When I noticed the time, it was about three o'clock in the afternoon and I was still about 200m east of the Norton Couloir. I was disappointed to see that my altimeter showed only 8,220m. I would have been delighted to have reached 8,400m for I had expended myself much more than I had done the day before. It was misty and snowing lightly. There was no question of going any further. My excuse was that I didn't know if there was a bivouac place higher up.

I was dead tired. Conscious of this, I had a job to make it to the next patch of rocks. I erected the tent earlier than planned. On a rock mushroom, safe from avalanches – snow slides would have branched to the left and right of it – I found a 2 × 2m spot which was almost level. I remained on my feet while firming down the snow. I asked myself how I would find my way back if the weather remained like this.

This doubt, and the knowledge of all that could happen, condensed into fear. Only when I was working was I inwardly calm. The light snow fall, the stationary clouds, the warmth – all this was sinister. Was it the monsoon or only anxiety? A change in the weather seemed to be on the way.

If I could not get back for days my reserves would soon be used up. The avalanche danger on the North Face and under the North Col was growing by the hour.

An hour later my tent was standing on the rock outcrop. Once again I anchored it with an ice axe and ski sticks. Here I could camp protected from the wind. Also, there was little danger here if there was a storm. I placed my open rucksack in front of the tent door and pushed the mat inside. Lumps of snow for cooking lay to hand around me. Everything was ready for the long night and a feeling of relief came over me.

I took only two pictures before I gave up photographing. It sapped my energy too much. And for what? Documentary proof, reports, all that had become meaningless. It seemed to me much more important that I made myself a drink.

That night I kept my clumsy, double-layered, plastic boots with all my clothing, for I could not allow them to get cold. My clothes felt strange and the layers between my skin and outer clothing were like unpleasant, stuffy air – hence the feeling of being in a strait-jacket.

As I lay in the tent, too tired to sleep and too weak to cook, I tried to imagine Advanced Base Camp. Nena would be making tea. Or was she looking straight up here? Had it cleared up meanwhile? Perhaps the weather would get better. Time passed too quickly and too slowly. Only when I managed to switch off completely, did it cease to exist.

On the evening of 19 August, Nena wrote in her diary:

It is 8 p.m. and twilight invades the narrow glacier valley. The snow began suddenly and still continues to fall. I could not see Reinhold the whole day. But I know he is up there, perhaps somewhere in the vicinity of the 'Second Step'. Tomorrow he will go to the summit. Hopefully the weather will improve again.

The heavy black clouds came from nowhere, towering up, spitting snow and sleet. What does it mean? I can do nothing but think of him constantly. If this flurrying doesn't stop he is lost. How much snow has fallen? How dangerous are the avalanches up there? How difficult is the descent in new snow? How long will it take him to get back to the North Col? Somehow I am sure that Reinhold will do the right thing.

But there is something incalculable in this man. His whole being is possessed, is energy, action. I am anxious but I don't mind. Above all I am vexed because the weather is playing him such a dirty trick. That's unfair. I sit in the empty tent and force myself to eat and drink. I try to read about medicine and inflammation of the lungs but my thoughts are up there in the whirling snow. I am madly excited and sad, both at once. I keep repeating the traditional Tibetan prayer 'Om mani padme hum', over and over again.

When it gets dark, I put on something warm and venture outside. Didn't I just know it! The 7,000m peaks are clearing, the clouds melting away. The wind is getting up. It drives the new snow off the ridges. I shout and scream. He does not hear me, cannot hear me. Nevertheless, I speak to him: 'I am with you!'

How does one live at this height? I was no longer living, I was only vegetating.

When one has to do everything alone, every hand movement takes a lot of will-power. With each chore I noticed the effect of the thin air. My speed of thought was greatly reduced and I could make clear decisions only slowly. They were influenced by my tiredness and pain when breathing. My windpipe felt as if it were made of wood and I detected a slight irritation in my bronchial tubes.

Although I was not able to prepare any really hot drinks, as water boils at a lower temperature at this height. I kept on melting snow. Pot after pot. I drank soup and salt tea. I was not very hungry and had to force myself to eat. Should I open these sardines or something else? The slightest effort required time, energy and attention. All my movements were slow and cumbersome.

I decided on bread and cheese, and chicken in curry sauce – a freeze-dried meal which I mixed with lukewarm water. I stuck the empty packet under the top of my sleeping bag. I would need it in the night to pee in. It took me more than half an hour to choke down the insipid pap.

Outside it was getting dark. The many small chores in the bivouac cost me as much

Traversing the North Face below the 'First Steps' and 'Second Steps'.

Reinhold Messner used
three yaks as far as Advanced
Base Camp (6,500m).

After a last clear view down to the Rongbuk Glacier (below) Reinhold Messner reached the summit of Mount Everest (8,848m) in thick, swirling cloud. As in 1978, he rested by the Chinese survey tripod. All photographs during his solo ascent were taken with an automatic self-release timer.

In the Gasherbrum ice-fall; Sia Kangri in the background is flooded with the first of the morning sun.

Approaching the Baltoro Glacier. The Balti porters added firewood to their loads.

On the snowy Baltoro Glacier on the way to Base Camp.

Base Camp was sited at the upper end of the Abruzzi Glacier. In the background from the left: K2, Broad Peak and the Gasherbrums.

Werner Herzog and Bubu Klausman (camera) accompanied us to Base Camp.

Hans Kammerlander on the summit of Gasherbrum II. In the background on the right is Gasherbrum I which he reached three days later together with Reinhold Messner.

Messner and Kammerlander climbed for a long time in shadow on the icy rocks of Gasherbrum I; when they got to flatter terrain, the snowstorm overtook them.

The descent from Gasherbrum I lasted three days in the snowstorm. Messner and Kammerlander were hypothermic, despairing and covered in ice. Nevertheless, they had realized their plan — the traverse of both eight-thousanders Gasherbrum I and Gasherbrum II.

Everest 1980: 'Twilight on Everest'.

Everest 1978: '200 kilometres per hour'.

Gasherbrum 1984: 'Here lies a dead man'.

energy as hours of regular climbing did. The difference between arriving at a prepared camp and being cared for there by Sherpas or comrades, and evening after evening of having to put up your own tent and cook is tremendous. Perhaps it is the essential distinction between the classic big expedition and the modern small expedition. Going to sleep is in itself a big exertion. Up here I could not simply get into bed, stick my head under the covers and fall asleep.

Once more I sat up in my sleeping bag. First of all I undid my boots. I wanted warm feet in the morning and boots that were not frozen stiff. So I changed my socks and put my boots back on. Once more I pushed my feet and boots right back into the sleeping bag and threw away the damp socks. Then, outstretched and propped on my arms, I stuck the rucksack under the mat for a pillow. I arranged the cooking equipment so that I could get at it the next morning from my sleeping bag. I had to shift my body a little constantly and keep my head up, not so as to sleep well but only so that I was able to endure the night.

These movements in the constricted tent made me breathless and I had to breathe deeply. In between I panted again. For hours I had had numb fingers. Despite the occasional sleep of exhaustion — an inadvertent dozing — I wasn't able to fall asleep properly that night. I was endless like the night.

In the morning I was just as tired as I had been the previous evening, and stiff as well. I asked myself whether I really wanted to go on. I must! For all that, I had too little strength to move my body. I knew from experience that I could go on for a time, but I tried to push these thoughts aside and to think of nothing — the state of mind which had allowed me to endure the night was prolonged. I had only to start moving and keep going to gain energy again but I lacked the will-power to make the first move.

When I opened the tent flap, it was already day outside. A golden-red glow lay over the summit pyramid. To the east were fields of clouds. Automatically I was reminded of the monsoon. It was ages before I was holding the first pot of warm water in my hands. There was ice in the tent. I couldn't eat.

As I fished lumps of snow into the tent, I stared up into the Norton Couloir. It was fairly steep. Smoky-grey clouds clung to the mountain sides. The air was crystal-clear, as if laden with moisture, and I was rather cold despite the favourable temperature. Ice lay on the edge of the rocks and on the hem of the tent. Cold during the monsoon was no problem on Mount Everest. I was pretty certain that it thawed in high summer when there was mist and no wind, even on the summit. My three layers of clothing — silk, pile suit and thin down suit — sufficed.

Two years before, in May 1978, I had endured −40°C at night. Now it was only as cold as −15°C, perhaps only −10°C. Nevertheless I must not be careless. So long as the sun wasn't shining, I kept my gloves on and boots laced up loosely. At this height frostbite can occur at a few degrees below zero.

I thought only about going on, as if retreat or failure had not crossed my mind. But what if the mist were to thicken? Should I still wait? No, that would be senseless. I was already very late, I must get outside. At this height there was no recovering. By tomorrow I could already be so weak that I wouldn't have strength for a summit attempt. Either go immediately or never. Either — or. I had to go either up or down. There was no other choice.

Bivouac tent at 7,800m.

Twice while waiting for the snow to melt I took my pulse. It was way above 100 beats per minute. I felt all in. There were no more chains of thought, only commands in my head. The night had been one long ordeal. There was pain in my joints and mucus in my throat. The morning was depressing.

This morning, 20 August, I left everything behind: tent, ski sticks, mat, sleeping bag; I also left my rucksack in the tent. All I took was the camera. Just as I was, I crawled out of the bivouac and drew my hood over my head. I buckled on my crampons with my bare fingers and pulled my titanium ice axe out of the snow. Had I got everything? It must be after eight o'clock already.

Without the load on my back I climbed more easily but I missed the ski sticks for balancing. I felt secure with my short axe in my right hand except when traversing.

When I climbed directly upwards my gloved left hand and ice axe fumbled in the snow beneath my head. I moved like a four-legged creature. While resting I spread my whole weight so that my upper body remained free. I knelt in the snow, laid my arms over the rammed-in axe and put my head on this pillow. In this way I could inspect the steep rise above me, orientate myself and weigh up difficulties. Luckily an uninterrupted snow gully ran up the Norton Couloir. As long as I could see and plod on, I was confident.

Once, before I had reached the bottom of the broad basin, I looked around for a spot for the possibility of a longer rest. The tent, a yellow speck, appeared as through a weak magnifying glass. Was that the light mist or were all my senses fooled? I made a note of the spot and then climbed the rise above me to the right. Pace by pace. Step by step.

Already after a short while I missed my rucksack like a true friend. It had been my partner in conversation for two days, had encouraged me to carry on when I had been completely exhausted. Now I talked to the ice axe.

A friend was little enough in this state of exposure. However, the voices in the air were back again. I didn't ask myself where they came from. I accepted them as real. Lack of oxygen and insufficient supply of blood to the brain were certainly the cause of these irrational experiences which I had got to know two years before during my solo ascent of Nanga Parbat. Up here in 1933, Frank Smythe had shared his biscuits with an imaginary partner.

My rucksack had been my companion. But without it I made better progress. If I had had to carry something now, I wouldn't have been able to move. I had decided to make this ascent because I could leave everything behind on the final day. In the driving clouds, following my instinct more than my eyes, I looked for the route, step by step.

Again I had a distant memory of this couloir. I was living in a sort of half-dark of mist, clouds, driving snow and the recognition of individual sections – 'I've been here before' – a feeling that even lengthy reflection could not dispel. An hour above camp I came up against a steep step 100m high. Or was it 200m that towered up in front of me?

The climbing was made easier by the snow. I always managed to get a hold for my whole foot without my crampons hitting the rock. For hours, repeatedly expending myself, dying, bracing myself, exacting my will, letting myself fall, collecting myself. The rock islands to the left and right of the great gully were yellow in colour with brighter streaks here and there. Often I had double-vision and was uncertain where I should

Second bivouac at 8,220m.

continue. I kept more to the right. The slope was now so steep that I rested in the climbing position. I was literally creeping along now. Only occasionally did I manage to do ten paces without stopping to gasp for air.

The view was disappointing. Yesterday morning it had still been impressive. When I looked down now on the long glacier with the moraine ridges, everything seemed flattened. The landscape was blunted, deadened by the new snow. Despite the swelling mist I lost all sense of distance.

Here, too, light powder snow was lying on top of a half-firm base. The rock slabs beneath, lying one on another like roof tiles and approximately as steep as a church roof, were almost completely covered in snow. I quitted the gully where it became broader and formed a pear-shaped bay. I took bearings on a blunt ridge up to the right; there it must be easier.

It became steeper. When I moved, I no longer pounded like a locomotive. I felt my way ahead hesitatingly. Jerkily I gained height. This climbing was not difficult but downright unpleasant. Often I found no hold in the snow and had to feel for the foot-holds.

I must not slip here. For the first time on this solo ascent I felt in danger of falling. It was like walking in increased gravity. This careful climbing with great concentration increased my exhaustion. Moreover, the mist was making things more and more difficult. All I could see was a piece of snow surface in front of me, and now and then a snippet of blue sky above the ridge. Everything moved very slowly and sluggishly. In spite of the enormous strain which each step upwards required, I was still convinced that I would get to the top. This I experienced now in a sort of anticipation, like a deliverance.

The knowledge that I was half-way there calmed me, gave me strength and drove me on. Often I was near the end of my tether. After a dozen paces everything in me screamed to stop, sit and breathe. But after a short rest I was able to carry on.

My worry about the bad weather had cost me additional energy. And there was the ever-recurring question of the descent. At the same time I experienced an inspiring hope in the thickening mist, something like curiosity outside of time and space. Not that demoralizing despair which a visible and unendingly distant summit often triggered; now it was all about the struggle against my own limitations. This became more distinct with each step; with each breath it resolved itself. The decision to climb up or down no longer bothered me, rather the irregular rhythm and the weakness in my knees.

I went on like a robot. Against all bodily remonstrances I forced myself upwards. It had to be! I didn't think too much, conversed with myself and cheered myself up. Where was my rucksack? My second friend, the ice axe, was still there. We called a halt.

The route up the Norton Couloir was logical and not as difficult as I had expected in the morning. I would find my way back. Up above it seemed to be somewhat flatter.

The fancy that I had climbed here once before helped me to find the right route time and again. The steep step shot through with brighter rock lay below me. Still I kept to my right. Shortly before an avalanche had gone down here. The snow was bearing my weight. Under the blunt edge it became deeper and my speed accordingly became slower. On my hands and knees I climbed up, completely apathetic. My boots armed with crampons were like anchors in the snow.

As I stood on the edge, I heard the wind between the stones. Far below, this rock ridge continued as a pillar. For a short while the mist was so thick that I could no longer orientate myself. More or less on the ridge, where the least snow lay, I continued for an hour until a dark, vertical rock wall barred my way.

Something in me drew me to the left and I curved around the obstacle. Still I held to the right. How long? I just kept on climbing up the slope. Time no longer existed. I consisted only of tiredness and exertion. I supposed myself to be near the summit, but the ridge went on for ever.

During the next three hours I no longer felt real. I was a creature shifting in space and time. Nevertheless, I kept moving. Every time blue sky broke through the thick clouds, I thought I would see the summit, that it would be there. But still there were snow and stones above me. The few rocks which showed above the snow were greeny-grey, shot through here and there with brighter streaks. Ghostlike, they moved in the thin clouds. For a long time I traversed upwards, keeping to the right.

A steep rock barrier barred my way to the ridge. I would have to pass to the right of the wall to get higher.

Arriving on the crest of the North-East Ridge, I sensed the cornices and stopped. Then I lay down on the snow. I was there! The ridge was flat. Where was the summit? Groaning, I stood up again and stamped the snow down. With my ice axe, arms and body burrowing in the snow I crawled on, continuing to the right and always going upwards.

When I rested I felt utterly lifeless except that my throat burned when I drew breath. Suddenly it brightened up. I turned around and could see down into the valley, right to the bottom where the glacier flowed. Breathtaking! Trance-like, I took a few photographs. Then everything closed in again. Grey, snow-drifts, completely windless.

Once again I had to pull myself together. I could hardly move. No despair, no happiness, no anxiety. I had not lost the mastery of my feelings – there were actually no more feelings. I consisted only of will-power. After each few metres this too fizzled out in an unending tiredness. Then I thought nothing, felt nothing. I let myself fall to the ground and just lay there. For an indefinite time I remained completely without will. Only then did I take a few more steps.

At most I thought it could be only another 10m up to the top. Below me to the left projected enormous cornices. For a few moments I espied the North Peak far below me through a hole in the clouds. Then the clouds parted above me too. Oncoming shreds of cloud floated past nearby in the light wind. I saw the grey of the clouds, the black of the sky and the shining white of the snow surface as one. They belonged together like the stripes on a flag. I must be there!

Above me was only sky. I sensed it although now, in the mist, I saw it as little as I saw the world below me. To the right the ridge still went up; but perhaps it only seemed to, perhaps I was deceiving myself.

There was no sign of my predecessors. It seemed odd that I could not see the Chinese aluminium survey tripod that had stood on the summit since 1975. Suddenly I was standing in front of it. I took hold of it and grasped it like a friend. It was as if I were embracing my opposing force, something that absolved and electrified at the same time. At this moment I breathed deeply.

The North-East Ridge in the vicinity of the summit.

In the mist and driving clouds I could not see at first whether I was really standing on the highest point. It seemed almost as if the ground went on up to the right. This tripod, which now rose scarcely knee-high out of the snow, triggered no euphoria in me. It was just there. Because of the masses of snow on the summit, it was much smaller than I had known it in 1978, plastered with snow and unreal. In 1975 the Chinese had anchored it to the highest point, ostensibly to carry out exact measurements. Since then they had given the height of their Chomolungma as 8,848.12m. I was thinking all these thoughts, up there. This artificial summit erection didn't seem at all odd. I had arrived!

It was after three o'clock. Like a zombie obeying an inner command, I took some

photographs. A bit of blue sky flew past in the background. Snow cornices towered up to the south, seemingly higher than where I was standing.

I squatted down, feeling as heavy as a stone. I just wanted to rest a while and forget everything. At first there was no relief. I was leached, completely empty. Nevertheless, in the vacuum something like energy was condensing. I was charging myself up. For many hours I had only expended energy. I had climbed myself to a standstill, now I was experiencing regeneration and a return flow of energy.

A shred of bleached material which was wrapped around the top of the tripod was scarcely frozen. Absent-mindedly I fingered it, then untied it, ice and snow stuck to it. I

had to take some more pictures but could not rouse myself to do it. Also I had to descend. Half an hour too late would mean the end of me. At this moment I was not at all disappointed that once again I had no view. For the second time I was standing on the world's highest point and could see nothing.

It was now completely windless. The light snowflakes danced and all around me the clouds swelled as if the earth were pulsating underneath. I knew not how I had done it but I knew that I could do no more. In my tiredness I was not only as heavy as a corpse, I was also incapable of taking anything in. My senses could not discern above and below.

Again a shred of blue sky passed and individual ice crystals shone in the sun. The mountains seemed far below and quite flat between the black-white of the valleys. This time I got the camera out too late. Then clouds, mist again; the primary colour of the valleys was now violet.

Was night coming on already? No, it was four o'clock. I must be off. No feeling of sublimity. I was too tired for that. And although at this moment I didn't feel particularly happy or special, I had a hunch that in retrospect it would be comforting, a sort of conclusion. Perhaps a recognition that I too would have to roll that mythical stone all my life without ever reaching the summit, if I myself were not this summit. I was Sisyphus.

After three-quarters of an hour, I had the strength to stand up; to get up and go down. It had got a bit brighter. My uphill track was still recognizable. That calmed me. How much easier the descent of this great mountain was! It cost only a fraction in strength and will-power compared with the ascent.

My whole energy now went into my senses. I found the smell of the snow and the colour of the rocks more intensive than in the days before, and jumped at the occasional sheet lightning that shot out of the clouds far to the west. I just wanted to get down. I climbed down — once facing inwards, then outwards again — as if I were in flight. I didn't ask myself why I had taken on all these strains in order to get to the summit. It would have been lovely to be down already. This long route was a burden.

What disturbed me most was my cough. It made my life hell. Even gentle coughing tore at my stomach. Besides, I had not eaten for many hours. I had to get to Base Camp as quickly as possible. Just before the onset of darkness I found my way back to the tent and my rucksack.

That night I hardly slept at all, and I could not bring myself to cook sufficiently. I drank a little snow water but again ate nothing. The warm flame of the gas burner, which buzzed near my face, was perhaps just to comfort me. I didn't put it out, although I couldn't sit up in my sleeping bag and fetch in snow. Every movement now took so much energy; energy which I had derived from climbing and the stimulus of having reached the top. Now it failed me. Lying there in the tent was like dying. Only my success kept me alive. I obeyed the law of inertia. Between waking and sleeping, surrounded by the living dead, the hours passed. I had no thoughts. I was still not out of danger.

Suddenly I was seized with terror. Was Nena still there? She didn't know where I was, that I would be down the next day.

She could not sleep either. That night she wrote in her diary:

Reinhold Messner a few metres from the tripod and the summit of Everest.

20 August 1980. Now I have accustomed myself to the fact that the snow and the clouds come and go; but I have not accustomed myself to sleeping here alone. I can do nothing else but worry about you, knowing you are somewhere above 8,000m. I hope that you are not suffering. Even here at 6,500m life is an ordeal, what must it be like up there? It snows more and more – 9 p.m.

My thoughts kept weaving uninterruptedly, always at the limit of consciousness. In the small hours I roused myself with the feeling that I had come to a decision, but I could not concentrate. Had I gone crazy? Had this emptiness sent me mad? Did I have altitude sickness?

When morning came I took to my heels. Without a drink, I left my camp, tent and sleeping bag – everything in fact except my rucksack. I pulled the ski sticks out of the snow and began traversing diagonally downwards and eastwards.

Eastwards I looked down into the snow basin of the Rongbuk Glacier as I reached the broad ridge just above the North Col. No tent stood there. Or was it just snowed up? The new snow was powdery and dry; it flew about when I stepped on it. It was bitterly cold.

Not only on the ascent but also now while descending my will-power became more and more dulled. The longer I climbed, the less important the goal seemed, the more indifferent I became to myself. My attention had diminished, my memory was weakened and my mental fatigue was now greater than my bodily fatigue. It was so pleasant to sit doing nothing and, for that reason, so dangerous. Death through exhaustion – like death by freezing – is a pleasant one. As I walked across the undulating ridge above the North Col, I felt as if I were returning from a nether world.

I let myself float on in my tiredness and in the knowledge that I had been to the summit. I offered no more resistance and let myself fall at each step. Only I must not remain sitting down. Day after day I had endured the loneliness of the undulating snow surface of the North Face. Hour after hour I had fought against the wind, which whipped up the sharp ice crystals. For an eternity I had travelled through the mist which deluded me that each block of rock was a friend. Every breath up there was an ordeal and yet I took it as a gift.

Now a feeling came over me of 'having survived', of 'having been saved'. Bit by bit I passed into something which one might call a 'place of fulfilment' or a 'saving haven'. Like the pilgrim at the place of pilgrimage, I forgot all the strains of the journey.

Nena did not know that I would be at the North Col soon. She, too, had been upset by the uncertainty of being alone these past few days. She filled her diary with soliloquies:

21 August 1980. Good morning, River. Thank you for being here and keeping me company. 'Hi', croaks the big black raven. For the tenth time I try to look through my telephoto lens. For an hour I have done nothing else, since sun up. But my eyes ache terribly. I have tried telling myself not to look for a while. I can't stop. The telephoto is like an obsession. Now even the rocks begin to move. Sometimes I see several people descending the North Ridge. Either he is just climbing down, or . . . I won't think further.

It is a glorious, warm day. I wash my face in icy water by the glacier. Reinhold,

Nena Holguin.

please come down. I don't feel too good, soon I must descend. If only I knew where you were! Later I fetch water from the stream between ice and moraine. As I stroll away from the river, I catch a fleeting glimpse in the bright midday light of a point, a dark moving point on the crest of the North Col. I am suddenly completely wild with excitement. Evidently Reinhold is not climbing with his usual surefootedness; it seems as if a drunken man is descending from the col, not the same man who went away four days ago.

I burst into tears. It is Reinhold, it must be! I run around like a mad woman. I shout up to him that I am coming. I know he can't hear me but nevertheless it helps. I must speak with him. Quickly I put on my top clothes, prepare myself to go to meet Reinhold on the glacier.

Bright swathes of mist rushed across the North Col. The seething sea of clouds over Solo Khumbu was blindingly white. The curved line of the North-East Ridge stood like a wall between the clear weather in the east and the monsoon to the south. With the certainty of a sleep-walker, I descended. Yet the snow did not please me, it was like jelly and made no firm bond with the firn base. It slid off the smooth ice slabs when I trod on it.

Presumably I was also now less awake because I expected no serious difficulties on the descent from the North Col and, therefore, was unprepared for them. When, still in a trance-like state, I slipped for the first time, my feet went from under me at once. I tried to brake but could not control the plunge. With the increasing speed of my fall, fresh strengths were unleashed, as was always the case when real danger aroused my abilities, and to such a degree that I asked myself from whence I had derived so much skill, stamina and energy so quickly.

Quickly I stood up again, gripped my axe more firmly and climbed down a steep snow slope facing inwards. My care was instinctive: no reflex flinching, no more sudden terror when the snow gave way; only a slow complaisance in my body. In my leaden tiredness there was no more hammering nervousness, but much more a sleep-walking confidence as to how to proceed. This sort of feeling of security was directly bound up with tiredness and danger.

The big transverse crevasse, into which I had fallen four days earlier on the ascent, I turned at and kept on my right, and now I was standing at the top of a dangerously steep slope. Avalanche danger! The morning sun had softened the snow. I experienced these alarm signals as searing pains in my body, not as thoughts in my head.

The drop beneath me was 400m high. Down below, the ice slope ran out into the glacier bottom like the splayed feet of the Eiffel Tower. Only brighter or darker shadows indicated crevasses, basins and domes.

I didn't hesitate for long, then continued my descent. Soon I had such numb fingers and tired legs, that I sat down in the snow and glissaded. I was dehydrated and thirsty but even the snow stuck like dust in my mouth. I sat down for a while.

After rousing myself for the final effort and without thinking, I traversed right, where a broad open crevasse forced me to take avoiding action. Too late I noticed that I should have gone left. I couldn't go back, I had to go on down.

Suddenly I slipped again unexpectedly, braked my fall with my axe and, as my arms refused to work, slid down the middle of the avalanche cone to the bottom of the wall. For a while I just lay there, then came to on the flat glacier floor. I got up on my knees, lay down in the snow again and then gathered myself up. Groaning, I staggered forwards, lost the ground under my feet and fell once more. All at once I threw everything away from me, rolled my face in the snow and shook myself. I was down!

I was happy and at the same time despairing. Then Nena came over the glacier ridge. She stood there, then advanced. Yes, it was Nena. I could no longer shout. Everything went black before my eyes. Slowly and not suddenly I dissolved. With each further step downwards, with the marker poles in front of me, the first moraines in sight, the whole world stood revealed in me, I saw my whole being from without. 'Here' was now somewhere else. I was transparent, made of glass, borne up by the world beneath me.

Nena said nothing. Or did I not hear her? Involuntarily I held my breath, stood still. I had difficulty staying balanced. I wanted to take hold of Nena and to be alone, to laugh and weep, to rest myself on her and remain lying on the glacier. Immobile and without a word I stood there, as fragile as a light bulb. A single word would have sufficed to destroy this glassy delicacy, this strange envelope which was all that was left of me. I could see through all my layers and knew that I was transparent for Nena too.

Propped on my ski sticks, I stared at her a while. Then I broke down. All my reserve was gone. I wept. It was as if all horizons, all boundaries were broken. Everything was revealed, all emotions released. How far had I to go before I finally broke in two? I myself was now the open book. The more I let myself go, the more it forced me to my knees.

Nena remained calm and took charge of me for the hours and days which followed. Now she made the plans, she got me to safety, she led the expedition. And she continued her diary:

Men always talk of the conquest of the mountains. And here he comes across the glacier, looks up only once, very slowly. He glances at me, comes on with sunken head, is no longer consciously there. Going up to him I say: 'Reinhold, how are you?' A few sobs are the answer. At the same time I can sense all his feelings. This moment I shall hold fast to for ever — without doubt the most profound feeling of union that I have shared at any time.

For a moment I hold him quite tight then, as he lies there, bend down to him and say: 'Everything's OK Reinhold. You are alright. The camp is over here.' 'Where are all my friends?', is his first question. 'I'm your friend, I'm here, Reinhold. Don't worry, we're going to our camp now', I reassure him. 'Yes, where is the camp actually?' He looks at me with tears in his eyes. His face is yellow, his lips are split and chapped. Probably he is suffering from heat stroke. I ask myself whether it is really he who has returned or only a part of him. Or more? I have to struggle to hold back my tears.

When he can stand up again, I take his rucksack, give him a ski stick. He staggers forward across the glacier. I have compassion for this man. He has so expended himself that only reaching the summit could have given him the strength to survive, to return. Here he is, the strongest person I know, totally at an end, leached even to the soul.

When we get to camp and are safe, Reinhold collapses once more on the stones in front of me. Yes, he was on the summit and people will say once again that he has conquered the mightiest mountain in the world. He has been successful, has attained his goal — but still more successful was the mountain. It has exacted its price from this man.

I know that Reinhold too sees the mountain thus. For him it is a giving and a taking in equal quantities, a sharing between the mountain and him.

# LIKE RENUNCIATION, ROUNDABOUT
# WAYS ALSO INCREASE UNCERTAINTY

After my solo ascent of Everest, there seemed to be no more logical goals on the eight-thousanders. Certainly, I could have climbed the highest mountain in the world by a more difficult route and again solo. But for me this would have been a repetition, not a new problem.

The consequent further development in my doings I already saw at that time in the combined traverse of two eight-thousanders, without descending to Base Camp in between or setting up depots beforehand. The chance of being able to traverse Lhotse and Everest from south to north, or the other way round, I judged to be minimal.

Therefore, I studied this project in the light of another, lower, pair of eight-thousanders, Gasherbrum I and II. For three years I carried this idea around with me, then suddenly I felt too old for such a hard route.

By 1984 I had at last the double permit. Hans Kammerlander, the young all-round mountaineer from South Tyrol, was my partner. It had been difficult to finance the crazy idea, for no layman could perceive the significance of this double traverse and the experts gave us no chance.

Having arrived in Base Camp, Hans and I decided to reverse the order because of the avalanche danger, thus climbing Gasherbrum II first. We renounced the descent of Gasherbrum I by the ordinary route from the outset because a French expedition was operating there. We wanted to climb and descend without outside help, without high camps, and without following or crossing the track of another group. Solely reliant on ourselves, we wanted to make that detour which, after my Everest solo, promised an increase in uncertainty, exertion and danger.

# The Roundabout Way as a Goal

## THE DOUBLE GASHERBRUM TRAVERSE

In June 1984 I travelled from Kathmandu to Rawalpindi with Hans Kammerlander. Shortly before, we had failed on Dhaulagiri and were hungry for success. For four weeks we had tried to climb the sixth highest mountain in the world by the North-East Ridge and in the classic expedition-style. On one occasion the miserable weather had hindered us, the second time it was the danger of avalanches, and then it was our indecision.

Hans and I were agreed: on the Gasherbrums we would be successful only if we were single-minded and persevering enough to endure the manifold stresses of an ordinary expedition. For months we had discussed the problems of our planned double traverse: the length of the route, 5,000m of ascent, the same amount of descent and climbing over a distance of 20km.

When we reached the lowest point between the two peaks (6,000m), would we be able to summon up the energy again to ascend another eight-thousander, after we had come down from one such high summit tired and exhausted? A rest between the two climbs would have been an extra strain for we would have had to carry more rations with us.

With thirty-five porters and a film crew directed by Werner Herzog, we marched for ten days to the top of the world. Hans and I waited for a period of fine weather, then began our climb from Base Camp at 5,200m. We climbed without maintaining contact with Base Camp and without pre-arranged depots. Without outside assistance and without the hope of help from below, we wanted to traverse two eight-thousanders by four different routes.

During the morning we had to give up on the South-West Ridge of Gasherbrum I. The slopes were too avalanche prone, so we descended to Base Camp. Hans hit on the splendid idea of reversing the traverse.

A few days later we set off again at two o'clock in the morning. In a sort of testament, before our departure I had handed over responsibility for the expedition to Werner Herzog in case we did not return.

It was as if, in the middle of my life, I had to prove to myself and the world that I was still capable of achieving more than I had done so previously and more than everyone else.

Hans and I climbed rhythmically without taxing ourselves. We had to have reserves of energy. The second summit would be much more strenuous than the first, both physically and psychologically.

The route (– – – – = concealed) of the Gasherbrum I–Gasherbrum II traverse. The overall length of the route was 20km with 5,000m of ascent and as much of descent.

Here and there the snow was knee-deep and there was no one to break trail for us, yet we didn't suffer. In three days in radiant weather we were on the summit of Gasherbrum II.

Hans and I were alone on the Gasherbrums. No other expedition was operating on our four routes. During our descent from the summit to our bivouac on the South-East Face, we buried an Austrian doctor who had been lying up there amongst the rocks for two years: that cost us time and energy.

The next morning we risked the dangerous descent into the Gasherbrum Valley. This route, between the French and Polish ridges, was steep and threatened by seracs. It was a dangerous risk and luck, a component in so great a venture as an eight-thousander double traverse, could not be relied upon. As far as the Gasherbrum Valley everything went quickly and smoothly. We were in blinding form. We still had provisions and fuel for a week or more and had not the slightest doubt that we could carry on. We felt more confident now than before on leaving Base Camp. We felt stronger too perhaps, although many strenuous days of climbing lay behind us.

Not only the radiant weather but also high spirits lent wings to my thoughts. Did one have to risk the apparently impossible in order to mobilize powers of which we are not otherwise aware? 'At forty, one must either give up great climbs or go a step further than before', I said jokingly to Hans. The idea for this double climb on two eight-thousanders had come to me because I had felt that I must either carry on more intensively and impudently than ever before, or give up. If my mountaineering became

242

routine, it was all over. This realization was confirmed on Dhaulagiri.

I believe this attitude holds good for every forty-year-old. Either he says to himself: 'OK, my life is behind me, from now on I'll stick to the beaten track' – in which case he begins to die – or, in the middle of his life, he discovers the possibility of heightening his game.

Naturally, risks increase with advancing age. One's speed diminishes, and ability to concentrate and skill are relative. Mental endurance does not suffice for survival at the limit of possibilities.

Early on the morning of 26 June, Hans and I crossed the flat Gasherbrum Glacier. The fear that an ice avalanche would be triggered off and come rolling over us from behind like a hundred express trains forced us on. Cold fear between the shoulder blades – I felt it tangibly. I dared not turn round for I knew how broken up the South-West Face of Gasherbrum II was. At any moment a serac up there might detach itself.

The snow was not yet softened but the hard layer covering the blue-green surface was so thin that time and again we sank in up to our knees, each time with the fear of having fallen into a crevasse. It not only cost us energy, it also undermined our morale. At a height of 6,000m, every step demanded the greatest effort of will.

Hans was leading. Stolidly, bent under the weight of his heavy rucksack, he turned off to the left in the middle of the Gasherbrum Valley. Without hesitation he started upwards in the direction of the Gasherbrum La. The traverse of both Gasherbrum eight-thousanders was about to become a reality.

Hans Kammerlander and Reinhold Messner at Base Camp. They were waiting for good weather for the traverse of the Gasherbrums.

Hans and I had discussed this moment for a whole year, longed for it, feared it. Here, at the lowest point between the two peaks the decision would be made. Only if we forced ourselves – exhausted, emaciated and without back-up – to venture the second peak, could we succeed in what no one had previously attempted – the combined traverse of two of the highest mountains in the world without rest and without outside help.

At a safe distance from the steep walls of the two Gasherbrums, Hans stopped. He took in our doubled rope so that I could move up to him. We said nothing about giving up or going on, simply threw off our rucksacks and sat on them. We were going to breakfast. Hans melted snow in a fist-sized pot on the gas cooker. It was a long time before we had prepared muesli and tea. Neither of us felt any hurry. We had time and would get to the Gasherbrum La, the col between our two peaks, before evening.

When I looked back at the ice-fall on the South-East Face of Gasherbrum II, down which we had climbed at first light, I was full of boyish pride. Sure, we had had some luck. When we had quitted our bivouac under the summit pyramid at three o'clock that morning, we had been both excited and anxious. As we traversed to the right and descended directly above the hanging glacier, which looked like the gateway to Hell, there was only one way to go: down into that deadly chasm! Up above hung these bursting seracs, several hundred metres high, ice ruins towering vertically above one another. The avalanche gullies in between, down which snow and ice swept like deadly missiles, acted as bob-sleigh runs.

The snow conditions on Gasherbrum II were good. The summit, in the early morning light, was often not visible; here it is still far away.

We had come down there to be quick and in good time to open up a new route, as well as to traverse our first eight-thousander, Gasherbrum II. No one before us had ever dared to pass through this hanging glacier. Going upwards would have been suicidal. From top to bottom, however, in the early hours, when the snow was hard and we were moving at the double, we had risked it and so had won time. This tactic had brought us success and helped to conserve strength. We had been lucky too.

Hans handed me a plastic beaker full of peppermint tea. With it we ate South Tyrol bacon and hard farm bread; our second breakfast. At 3 a.m. we had each sipped a half-litre of 'prima colazione', a drink which Italian nutritional experts had worked out specifically for our traverse: a mixture of cocoa, rolled oats, mineral salts and vitamins. This gave us sufficient calories for a minimal weight and guaranteed that we would not suffer any deficiency symptoms.

The choice of the correct foods made up only a small detail in the mosaic of our expedition preparations. Much more important was our motivation. And that grows only out of enthusiasm, perhaps even a blind fanaticism. It can also give rise to the realization that life is a game. Time and again the player gets himself worked up about an idea, risks his 'certainties', stakes his life every day to the hilt.

Not only bodily but also spiritually, through this outlook, much strength and impetus had accrued to me. Now a feeling of a life free of old age filled me. I would have been able to hold my own with twenty-year-olds. I had just as good ideas as they; I had as much strength as they; above all, however, I had enthusiasm and readiness for action. I

A few metres below the Gasherbrum II summit. With that the first quarter – the easiest – of the tour de force was overcome.

didn't feel old, I felt strong. The twenty-six-year-old guide Hans Kammerlander was an ideal partner for me. With him I would be able to realize many plans.

In this mood I had prepared for the Gasherbrum traverse and this mood had carried us both this far. I had wanted to do something that not once young, leading climbers had dared to think about.

We bore the responsibility ourselves, each his own and we knew exactly that neither one of us would get far without the other. As far as the next big crevasse perhaps, or to the first overhang. And if we did not get on well together, it was too bad – we were stuck with each other.

After an hour's rest we continued. Our rucksacks now each weighed about 15kg less than when we had originally set off. The sun began to soften the snow.

Just above the marginal crevasse – a hidden crevasse which marked the start of the steep wall up to the Gasherbrum La – we unroped and climbed each for himself, resting independently. Hans moved slowly and for as long as possible without stopping. I climbed fast, hyperventilated and rested frequently after every twenty to thirty paces, as I had learned from the Sherpas.

The ice under the two-fingers-thick snow crust was hard. My blunt crampons no longer gripped well and the blade of my ice axe was no longer razor-sharp after days of climbing. But we had no file with us and so could not sharpen our equipment.

I climbed up the fall line extremely carefully, observing Hans meanwhile as he zigzagged higher. In so doing I caught sight of a bit of the western sky and a shock wave

The second ascent day on Gasherbrum II. Messner and Kammerlander alternated the lead. Masherbrum is in the background.

went through my brain: bad weather! Thin, fish-shaped, cirrus clouds were driving in on the horizon; in between, dark blue.

Hans also saw the threat but he went on; he didn't want to think about it. We both avoided talking about it. At this height, every word cost lung- and will-power. The ascent took hours but we were convinced that it was not in vain. Only on the edge of the Gasherbrum La, at 6,600m, did we attempt to assuage our fears with commonplaces:

'The weather will hold for a couple of days.'

'In an emergency we can always go down.'

Then we dug a platform on the slope for our bivouac tent, 2.1m long and 1.6m wide. Each pushed his sleeping mat inside the tent, then his rucksack. Finally we crawled in. This accommodation weighed only 1.5kg and was tested in a wind tunnel to resist storms up to 180kmph. We dismantled it each morning, stowed it away with the rest of our belongings in our rucksacks and carried on climbing. It must not fail, nor might we lose it – we had no replacement.

The night passed quickly. In contrast to higher up, here we slept well. So well that we set off too late the next morning. The weather seemed to have improved, except for the gusts of wind which attacked us from the west and tore at our rucksacks. For hours we climbed directly up the North Face. In the middle we came across some frayed fixed ropes which an American team had had to leave hanging there in 1982. Because we had to concentrate completely on the climbing on the one hand and had hardly any view southwards on the other, we didn't notice the grey sky until nearly midday.

Hans Kammerlander cooking on Gasherbrum II. In the background is the symmetrical pyramid of Gasherbrum IV.

At the lowest point (*c.* 6,000m) between the two Gasherbrum summits Messner and Kammerlander did not hesitate for a moment; they carried on with their traverse.

When we reached a small saddle at 7,500m in the early afternoon, Hans and I knew that we were in a trap. Suddenly it became uncannily gloomy. The storm increased to hurricane force and shreds of mist flew away over us like huge bats. Only with difficulty were we able to erect the tent on a small patch of snow out of the wind. We considered whether and for how long we could wait it out. As if we would have had the strength to go for the summit after three days of storm!

In the evening it got up once more. We cooked and drank. The whole night through the storm raged over the ridges, so that I found it difficult to follow a chain of thought through to the end. The constricted bivouac was claustrophobic and we left the tent entrance open an inch or two. So much snow-dust flew in that I buried my head in my sleeping bag. There was no point in talking for, with the flapping of the tent walls, we couldn't hear ourselves speak. By morning the snow lay 5in deep on top of the sleeping bags. The storm howled on.

In my consciousness our tiny tent had grown to the size of a room. Hans babbled something about a second tent nearby. There was another party there, he said. As far as I was concerned, his remark fell on stony ground. For hours now, the feeling that a third man was lying in the tent had become 'reality', irrefutable. Thus hallucinations tormented us.

We drank tea. Then we dismantled everything and set off upwards again, despite the bad weather. To have climbed down would have been just as dangerous in the strong wind and fresh snow. We kept to the rocks all the time and committed to memory

The serac zone on the ascent to the summit of Gasherbrum I. The technical climbing difficulties weighed less than the heavy rucksacks.

individual towers, so as to be able to find the way down again should we not be able to descend by our planned route. Route-finding was extremely difficult, together with our helplessness in the driving snow. When one stares into the mist for hours, the eye dulls. We only knew that as long as the ground rose we were not on top.

After climbing more than ten paces each time, my chest pained me. I stopped, coughing, body propped on my ski sticks, mouth wide open and eyes shut. I had to saturate my lungs with air in order to come to again. Thus I stood still for a while and everything retreated far from me. My head was empty, my chest relaxed. These were moments of relief which produced a long after-effect. Then I straightened up again, firmly determined to go on, to torment myself further. There was only one course of action — we had to continue! By the afternoon we could recognize the South-West Ridge to the right of us; it could not be far to the summit. As an aid to route-finding on the descent, Hans stuck a ski stick upside-down in the snow. We went on climbing for another hour over a very steep snow field which seemed endless. In the middle of it Hans left a second ski stick behind. Then suddenly we saw rocks above us again. Above that, a snow ridge and above that, space.

Columbus must have felt like we did then when he discovered America. The ridge climbed away to the right, so we carried on. Our goggles were iced up, our faces numb. If we took off our glacier goggles, our eyes burned, so sharp were the snow crystals which the hurricane drove before it. At last, behind a cornice was the summit! The second eight-thousander within four days!

Hans Kammerlander during descent to the Gasherbrum Valley. The snowstorm had armoured him and Messner with a crust of ice. Mostly they climbed unroped.

From now on it was all downhill. That was the sum total of our happiness. There was no photograph with a flag and no hurrahs. Only the question: 'How shall we ever get down again?'

Hans started back down first. Just below the cornices on the summit ridge, I lost my grip. A moment of carelessness, a gust of wind – I fell backwards. 'Hans!' I screamed. At the last moment I was able to regain my balance.

We climbed down to the planted ski stick and moved valleywards along the West Ridge, the edge of which served to orientate us. At a height of 7,400m we bivouacked again. This night was worse than the previous one. Only total exhaustion allowed us to fall asleep for minutes at a time.

Our descent into the Gasherbrum Valley the next day was carried out in trance-like indifference. The snowstorm continued unabated. Now and then we abseiled, anchoring the rope to rock spikes. Mostly, however, we climbed unroped, each for himself.

Sometimes I waited for Hans, sometimes he for me. We were both coated with an armour of ice and were as slow as snails in our movements. Often we rested for too long. Had we sat down to rest for two or three hours, we would hever have got on our feet again. Perhaps we would have fallen asleep for ever, like that Austrian whom we had found up above a few days earlier.

When on one occasion I found that Hans was not following me, I waited in despair. Suddenly a piece of bluey-white rock detached itself from the almost vertical wall above me. I looked for cover. Yet the stone-fall failed to materialize. Hans, who while resting had squatted like a part of the rocks, came on as surefootedly as a chamois. Instinctively he was nestling into the wall when a gust of wind came and quickly he moved to one side as a snow slide started.

For many hours we descended thus. Only once, on an avalanche slope, neither of us trusted the other to go ahead. The drifted snow lay chest-high, hence there was danger of snow slabs. The flank below us was as steep as a church tower roof and below that the world broke off into bottomless depths. After a lengthy detour, we finally passed this danger spot.

On the evening of the seventh day of climbing we were down in the Gasherbrum Valley, tired but alive. A stone avalanche, wide as a motorway, which had swept over our descent route a little earlier, just after we had come down, now gave us a feeling of invulnerability. We wanted to get down to Base Camp that same day. We had to be safe at last, no longer riding our luck, sleeping.

The ice-fall was soft. In the diffuse light we could not distinguish the firm ground from the crevasses. Again and again one of us sank into concealed holes in the snow. It was very dangerous and strenuous.

Half a dozen times we thought of giving up and bivouacking, yet each time disquiet drove us on. In the middle of the ice-fall – as I was trying to direct Hans from behind, checking the guiding rocks in the crevasse labyrinth – I saw him disappear at the edge of my field of view. I knew what had happened but reacted too slowly. I took in the rope, was yanked forward a few steps, managed to get a hold and threw myself on the ground.

When I had hold and looked around, all was deathly still. The rope was tightly stretched and there was no reply to my shout. I managed to get a titanium screw out of my rucksack and push it into the ice. Meanwhile a quarter of an hour had elapsed. As I fixed the rope to the karabiner, Hans's head emerged from the crevasse. He said nothing, just fished his rucksack and goggles (which had got hung up on a snow bulge) out of the black hole and carried on. Then, on the first flat spot, we bivouacked for the last time.

We drank unsugared tea; there was nothing left to eat. On our descent from Gasherbrum I, we had left almost all our rations behind so as to be quicker. We had been able to carry them no longer.

'If you don't pay attention next time, we shall both be dead', Hans said suddenly, stonily. I accepted his legitimate reproach and we spoke no more about the incident.

On the morning of 30 June we approached Base Camp. The tents were recognizable as bright specks on the dirty-grey moraines of the Abruzzi Glacier. We could even see tiny human figures. Our cook, Ros Ali, the liaison officer and Werner Herzog with his film crew, who were shooting a documentary film about our climb, came towards us as far as the edge of the glacier. We had no answers to their questions, as if our experience up above had been wiped out in the instant we returned to the security of semi-civilization.

It was impossible to film what Hans and I had experienced in those eight days between Base Camp and Base Camp, only fragments could be captured in words and pictures. Our fears, our hopes, our mission and our despair were too great for the two of us to have been able to carry them down into the valley.

# The 'Snow Lion' as Symbol of Challenge

Our traverse of the two Gasherbrum eight-thousanders has not been repeated yet. A few groups announced a similar plan but failed in the attempt because of the length of the route. In the meantime, moreover, it has become almost impossible to carry through such a complex traverse totally under one's own steam. The run on the highest mountains in the world has become so great that each summer, on average, a dozen or more expeditions share the permits for Gasherbrum I and II. Meeting up with other climbers setting up high camps and fixed ropes, would be unavoidable.

The Snow Lion, a Tibetan creature of fable.

This accumulation of mountaineers on the eight-thousanders is one of the reasons why I have withdrawn from this sort of adventure. For me, silence, self-reliance and self-justification are the basic assumptions for the experience I seek in the mountains. Nowadays all this is to be found much more on the six- and seven-thousanders of the Himalaya and Karakoram than on the overrun eight-thousanders. One of the outstanding pioneer feats of recent years was accomplished by the Yugoslav, Tomo Česen, quite logically on a high seven-thousander: Jannu in the Kangchenjunga group. Alone and alpine-style, in 1989 Česen climbed the difficult and dangerous North Face, a wall on which some large expeditions had failed.

The large-scale traverse of the four Kangchenjunga summits by a team from the USSR was the 1989 exception on the eight-thousanders. Of course this expedition was in its ways and means a mammoth undertaking; yet, on account of the length and difficulty of the route, it was justifiable. Like the new route on the East Face of Everest, put up by four Americans in 1988, the Kangchenjunga traverse is proof that advances are possible in Himalayan mountaineering, if we take up the problems offered.

In order to promote high-altitude mountaineering, and to make clear to laymen the distinction between a pioneering feat and mere show, in 1990 I set up a money prize, the 'Snow Lion', which is to be awarded each year for an ecologically-sound, creative feat. The prize money is to match the current cost of a small expedition to the Himalaya. In this way impecunious young climbers can realize their dreams too and, above all, become more active than they might be with sponsors.

The 'Snow Lion' is not to be a mark of the best, rather a stimulation to look for new ways and to complete routes without leaving behind rubbish and aids for others. In the long run, adventures will only be possible if we all leave the mountains as wild as we have found them.

For the Tibetans the snow lion is a creature of fable. For us it should be a challenge to give back to the great mountains that mystery which was and still is the basic assumption for being able to grow as a person on high.

**For the picture on page 33 – Nanga Parbat 1970: 'Frantic on the Diamir Glacier'**
I could not grasp that Günther was dead. For a day and a night I searched for him. In the midst of this ghostly glacier world, amongst the ice ruins, dehydrated, and with frostbitten hands and feet, I experienced madness for the first time. I no longer knew who I was, what I was doing. Nevertheless, I continued my descent, crawling downwards. It took me many years to get over this Nanga Parbat expedition and the death of my brother; to understand his death as part of my life.

**For the picture on pages 34–35 – Manaslu 1972: 'The greatest ice desert in the world'**
After I had gone around in a circle a few times, I knew that I had no chance of survival if I did not hit on the tent soon. The hundred visible square metres around me became the greatest ice desert in the world. I was lost. It was impossible to recognize any clue in this inferno of storm. I owe my life to a single clear thought: to move directly against the storm, then climb up to the ridge and thus perhaps to find my way back to the tent.

**For the picture on page 36 – Hidden Peak 1975: 'Nirvana'**
Up on the summit I experienced a deep inner peace, a nirvana. When I returned to the valley, my attitude to life had markedly altered. I had felt this even more strongly in 1970 after I had lain completely exhausted at the foot of Nanga Parbat in the Diamir Valley. Then I had accepted death for the first time, and this had material consequences for my future existence. Today I know man is not an indestructible something, rather a process, a variable condition. I have of life just as little fear as I have of death, and best of all would like to be unrestricted, to know of nothing that I have not experienced.

**For the picture on page 221 – Everest 1980: 'Twilight on Everest'**
This dangerous incident had only shaken my body and not that identification which for weeks had constituted my being; my identification with Everest. My fall into the crevasse had jerked me into a state of alertness which far exceeded my normal state. As I reached the top of the col I suddenly felt a strong westerly wind in my face. I caught my breath and my eyes watered. I stopped briefly, looked around, breathed more quickly and intermittently. Then a regular rhythm returned once more.

**For the picture on pages 222–223 – Everest 1978: '200 kilometres per hour'**
Anxiously the two Sherpas lay next to me. The hurricane roared over our campsite at a speed of almost 200kmph. The temperature was below −40°C. We had no oxygen apparatus and had not slept much. Had the tent ripped, it would have meant death for us. It is these particularly extreme experiences which provoke new adventures. I have never fallen, it is true, but often I have been near to death. At least once I did 'die' but I am still alive and since that time I climb with a different outlook on the world, on death and on myself.

**For the picture on page 224 – Gasherbrum 1984: 'Here lies a dead man'**
During our descent from the summit to our bivouac, we buried an Austrian doctor who had lain there amongst the rocks for two years. This cost us time and much effort. Then came the dangerous descent into the Gasherbrum Valley. As I looked back at the ice-fall on the South-East Face of Gasherbrum II, down which we had climbed at first light, I was full of boyish pride. We had been lucky too. Luck is that component which can bring about such a great venture as an eight-thousander traverse but it cannot guarantee it.